on track ...

Stackridge

every album, every song

Alan Draper

Foreword by Mutter Slater

SONICBOND

sonicbondpublishing.com

Sonicbond Publishing Limited
www.sonicbondpublishing.co.uk
Email: info@sonicbondpublishing.co.uk

First Published in the United Kingdom 2022
First Published in the United States 2022

British Library Cataloguing in Publication Data:
A Catalogue record for this book is available from the British Library

ISBN 978-1-78952-232-7

Typeset in ITC Garamond & ITC Avant Garde
Printed and bound in England

Graphic design and typesetting: Full Moon Media

on track ...

Stackridge

every album, every song

Alan Draper
Foreword by Mutter Slater

SONICBOND

sonicbondpublishing.com

Acknowlegements

My heartfelt thanks go out to everyone who has helped and supported me with this book, especially to Mutter Slater for kindly providing the foreword; Dave Baxter for spending hours sifting through countless photos from Stackridge gigs; Ade Macrow for our passionate conversations about the band throughout the years; Tim Scott – my longtime friend and bandmate – for initially pointing me in the direction of Sonicbond Publishing; longtime Stackridge manager Mike Tobin for his encouragement and assistance; James Warren for giving a thumbs-up on this project; my sister Diane Perry for providing photos and sharing all those brilliant Stackridge gigs with me back in the 1970s; my brother Bruce for his constant encouragement and support; Stephen Lambe for offering me this book commission, and to my beautiful wife Radiance for her everlasting patience during the writing of this book.

Much of the information in this book has been gleaned from my own *Stackridge Diaries* and through the many conversations with fans, band members and their associates throughout the many years that have passed since I witnessed my first Stackridge gig all those years ago.

An indispensable reference resource was Ade Macrow's *Stackridge and Co. Complete Gig Guide*, which logged all the gigs performed by Stackridge and its offshoots throughout the years: complete with useful trivia notes on various dates.
Ade's *Stackridge – Radio and TV Sessions Guide* proved to be another valuable resource for my research.

Finally, I would like to dedicate this book to Rhubarb Thrashers everywhere, with love.

Foreword

It inevitably comes as an unexpected surprise when someone expresses an interest in something that resulted from a fluke of fate when I was that young man over 50 years ago. Yet, here I am rummaging through a clutter of dusty memories in an effort to write something pertinent as a foreword to this encyclopaedic reference book (scrupulously compiled by Alan Draper) which guides us informatively through all of Stackridge's recordings, on to The Korgis and beyond.

So, what can I add to this already comprehensive history? What led Stackridge from being a minor Bristol band to one that knocked on the door to premier-league success? (If only we'd found the key to that stubbornly immovable door.)

We didn't really know what we were doing. The success that did come our way was fallen upon by accident as we bundled our way up and down the country playing gig after gig. If we were guided, it was by a combination of blind cussedness, a lack of anything better to do, and mere happenstance. As you will read, the personnel who recorded the first three albums and various singles for MCA (some say the classic Stackridge lineup) came as a result of chance meetings, random departures and cavalier experimentation during countless rehearsals, dotted with the occasional minor local gig. This half-assed method was rendered the success it became by us intuitively knowing when something we hit upon showed promise, and this was reinforced by the positive response from the growing audiences after we ventured out from Bristol and hit the highways in our mustard-coloured Ford Transit. In other words, you, dear reader. I thank you with all my heart. We've all had a lot of fun with music and gigs along the way (Indeed, I continue to do so). I hope you'll bear the jollity in mind as you absorb the intriguing facts and statistics enshrined in this book.

Mutter Slater, 2022

on track ...

Stackridge

Contents

Introduction

In the late-1960s, the British blues boom was in full swing – a back-to-the-roots movement led by bands such as John Mayall's Bluesbreakers, Fleetwood Mac, Chicken Shack and Savoy Brown, which saw the deification of a new breed of guitarist, spearheaded by Eric 'Slowhand' Clapton and the sublime touch of Peter Green: leader of Fleetwood Mac. Over in Bristol, two acolytes of Peter Green's playing were guitarists Andrew Cresswell Davis and James Crunberry Walter. In 1968, their mutual respect for the blues brought them together and they formed the band Griptight Thynn: a name chosen in honour of a character from the influential 1950s radio programme *The Goon Show*. Davis had previously learnt his chops as a member of holiday-camp specialists The Blue Crew back in 1966 and The Kynd in 1967, while his erstwhile partner – using the first-name appellation Crun (yet another *Goon Show* reference!) – had plied his trade with local bands The Mike Gray Quartet in 1966 and Sunken Rake in 1967. The new blues-powered Griptight Thynn consisted of Andy Davis on guitar and vocals, Crun Walter on guitar, Duncan Graham on bass, and drummer Dave Fortune, and they became regulars at Bristol haunts The Dug Out and The Granary, where they supported upcoming acts like Caravan and jazz rock band Heaven. On one occasion in 1968, they were supported by local band Obsession, whose singer Mike Tobin would end up managing Davis and Walter in Stackridge a few years down the line.

By the summer of 1969, the two Griptight Thynn guitarists jointly felt like they wanted to expand musically into more exploratory territory, and quit the band with plans to form a new, more adventurous unit, no doubt influenced by the evolution of psychedelia into a new underground that was later christened progressive rock. Initially using the name The Vera Lynn Experience, the new band soon adopted the moniker Stackridge Lemon, as Crun Walter swapped to bass guitar, Andy Davis remained as singer/guitarist, Bob Thompson was drafted in on keyboards and Tony Fennel (ex of East of Eden offshoot Barnaby Goode) sat in on drums.

Many personnel reshuffles took place over the next year, and at times the band resembled a musical roundabout. The legendary Murray Smith came in on slide guitar during 1969 – as later immortalised in the song '32 West Mall': a Bristol address at which the band were tenants that year. Murray Smith's tenure with the band didn't last the year out, though, despite his legend living on. The timings of various band inductees appear nebulous through this era, differing with alternate accounts. But Andy Davis had befriended James Warren earlier in 1969, as their respective bands Griptight Thynn and Dawn (not Tony Orlando's crew, but an American West Coast-influenced outfit plying the Bristol Scene in 1969) were both habitués of The Dug Out and The Granary.

The first important gig for Stackridge Lemon was their debut at The Granary on Christmas Eve 1969, and it seems by this time they'd settled the drum position with Bill Bent, who was by now incumbent. They would also soon pick up prize asset Mutter Slater, who was previously gigging as part of a duo called Mick and Mutter. The pair had earlier been booked by Mike Tobin via the Plastic Dog Agency as support for a band called Marsupilami for a gig at Glastonbury Town Hall. Slater evidently made a strong impression on Tobin, as he was subsequently invited to join the latter's latest band, who were eventually christened Pudding and who ended up sharing the bill with Stackridge Lemon at The Granary gig. As the Pudding lineup was in the process of dissolving, Crun Walter suggested to Andy Davis that they join forces with Slater. As a result of his addition to Stackridge Lemon, a key part of the band's sound was now in place, as Slater's flute turned new extended Walter/Davis compositions like 'Purple Spaceships Over Yatton' and 'Slark' into something magical.

As the band moved into 1970, James Warren was also now in place, with his extensive portfolio of songs bringing a welcome contrast to Davis and Walter's style, and giving the band a broader base and more scope to achieve their manifesto of forging an individual, eclectic mix of influences from as many genres as possible. The final piece of the Stackridge jigsaw was also soon in place through a chance pub encounter. This time it was tweed-jacketed Mike Evans who – with violin case in hand – strolled into a bar and struck up a conversation with the imbibing band members. Andy Davis' reaction was along the lines of 'Ah, a violin. We don't have one of those yet', and Davis and Warren immediately invited him to join the band, to which he replied in the affirmative.

The addition of Evans brought the classic lineup into being: just as they dropped the 'Lemon' to become simply Stackridge. Mike Evans was a virtuoso violinist who'd performed with symphony orchestras and had forged a strong identity in Bristol's folk clubs with outfits such as The Westlanders and The Moonshiners. Most importantly, he had an open musical mind, and was more than willing to attack any genre with his considerable skill and versatility.

Stackridge commenced a busy gigging schedule starting at a London venue called The Temple on 6 February, followed by Dagenham Roundhouse on 28 February, supporting Family. Every month, the gigs increased, taking in all corners of England and Wales as the band developed their presentation and started to pick up a following, eventually completing 60 gigs by the close of the year. The early set was comprised of less than a handful of numbers, which were liberally stretched out with improvisation, sometimes to 15 or 20 minutes. These included compositions such as 'Teatime', 'Purple Spaceships Over Yatton' and the usual set closer 'Slark'. One of the most notable gigs from this period came on 19 September when Stackridge opened the first Glastonbury Festival, and – when The Kinks failed to turn up – closed said festival on 20 September. Then, on 4 October, the band played London's Marquee Club supporting Genesis, who happened to be between guitarists at the time – Anthony Phillips having quit, and Steve Hackett not yet being in place, so guitarist Mick Barnard was filling in. Another interesting date in Stackridge's 1970 gig list was on 13 December when they played Bowes Lyon

House Youth Club in Stevenage, Hertfordshire, with a bill of Stackridge, Yes and Iron Butterfly, which must've been some gig!

By 30 November, the band played their first topping gig at the Marquee with Bristol band First Light, who supported them on their autumn/winter tour. According to Mike Evans, this was the gig when MCA Records first registered an interest in signing the band, and when they returned to Bristol on 22 December to play the Victoria Rooms, David Howells from MCA signed them up for a three-year/three-album deal. At last, Stackridge had landed that prized recording contract: the holy grail for bands at the time. This was a magical period when major companies were more than willing to sign interesting young bands and give them the time to develop musically with minimal interference: a more open and enlightened era when the music was indeed the message.

It was December when the band had the first of many future personnel reshuffles, as Crun Walter quit to return to his previous occupation of bricklaying. He would eventually return to the fold, but it wouldn't be for another 16 months. The band's practical solution was for James Warren to return to his first instrument the bass, as the new-look freshly signed Stackridge slimmed down to a versatile five-piece. 1971 was fast approaching, and the future was looking bright for this enigmatic West Country band.

It's impossible to discuss Stackridge without mentioning their remarkably dedicated fan base, which by this juncture was already expanding. Somewhere around this era, fans of the band started to be referred to as Rhubarb Thrashers – a term that appears to have originated from the lyrics of the James Warren song 'Marzo Plod' (discussed in the next chapter). Many fans did indeed bring sticks of rhubarb to gigs to thrash along to the music, and the term 'Thrashers' for Stackridge followers stuck, and became currency when discussing other fans' reactions-to and thoughts-on all things Stackridge. I've taken the liberty of employing this term when referring to the fan base reactions to various recordings in the main text. From 1971 onwards, hardcore Thrashers organised themselves into many groups – often referred to as mobs, and usually based on geographical area: some of the most prominent early-1970s ones being The Guildford Mob, The Kingston Mob, The Bathampton Mob, The Redbridge Mob, The Leeds Lummy Days Society, The City Arms Mob, and The Newham Thrashers (an East London aggregation of which I was a prominent member). A common feature of many Stackridge gigs in this era – especially in the summer – was a pre-gig football match, as Stackridge challenged various mobs of Thrashers to a game. The Newham Thrashers played them several times, and Stackridge usually ran out as clear victors, mainly thanks to Crun Walter's dubious tactical approach to the beautiful game! We had a lot of fun.

Thrashers were an integral part of any Stackridge performance, interacting via humorous homemade signs and customised metal dustbin lids. (Ours were painted orange with 'Newham Thrashers' emblazoned on them in purple!) When the band cut loose with their fiddle extravaganza 'Let There Be Lids', the front rows were often ablaze with Thrashers thumping lids together, along with Mutter Slater, Crun Walter and roadie Pete Donovan doing likewise on stage as Mike Evans sawed away ever faster on his violin. The fan base developed its own subculture as time went on, with newsletters, fanzines and meetups. And indeed, it thrived once more after a gap of 23 years from when the last 1970s lineup dissolved in 1976 to the Stackridge renaissance from 1999 onwards. As the millennium came and went, original 1970s Thrashers came out of the woodwork, soon to be joined by new, younger enthusiasts, as the fanzines flourished and fans organised quaintly-named 'Un-convention''s where Thrashers would come from near and far for a meetup to discuss the band – occasionally joined by various band members for a game of football, a drink and a general good time. Your average Thrasher was generally musically literate, intelligent and fun-loving, and this shone out both in the band's 1970s heyday and their later rebirth. It's true to say that few bands inspired such deep and long-lived devotion from their fan base as Stackridge engendered. So now, let's take a trip through the recorded legacy of the band and its various offshoots and solo albums, spanning half a century of recording.

Stackridge (1971)

Personnel:
Andrew Cresswell Davis: lead guitar, piano, harmonium, acoustic guitar, acoustic bass ('Essence Of Porphyry'), plucked piano strings ('Percy The Penguin'), vocals
James Warren: bass, acoustic bass, acoustic guitar, vocals
Michael Slater ('Mutter'): flute, alto flute, vocals
Michael Evans: violin, vocals
Billy Bent: drums, triangle
Plus, three trumpets ('The Three-Legged Table', 'Essence Of Porphyry'); three cellos and one oboe ('Essence Of Porphyry')
Recorded: De Lane Lea Studios, London, 22 March to 10 April 1971
Producer: Fritz Fryer
Engineer: Martin Birch
Label: MCA, Edsel/Demon, Angel Air
Release dates: 6 August 1971 (MCA), 1997 (Edsel/Demon CD), 2006 (Angel Air CD)

Celebrating a new record deal with MCA which was signed, sealed and delivered in January 1971, the five-piece Stackridge forged boldly forward. When it came to the decision of what to present on their debut album, they chose the adventurous route and opted to go for mostly new, untried material not featured in their contemporary setlist. Apart from a few previous stage favourites, a good deal of the album was freshly minted. On 22 March 1971, the band entered De Lane Lea Studios to record their first album. With a healthy and very busy gigging schedule in place, Stackridge only had 13 free days during the period booked for the recording. Ten tracks were committed to tape – nine appearing on the album, and one on the B-side of their first single. No outtakes have so far surfaced from these sessions.

Having recorded their debut album, the band commenced an intense period of gigging throughout the remainder of 1971, including a tour of English cities, supporting Wishbone Ash in June. The two bands were MCA labelmates and were big fans of each other. James Warren has recounted that when travelling to gigs in 'Bessie' (their faithful band wagon), they would often amuse themselves by performing *a cappella* vocal versions of classic Wishbone Ash guitar duets. Also featured on the tour were Glencoe – a band that much later evolved into Ian Dury's backing band The Blockheads. On the final date of the summer tour, all three bands could be seen jamming together at Nottingham's Albert Hall: that must've been quite something to witness.

Stackridge had been prepared to promote the new album on the Wishbone Ash tour, but due to production delays, it wasn't available until August 1971, when it finally hit the record stores. The band did manage their best annual tally of gigs so far in 1971, though, completing 174 live dates, including a jaunt to Denmark.

In the summer of 1971, Andy Davis found himself heading for an unlikely session after an accidental meeting on the street with fellow Bristol musician

Rod Lynton, who was hurrying by with guitar case in hand. He was on his way to sessions for the new John Lennon album *Imagine,* and suggested that Davis grab a guitar and come along. And so it was that the two Bristolians contributed acoustic guitar to several Lennon tracks in July that year. The tracks Davis finally played guitar on, were 'Gimme Some Truth', 'Oh Yoko' and 'How Do You Sleep?'. An amusing anecdote he's told about this time is that he was invited to stay on after the sessions, as both George Harrison and Ringo Starr were on their way in. But Davis had to skedaddle, as he had a gig to play with Stackridge that evening. So it was that Davis gave up the chance to play with three of The Beatles in favour of a Stackridge gig at the Winter Gardens, Cleethorpes, on 23 July. To rub it in, drummer Bill Bent collapsed with appendicitis at that gig and had to be rushed to hospital! Such a high-profile session was still a nice one for the Davis portfolio at the time, though.

The following month finally saw the release of the delayed debut album, and once Bill Bent had recovered, they hit the road once more to promote the new record. Manager Mike Tobin was now in place and would guide their career through to 1975.

The *Stackridge* album cover artwork shows a vista of strangely eyeless seagulls in flight, set against an azure sky with a pink horizon, and is, in fact, based on a bathroom wallpaper design. The gatefold sleeve opens up to reveal a sepia-tinted portrait of the band, covered with James Warren's spidery handwriting in white, making it a bit difficult to read. The cover design was courtesy of those doyens of early-1970s album covers: Hipgnosis. Also featured on the inside gatefold is an image of the famous 'Stackridge Gnome': a spindly-looking character with one hand behind his right ear as if listening intently and attired in a ragbag of clothes including tight half-mast trousers, a buckled shoe on one foot, and horizontally-striped socks. The distinctive gnome image also featured on Bill Bent's bass drum skin, and at the early Stackridge gigs, it appeared as if the gnome was tapping one foot in time with the beat. Whether this was intentional or not, I was never certain of, but it was a nice touch! In the album credits, Andy Davis employs his full triple-barrelled name, while Mutter Slater and Mike Evans are both listed under their full first name: Michael.

On release, the album was snapped up by their ever-growing fan base, shifted around 4,000 copies at the time, but became a steady catalogue seller in the years that followed. The album was re-released on CD on the Edsel/Demon label in 1997 and again in 2006 by Angel Air, with two bonus tracks – the single version of 'Slark' (covered later in this chapter), and a version of 'Let There Be Lids' from a recording session in 1973 (covered in the chapter on *The Man in the Bowler Hat*).

'Grande Piano' (Davis, Warren)

This joint composition by the two main Stackridge songwriters opens the band's eponymous debut album with a flourish. Despite the five-man personnel listed for the *Stackridge* album, this track is virtually a trio performance driven by Andy Davis' piano, James Warren's tremendously-motoring bass, and an exceptionally fine and powerful contribution from the drum kit of Bill Bent. Both Mutter Slater and Mike Evans appear to be absent from this studio take of a song that served as a regular Stackridge set opener up until the autumn of 1972.

Tagged 'Heavy West Country' by journalist Steve Turner – writing for *Beat Instrumental* magazine at the time – 'Grande Piano' displays the Warren/Bent rhythm section at its finest. James Warren opens with some impressive bass note bending before hitting the pulsing groove that propels the song along. Bill Bent's hi-hat and cymbal punctuation, in particular, enhances the rhythmic thrust of the song and his drum fills are absolute perfection, constituting one of his best performances on record. Andy Davis' verse vocals are filtered through an EQ accentuating the hi-mids and squashed into the left-hand channel of the stereo picture. The verse melody and tempo are somewhat reminiscent of the Everly Brothers' 1965 hit 'The Price Of Love'. The filtered vocal trick on the verses works a treat, as when the middle eight first swings in, the vocal suddenly opens up across the stereo spectrum in a glorious sweep akin to the sun bursting out from behind the clouds: an effect heightened by some sparkling Warren backing harmonies on the middle-eight repeat.

The lyrics are probably more likely to be the work of Warren rather than Davis, as the latter rarely seemed to get involved in the lyrical side of writing for Stackridge in the early days. As for the subject, this is best left to the imagination of the listener, as Davis' vocals invoke images of the composer Handel and 'major-7th interludes', mixed up with a surreal dream sequence. There are also some neat Davis guitar fills pushed off to one side of the stereo mix by producer Fritz Fryer.

Always one of my personal favourites from the first album, 'Grande Piano' remains a slice of prime Stackridge, wonderfully engineered by Martin Birch, who was concurrently working on Deep Purple's *Fireball* album during those months.

'Percy The Penguin' (Davis, Warren)

The first recorded example of the strange and often animalistic characters that would colour many a Stackridge lyric over the years, 'Percy The Penguin' also demonstrates their penchant for attributing anthropomorphic qualities to these creatures, perhaps to illustrate human foibles. Musically, this sounds like a straight 50/50 collaboration, with the simpler verses sounding more in Davis' style, while the chord shifts of the middle eight sound more like Warren's work. Performed in a laid-back manner on acoustic guitar with bass and harmonium underpinning, Davis plucks the melody on the strings of a piano while Bent plays bongos. James Warren's lead vocal is supported by Davis and Slater's fetching harmonies on the later verses and is slightly underplayed in the mix.

Towards the end, sound effects of wheeling seagulls and breaking waves add to the atmosphere as the sad tale of Percy's plight unfolds.

Born with 'cucumber wings', our hero longs to take flight, and carries his quest to the sage of the polar region – Polo the bear – though it's never explained how a native of the North Pole came to be on hand to a South Pole native like a penguin unless Percy was one heck of a good swimmer! Polo proffers Percy some wonderfully poetic advice on the nature of the air, with the couplet 'The substance is void/Its quintessence is bright'. But despite this enlightenment, poor Percy remains Earthbound. Perhaps a metaphor for all the hopes and dreams beyond achieving that we humans harbour, it all ends in tears as he dies from a broken heart. Touching or completely daft – depending on your disposition – it remains somewhat neglected in many Thrashers' affections. Despite this, it has its place in the Stackridge canon, and in the context of the album, it works well as a change of pace and mood after the rockier opening track, setting out an agenda of disparate influences that would be the hallmark of this great band throughout their career.

'The Three Legged Table' (Warren)

The centrepiece of side one – speaking in vinyl terms – is this multi-movement suite clocking in at 6:45 in length. It's a James Warren masterstroke, cunningly devised in four discrete sections, each one building in intensity and excitement following the gentle, poignant opening, which faintly recalls Paul Simon's 'The Sound of Silence' in its acoustic guitar arpeggio. The lyrics are early examples of Warren's word games – intriguing and atmospheric, conjuring images of distant places in the context of a daydream.

For the first time on this album, Mutter Slater's flute and Mike Evans' violin come into full play, weaving beautiful tapestries around Warren's vocal on the second verse. The music gradually becomes more pensive, heightened by the use of a pedal harmony in the bass, holding against the changing chords, creating and releasing tension as the flute and violin stoke the intensity. This is only released when the rhythm shifts to a resigned shuffle, Bent making use of his brushes to push the track through this section until a more-dramatic change of mood is ushered in by a boogie-like close-harmony vocal passage featuring a rocky bass line.

The lyrics depict a passing American landscape, as if describing a kaleidoscopic impression of touring across that continent – something Stackridge never got around to doing at the time, unlike many of their contemporaries. The music's forward motion is spurred on by some searing guitar licks from Davis, while Evans bounces his bow off the violin strings to fabulous effect. The whole arrangement explodes in a flurry of tambourines and Mexicali trumpets for the final excitingly energised section, topping off a fine piece of arranging by James Warren. With wonderfully surreal lyrics that mean everything and nothing at the same time, at the closing rhythmic accent we're left pondering the memorable phrase, 'The three-legged table is one'.

'Dora The Female Explorer' (Stackridge)

Hopeful of scoring a hit with the band's first single, MCA released this ebullient track in the summer of 1971. Despite some airplay – notably from Johnnie Walker on Radio One – it failed to dent even the lower reaches of the charts. It seemed an ideal choice, distilling all the virtues of the band's more commercial-sounding side into one exuberant conga-friendly rave-up.

'Dora' positively stomps along, given a great head of steam by Mutter Slater's chugging harmonica and Mike Evans' insistent violin riffs working in tandem. This irresistible forward motion is spurred on by Warren's bass line and its notable descending-quaver runs that lead the listeners' ears into several of the catchy choruses. He throws in an occasional double repeat of the first half of this run on a few choruses: a simple ear-pleasing variation that demonstrates what a masterful bass player he is. Warren also takes the lead vocal, with Davis supporting him on the rousing choruses. The choral refrain is repeated three times on each chorus, and the single might've benefitted from editing this down to a more logical two refrains per chorus, compacting the track a bit and adding to the catchiness quotient, as the ears tend to naturally expect two rather than three refrain repeats. The triple refrain has the psychological effect of making the track seem more drawn-out with less hit-potential. Interestingly, the millennium lineup distilled 'Dora' in exactly this manner when they added it to their 1999 touring set, performing many a power-packed version, much to the delight of Thrashers everywhere. The 1971 version has a feature not shared by any later live variants – in the drifting, ambient piano-led coda that fades off into the distance.

Another example of the Stackridge penchant for story songs, 'Dora' is the only official recording sporting a 'Stackridge' writing credit, being presented as a group effort. How much each member contributed is open to debate. To my ears, it sounds basically like a James Warren song: an impression reinforced by the fact that Warren also takes the lead vocal. Perhaps it represented a band decision to democratically share any royalties from a potential hit single.

'Essence Of Porphyry' (Warren)

Various members of the band have since commented on the large amount of material that the young James Warren brought to Stackridge when he joined the group in 1969. No surprise then that he ended up contributing to all but one of the first album's tracks. Andy Davis has since mentioned that many of Warren's early offerings were often in four or five movements, which is indeed the case with this, the album's most startling track.

This somewhat inexplicable collection of variations divided Thrasher opinion at the time, many fans lauding the song's ambition and originality, others accusing the band of self-indulgence: an epithet often bandied around by the music press of the time, particularly when attempting to denigrate any work displaying a vaunting ambition. In the early-1970s (the age of progressive rock), music critics often cried 'Pretentious!': sometimes justified, but often misdirected.

The track in question is a case in point. Showing the clear influence of the work of American iconoclast Frank Zappa (a band favourite), 'Essence Of Porphyry' seamlessly combines this with much more English strands of influence, such as light classical and soundtrack music. Arranged by James Warren and featuring three trumpets, three celli and an oboe in addition to the group lineup, this is the first of the band's bold orchestral experiments. Broaching territory later more the province of Andy Davis, 'Essence Of Porphyry' opens with a peculiarly sideways-sliding theme that instantly cries 'English music', and raises a mental image of a collection of the band's animalistic characters capering around in a West Country meadow! The music soon settles into a more gentle, pastoral theme with some lovely interplay from the band's two virtuosi: Slater's flute and Evans' violin fluttering around each other like a couple of butterflies over Warren's guitar arpeggio.

Like a series of film scenes, the music shifts between the playful and the pensive, occasionally interrupted by various blasts and trumpet fanfares when the listener least expects it. Displaying a kind of warped logic, the music manages to make sense of the disparate sections that flow or sometimes jar into each other. Davis borrows Warren's acoustic bass on this number, leaving the higher acoustic guitar parts to the latter. Mutter Slater is listed as playing both flute and alto flute, and as the whole thing appears to come to a climax in a series of blaring trumpet fanfares, there's a slight pause before the slippery opening theme returns to introduce an unexpected coda. This time, drummer Bill Bent brutally hammers the opening theme into a strictly swaying tempo, entering a cello-driven passage which states an inspired oboe-led counterpoint before embarking on a storm-tossed unison celli cadenza over Davis' pedal-note bass pulse. Ending in a satisfying classical cadence, 'Essence Of Porphyry' marks out the spirit of musical adventure abroad at that time and can be viewed as either a bold statement of the band's musical manifesto or perhaps as an elaborate musical joke.

'Marigold Conjunction' (Warren)

The opening track on side two was considered for release as the group's debut single before the more obvious choice of 'Dora' won out. 'Marigold Conjunction' would've been a strange choice, densely packed as it is with Warren wordplay, and may have served only to confuse the public at large. A steadily-paced pop/rock tune, it creeps in and stalks out like a slowed-down little finger shuffle boogie, reminiscent in feel to The Beatles' 'Come Together'.

Following this intro, James Warren's lyric takes us on a trip through a succession of very English characters, including one 'Ebeneezer Lemon Tweezer' who appears in the choruses: perhaps a reference to the band's earlier moniker of Stackridge Lemon. The vocals are sung mainly in two-part harmony, sounding like Warren double-tracked but listed in the sleeve notes as by both Davis and Warren, with a third harmony part supplied by Slater on the final verse. The vocals are oddly placed in the mix, panned out to each side of the stereo picture, which tends to give the impression of underplaying them slightly in the mix and reducing their impact.

The track mooches along pleasantly enough, and there's plenty of musical interest to make the journey worthwhile – particularly Warren's ear-catching bass-playing which engages well with Bent's drumming: the latter's kit being very well-recorded and up-front, with a satisfying thud to the bass drum and some interesting side-to-side stereo panning on the sizzling cymbal splashes. He gives a tight performance but audibly clashes his sticks together as he goes into a fill during the middle eight's second repeat. Davis provides some nice double-tracked, down-home guitar picking in the middle, making a break from the somewhat breathless wordiness, and the violin and flute are subtle rather than full-on, which gives the track character. Without being a major Stackridge composition, 'Marigold Conjunction' holds its own as another unique facet of the band's musical eclecticism.

'32 West Mall' (Davis, Warren)

A legendary piece of Stackridge folklore is enshrined in '32 West Mall', being the address of the Bristol flat the group members shared in their early days. Lyrically quite unusual for Stackridge – dealing as it does with a real historical event rather than some fantastical yarn – this endearing snapshot from a day in the life of the band is beautifully rendered by Davis, Warren and Slater, and features winning three-part vocal harmonies, with some interesting filtering and panning on Andy Davis' lead voice on the first chorus. As the tale proceeds, Murray Smith – their one-time slide guitarist – gets a mention in the line 'Murray's joined us for our breakfast too'. The vocals are accompanied by just Davis on finger-picked acoustic guitar and Warren on bass, and there are also some interesting sound effects of a thunderstorm, rain falling on the roof, and a tinny radio transmitting on the fade-out. The charm quotient on '32 West Mall' is high, and it has remained a big favourite of both Thrashers and the band. The millennium lineup revived the song three decades later: still sounding as fresh as it does on this first album.

'Marzo Plod' (Warren)

One of the characters that loom large in the Stackridge legend must be that eternal Rhubarb Thrasher 'Marzo Plod'. An invention of the fertile and decidedly-odd mind of James Warren, Marzo is depicted as a strange human/animal hybrid of great longevity, having been born in 1563, but still evidently alive and thrashing his rhubarb when this song was minted in 1971! As the song that gave birth to the whole rhubarb-thrashing movement, it finds Stackridge in best storytelling mode. It mentions in passing, several other characters inhabiting that peculiar parallel universe the band have created, including Marzo's best friend Tinlips, and those mysterious aliens who visited the West Country in their purple spaceships, consuming the steel-plated beans fried for them by Mr. Plod, and no doubt firing up the warp cores of their spaceships with the purple mineral porphyry, or at least the essence of it!

The music plods along with an engaging gait, featuring Warren's marvellous up-front bass-playing as the musical pivot, again tying in firmly with Bent's drumming, accompanied by all sorts of wonderfully-fluent jamming on guitar, flute and violin, cascading around behind Warren's lyric: his voice somewhat comically pushed into the right-hand channel. He appears to be stifling a fit of the giggles, and at one point, a clearly audible grin can be heard – on the final word of the line 'No one would believe' – giving the feeling that this was a fun session. The instrumental interludes between the verses have a kind of folk/jig feel, and there is much on this debut album that bolstered the early belief that Stackridge were some kind of weird folk group. Of course, they were always much more than that.

Decorated with a series of sound effects – such as a stick of rhubarb being thrashed, a steel-plated bean rolling from speaker to speaker, and a purple spaceship landing – 'Marzo Plod' is an absolute delight when listened to in headphones. It's the sort of daft ditty that causes lovers of the flippant and playful to grin from ear to ear and those with an overly-serious turn of mind to possibly run for the hills.

'Slark' (Walter, Davis)

Ex-bass player James Crunberry Walter's only writing contribution to this album was the lyrics to this ultimate early-Stackridge epic. The lyric delineates the tale of a mythical West Country dragon that swooped down to scoop the song's narrator from his creosote car whilst he was careering from Kebeeble (whereabouts still unknown) to Kenn (a small village near Yatton in Somerset). Firmly in the folk-tale realm of the fairy story, the words tell only half the tale, as Andy Davis' music – mostly based around or extrapolated from the timeless minor-key riff that provides the unforgettable opening hook – is often as descriptive as the lyrics.

The band's live blockbuster in the early years, it usually occupied pride of place at the end of the set, and sometimes stretched out to 20 minutes or so, extended by Mutter Slater's extraordinary mime sequences which preceded the song's development section. An ideal vehicle in the age of progressive rock, 'Slark' live could be an overwhelmingly powerful experience. The album version was an attempt to replicate the mighty live version. But as with all studio creations, the essential element of frisson with a live audience, and the excitement and adrenaline that this generates, is inevitably lost. That aside, this version runs for over 14 minutes and brings back a vestige of the drama and emotion that 'Slark' could generate in a live setting.

Opening with Mutter Slater's reverb-treated flute playing the classic riff, it's joined by Mike Evans' harmony violin riff on the next round before Andy Davis begins the tale of an apparently doomed individual that the monster Slark scoops up and carries away. Warren joins Davis with a vocal harmony for the following verses, as the flute and violin slowly stoke up the pressure with their insistent riffs between each verse. The song part then gives way to a plaintive violin and flute melody as the chord pattern changes, before falling gently into one of Slater's most affecting flute passages, cascading up and down the scale in wondrous waves of great beauty. This relaxing interlude is interrupted by a shorter version of his mime sequence, in which he deploys his flageolets: played two at once (a bit of a Roland Kirk influence here!), using all sorts of snorting, gurgling and yelping noises through his flute to depict the trepidation and terror of the dragon's victim, ending up with some little-boy-lost Echoplexed cries for his 'Mummy!'.

A *raspberry* blown into the mic marks the end of this sequence. The development section that follows is one of the most exciting tracts of Stackridge music ever and was always guaranteed to raise the hairs on the back of the neck of die-hard Thrashers in a live setting. Using half of the classic opening riff, the flute settles on a crotchet pulse note, while the other instruments entering one by one then join in the pulse – Warren's bass, Davis' guitar, Evans' violin and Bent's drums – to create a spine-tingling suspension. With the tension at a peak, the music cleverly moves through several key modulations before exploding into a wonderful rising four-chord sequence topped by a wild violin improvisation from Mike Evans. After several rounds – the second of which features a rippling, multitracked violin duet over the rock beat – the simple folk melody expands to symphonic proportions as the flute and violin perform a call-and-response routine and the rhythm section pile in enthusiastically to drive the track forwards. The climax is reached in a series of dynamic, stop-time punctuations with pregnant pauses before the song section returns for two final verses. Just listen to Warren's great bass-playing on these verses: a master at work indeed!

It all ends with a studio sing-along on the riff, which maybe goes on a bit too long for a studio creation. Another attempt to ape the live vibe was the added tape of applause at the end. This is cut short, and a sequence of somebody walking away whistling the riff (allegedly sound engineer Martin Birch) was recorded in a multi-storey car park and tacked onto the end. So ends the first Stackridge album – a varied, eclectic and distinctly odd collection of nine tracks, with James Warren as the dominant writer – a position he would hold for the first two albums, after which Andy Davis would be in the ascendant as the chief Stackridge songwriter, ably supported by Mutter Slater's compositions as time went on.

Additional Material

'Everyman' (Davis, Warren)

This overlooked gem was a remnant from the sessions for the first album and appeared as the B-side of the 'Dora' single. A joint composition between Davis and Warren, the opening fingerpicked minor-key sequence decorated by a lovely flute and violin counterpoint, gives way to a major-key verse that sounds typically like Andy Davis' work. The lyrics are very much in James Warren territory – very thoughtful and reflective, less whimsical than he's usually prone to be, and genuinely moving in concert with the very hymnal music. There is some particularly lovely violin-playing from Mike Evans behind the vocals: very emotive. The opening theme reappears for the extended coda, this time accompanied by the group chanting like penitent monks, adding to the track's general ecclesiastical feel. The end section builds from a gentle beginning to a more wind-whipped feel, bringing to mind a band of pilgrims in a sailing ship, on their way across the ocean in search of a new start, in the manner of the Pilgrim Fathers on the Mayflower. As the swaying coda rhythm progresses, Davis adds some Leslie-speaker guitar licks, and Slater improvises impressively on flute as the track begins to fade. A worthwhile recording that will reward your attention, 'Everyman' is one of several early Stackridge tracks that were only available as B-sides until compiled for the 1976 *Do the Stanley* compilation album.

1971 Radio Broadcast

Personnel:
Andrew Cresswell Davis: acoustic guitar, vocals
James Warren: bass, vocals
Mutter Slater: flute, vocals
Mike Evans: violin, vocals
Billy Bent: drums, percussion
Recorded: Maida Vale, Studio 4, London, 21 September 1971
Producer: John Walters
Engineer: Bob Conduct
Broadcast: John Peel Show, Radio One, 20 October 1971
Label: BBC Worldwide, Strange Fruit
Release date: 1997 (Included on The Radio One Sessions compilation CD)

'Three-Legged Table' (Warren)

A startlingly different arrangement of the energised final segment of 'The Three Legged Table' was broadcast on Radio One on 20 October 1971. More than a decade ahead of the pack, Stackridge were pioneering what was later dubbed 'world music' with this remarkable reinvention of James Warren's ditty. Coming on like a collision between calypso and an authentic afro rhythm, the band harmonise the lyric over churning acoustic guitars, while on the choruses what sounds like the larynx of Mike Evans replicates a cross between a yodel and the bloodcurdling cry of a Zulu warrior, in a quite remarkable and amusing performance.

'Slark' (Walter, Davis)

A full-length version of 'Slark' was also recorded at these sessions, and broadcast on the same evening. At almost 15 minutes in duration, there are several interesting differences from the studio version. Someone appears to be quietly whistling along with some of the opening riffs, and then singing along with later riffs in a deep voice, and this was rumoured to be John Peel himself, who was a big Stackridge fan. Mutter Slater performs some subtle flute variations on his lovely triplet passage following the opening verses, and he also expands his *mime* sequence, which stretches to three minutes here. This includes some Echoplexed flute/vocal tomfoolery: at one point sounding as if he has a wasp trapped inside his flute! Though this section is less voluminous than the epic live performances, he still manages to throw in Laurel and Hardy's 'Dance Of The Cuckoos' on his flageolets before the development section sets in. The energised passage that follows is somewhat less powerful than it was wont to be in a live setting, and the flute/violin call-and-response section is replaced by Mike Evans shimmering notes behind Slater's rising flute riffs. After some ironically weak applause from the band members, someone can be heard mumbling 'Thank you' at the end.

1971 Rockfield and De Lane Lea Studio Sessions

Personnel:
Andy Davis: piano, Mellotron, vocals
James Warren: bass, vocals
Mutter Slater: flute, vocals
Mike Evans: violin
Billy Bent: drums, percussion
Orchestral arrangements: Tony Cox ('Slark'), James Warren and Mike Evans ('Purple Spaceships')
Recorded: Rockfield Studio, Monmouth, Wales (23, 24, 25 November and 4 December); De Lane Lea Studios, London (2 December)
Producer: Fritz Fryer ('Purple Spaceships'); Tony Cox ('Slark')
Label: MCA
Release dates: 5 May 1972 (MCA single), 1976 (Both tracks included on Do the Stanley MCA compilation LP), 1996 (both tracks included on Friendliness Edsel/Demon CD re-release), 2006 ('Slark' included on Stackridge CD re-release, and 'Purple Spaceships' included on Friendliness CD re-release on Angel Air)

As the 'Slark' b/w 'Purple Spaceships Over Yatton' single more properly belongs in the five-piece Stackridge era, I have dealt with these two tracks here rather than in the *Friendliness* chapter, although the sessions display a slight overlap with a few recordings used on that album. Fritz Fryer is still in evidence co-producing on 'Purple Spaceships', which possibly indicates that this may have been the first track recorded at Rockfield Studios, as the first recording sessions took place there, though it's unclear whether Martin Birch was still in attendance as engineer. Judging by the sound of the track, I would guess he probably wasn't. By the time of the 'Slark' re-recording for the second single, Tony Cox had been drafted in. His previous work included orchestrations on the Yes album *Time And A Word*, which raises the suspicion that he may have had some input in the heavily-orchestrated version of 'Purple Spaceships' as well.

'Purple Spaceships Over Yatton' (Walter, Davis)

This was one of the instrumental blockbusters of the early Stackridge live set. This cosmic epic – though often a brilliant ensemble group performance – was really a spotlight for Mutter Slater's flute pyrotechnics, giving him the chance to stretch out and improvise a bit. The composition – credited to then-absent bass player Crun Walter and Andy Davis – is simplicity itself, and shares a lineage with bands then working at the atmosphere end of the progressive rock spectrum, such as Pink Floyd.

Calling upon the dynamics of classical music to inform its construction, 'Purple Spaceships' consists of three basic sections, all led by the flute in a live setting. Oddly, the plural 'Spaceships' became a singular 'Spaceship' when it appeared on the B-side label of the re-recorded 'Slark' single. This may have just been a misprint, and was corrected on subsequent releases.

When it came to transforming what could be an overwhelmingly powerful and moving live experience into a studio creation, the band opted for a heavier, more orchestral feel. Although the studio version has an extreme dynamic range from almost inaudible to blaring, much of it sounds somewhat muted, the first section, in particular, lacking the airier feel of the live arrangement. After an introductory stanza which sets a three-note rhythmic phrase firmly in the mind, the first section settles into its template of three repeated minor riffs over a pedal D drone. The band drafted in an orchestra for this auspicious occasion, and with Fritz Fryer apparently still engineering, they presented their new arrangement, taking into account hastily-scribbled strings and brass score. The orchestral intrusions on this first section lend the track an uncharacteristic weight that the live version never really had, and Mutter Slater's flute riffs leading this opening movement – which could be so emotive and atmospheric in a live setting – lose some of their lustre, being swamped by the heavy orchestral tones. With the lightness of the live version absent, the music is left with a somewhat heavier sound and a much darker feel. Perhaps this is what the group were aiming for, but for lovers of the live version, like me, it doesn't quite compare.

The following plunge into almost absolute silence for the start of the buildup section, could convince the casual listener that the track has ended prematurely, such is the minuscule volume of the passage's first 30 seconds. An exceptionally exciting experience live, this dynamic dip usually gave the band a chance to improvise and mould the piece into whole new areas, sometimes sounding quite avant-garde. The studio version eschews Slater's marvellous flute variations in favour of a creepy horror movie-type orchestral buildup, initiating the famous Morse code SOS rhythm, which forms the framework of this middle movement with its insistent one-note hammering out of this rhythm. As the music gets louder and louder, the bass notes of Andy Davis' piano join in to add to the menace which reverberates throughout, finally exploding in a scything strings riff, followed by a heavy pounding passage with both group and orchestra hammering away at the SOS riff for all they're worth. As the entire orchestra takes up an Eastern-sounding descending melody, one gets the impression that this particular alien invasion signals the crack of doom – an effect that the climax to this passage exacerbates with its wincing discordant brass stabs and dissonant strings. The harsh tritone-based sound here is reminiscent of the more-abrasive passages of 'Mars, the Bringer Of War' from Gustav Holst's suite *The Planets*, and the Holst masterwork is an obvious influence on the whole structure of 'Purple Spaceships': a fact Andy Davis acknowledged at the time. On first hearing, I put this heavily-dissonant climax down to an ambitious attempt to create a Stravinsky-like passage to jolt the listeners' sensibilities, but the truth lay elsewhere. As the composition was credited to Walter and Davis, it seems strange that Warren should enlighten us on the genesis of this dissonant section, stating that the reason it ended up sounding this way was because *he* was arranging the orchestral parts, and having only a passing familiarity with musical notation, gave instructions to the more musically literate Mike Evans to scribble out the notes he asked him to. What the violinist failed to realise was that Warren was also unfamiliar with transposing instruments such as brass, which are set at a certain pitch, and the usual written notes need to be transposed to make the brass sound in the same key as the rest of the players! Why Mike Evans failed to spot this, is also something of a mystery, but perhaps he put it down to the fact that Warren may have been expressing one of his eccentric musical ideas. The fact that this passage replaced one of Mutter Slater's most wonderfully-climactic live flute parts was something of a disappointment.

The final more-relaxed and floating section most closely resembles the live version, as Slater is at last permitted to stretch out on his flute, here double-tracked. Even this is somewhat truncated, and the whole track is two or three minutes shorter than the average live version. Slater opens the coda by stating the simple melody over a repeated four-chord sequence, and the Bee Gees later seemingly appropriated and sped up part of this tune for their 1979 hit 'Tragedy' (Probably coincidence rather than plagiarism). After some fluttering-if-somewhat-curtailed flute improvisation, the track resolves on several repeats of the melody, with the violin providing a harmony line.

All in all, the studio version of this epic sounded like something of a missed opportunity, although – strangely and somewhat perversely – Mutter Slater pronounced himself pleased with it at the time, despite the fact it neglected to utilise all of his incomparable flute parts that were so integral to live versions throughout the years. The sad thing was that we never did get the definitive live arrangement of 'Purple Spaceships' on record – at least not with the classic lineup – and the other available renditions of this jewel in the Stackridge tiara will be discussed in due course.

'Slark' (Walter, Davis)

The decision to re-record what became the band's most famous track for release as a single was, on the face of it, a strange one. Basically, a fairly simple song in the folk ballad mode, the live arrangement – as replicated on the first album – saw this folk tune expanded to epic proportions, posing a thorny problem for the band in editing down such an arrangement to accommodate the three-minute-single mentality of radio programmers. A drastic rearrangement was called for, and the group are to be applauded for their imaginative reinvention of this classic Andy Davis tune, which is brilliantly condensed into a more radio-friendly four-and-three-quarter-minute duration – still slightly too long to tempt most of the daytime radio DJs of 1972 into giving it airplay though. Whether it would've stood much of a chance of chart success – even with more airplay – is debatable, although the riff is undeniably catchy and may have just been enough to hook into the brains of the general public. Such questions are rendered academic, as the single received minimal airplay on its 5 May 1972 release and shared the fate of every other Stackridge single: seeing no chart action whatsoever. This was a pity, as the 'Slark' single certainly deserved a wider audience.

Where the album version had been based around an acoustic guitar matrix, the single version is mainly piano-driven, proving that its durable riff sounds great on whichever instrument that plays it. To compact the arrangement, the riffs are only played once between the opening verses, as opposed to twice on the longer version, and though flute and violin are still much in evidence in this arrangement, Andy Davis' piano dominates the feel. Tony Cox's production brings in a grand orchestral swell after the first three verses, using the rising chords from the long version's development section to build the tension, before delightfully-skipping reggae-tinged passage skanks along, with Slater's whimsical flute providing some grin-inducing asides to the main melody, as Davis *raps* the next two verses of Walter's lyric over the descending final chord at the end of each rising sequence. This finally resolves in a harmonised last verse sung by Davis and Warren before the inevitable sing-along on the final riff melody; the newly acquired Mellotron giving the coda a floating feel with its simulated strings. Ending on a strong minor chord, the 'Slark' single remains an edifying slice of classic Stackridge, and a worthwhile re-evaluation of a great tune.

Friendliness (1972)

Personnel:
Andy Davis: keyboards, guitar, vocals
James Warren: guitar, bass ('Keep On Clucking'), vocals
Mutter Slater: flute, piano ('Story Of My Heart'), percussion, vocals
Mike Evans: violin, cello
James Crunberry Walter: lead guitar ('Keep On Clucking'), bass
Billy Sparkle: drums, percussion
Andy Leggett: saxophone ('Anyone For Tennis')
Recorded: De Lane Lea Studios (2 December 1971) and Sound Techniques Studios, London (August-September 1972)
Producer: Vic Gamm, Stackridge
Engineer: Vic Gamm (Sound Techniques)
Label: MCA
Release dates: November 1972 (MCA), 1996 (Edsel/Demon CD), 2006 (Angel Air CD)

Several tracks later emerging on the *Friendliness* album also appear to have been started at the November/December 1971 sessions – particularly 'Father Frankenstein Is Behind Your Pillow', which was almost certainly recorded at De Lane Lea on 2 December and is credited to this studio on the LP sleeve. Additionally, Andy Davis claims that the title track was at least partially recorded at Rockfield Studio too. It's debatable how many other Friendliness tracks were started at these 1971 sessions, but Mutter Slater's 'Story Of My Heart' is another strong possibility, as it was performed with an almost identical arrangement to the album version on the Radio One John Peel session on 20 March 1972. All this raises the obvious question of which tracks bassist Crun Walter did or didn't perform on, as he only returned to the band on 30 April 1972. He is credited with bass on the entire album, except for 'Keep On Clucking', on which he swapped bass for guitar, but logic would dictate that the superb bass-playing on 'Father Frankenstein' is more likely to be James Warren at the earlier De Lane Lea session. Quite why 'Father Frankenstein' and some of the other partially recorded tracks were left in the can for so long (until the band reconvened at Sound Techniques in August 1972) is something of a mystery. Perhaps the band's legendary live workload prevented them from returning to the studio to complete *Friendliness* until then, but a nine-month gestation period was extremely rare for a recording project in those more prolific times.

They may have been debating over a producer but finally settled for co-production with engineer Vic Gamm, who entered the picture at the Sound Techniques sessions in August 1972, when, according to James Warren, the band recorded the rest of the album in ten days working from 2 p.m. to midnight: 70 hours of recording and 30 hours of mixing. According to their manager Mike Tobin, the final mixing session was on 9 September 1972.

Friendliness hit the stores in November 1972, just as bassist Crun Walter was struck down with appendicitis, causing the band a promotional conundrum. This was solved by drafting in local musician Paul Anstey on bass, just in time for the December Christmas Pantomime Tour with fellow West Country band The Pigsty Hill Light Orchestra. Members of both bands starred in an adaption of Robert Louis Stevenson's *Treasure Island*, and much fun and hilarity abounded at these gigs. I managed to catch the band twice on the Pantomime Tour, where they still managed to fit in their regular set amongst the bedlam and chaos that was the pantomime – which featured, amongst other things, corny jokes; Mutter Slater as 'The Parrot'; a custard-pie fight, and James Warren narrating the whole shebang. By the time the band wound up at London's Marquee Club for their New Year's Eve party (What a gig that was!), they'd amassed a 1972 gig tally of 112 dates. A comic specially produced to promote the *Friendliness* album was distributed at gigs and proved to be an amusing read.

The album's sleeve was designed by local Bristol artist Dave Borthwick, who later became one of the leading animation directors in his field. The front cover portrays an old rustic-looking man in a hat and overcoat, wearing odd shoes and sitting against a hedge. A flock of birds flutter around his head and alight upon his open hands: an image that really sums up the album title, which forms a curved arc below his feet. The charming band portraits on the back cover are presented with three on each side of the printed song lyrics, and they are beautifully rendered, making *Friendliness* a complete package and complementing the music within.

Friendliness remains a band and fan favourite, and for me, it comes closest to defining the adventurous musical eclecticism and questing spirit that was the hallmark of the classic Stackridge lineup. Edsel/Demon Records re-released the album on CD in 1996, with three bonus tracks – the single version of 'Slark', 'Everyman' (B-side of 'Dora') and 'Purple Spaceships Over Yatton': the 'Slark' single B-side (with misprint corrected!). In 2006 it was again made available on CD via Angel Air, this time with bonus tracks 'Everyman', 'Purple Spaceships', 'C'est La Vie' and 'Do the Stanley': the latter pair covered in the next chapter, as they came from 1973.

'Lummy Days' (Davis)

Rightfully regarded by the vast majority of Thrashers as the all-time Stackridge anthem, 'Lummy Days' opens side one of *Friendliness* in the grandest style imaginable. An early peak in Andy Davis' composing career, this legendary track manages to compact a plethora of different emotions into less than three and a half minutes and is a veritable pocket symphony.

Starting out as a marching tune bearing a passing resemblance to the theme from the early-1970s children's TV show *Hector's House*, Mike Evans' violin is dominant, stating the opening section's memorable theme, while Davis' piano marks time in the righthand channel, and Slater's flute is panned to the left. The newly christened Billy Sparkle (after a name change from his former moniker Bill Bent) provides some bouncing drumming to drive this section along, and he locks in well with the recently returned Crun Walter on bass: announcing the new Stackridge rhythm section to the world. As the melody on this first section rises, Warren adds some precise electric guitar notes that seem to offer a comical reply to the main tune; even on an instrumental, the Stackridge humour shines through brightly! The second repeat of this brilliant opening section features a somewhat wheezy-sounding flute and organ passage, highlighting the album's production as being less technically perfect than the first album. Not that this detracts from the track's wonderful feel – not one iota in fact – and as the drums bounce back in after this fairground-style section, the joyous feel is tangible in its spirit-lifting verve.

A short passage with a slightly darker colouring follows, reminiscent in feel to 'Barwick Green': the theme to the long-running Radio Four series *The Archers*. Davis' see-sawing piano riff links this to the poignant violin-led middle movement that's a masterclass of compact composition in a neoclassical style. Dazzlingly performed by Evans, over elegantly-constructed piano chords, the way this central movement leads back into the stomping martial theme is ample evidence of musical genius at work and has the effect of making this listener want to punch the air with sheer joy as the opening melody returns once more. This theme is then cleverly stretched over twice its original length on its final repeat for the coda, as Sparkle beats out a thumping rhythm on his drums, and Slater's flute describes great cartwheels of flurrying notes behind the stately piano melody. One final repeat of the darker-hued melodic part sees Evans adding cello to his musical arsenal – perhaps the only time on a Stackridge recording that he did so. The return of the see-sawing piano, followed by nine magical climbing notes on the same instrument, end in a perfect cadence as the whole ensemble hammer out a final definitive two-note statement, to which Davis adds a comical punctuation mark on the bass end of the piano. This final act of ingenuity completes an exceptional piece of music that remains a high watermark in Andy Davis' writing career.

'Friendliness (Part One)' (Warren)

Often accused of an inherent flippancy by their detractors, Stackridge were viewed by many as a bunch of daft yokels who just traversed the country, thrashing rhubarb and banging dustbin lids. Those of us who fell under their beguiling spell knew differently of course, and the two-part title track is ample demonstration of an extremely thoughtful band at work.

Though much of his writing displayed a frivolous, playful side, James Warren was also capable of distilling a more philosophical brew in his lyrics, and the simple wisdom expressed in 'Friendliness' – promoting kindness and amity over greed and enmity – strikes just the right tone to be heartfelt without appearing mawkish. Set against a backdrop of acoustic guitars and harmonium, Warren and Davis' lush, creamy harmonies reflect the influence of American

West Coast music: particularly The Beach Boys and Crosby, Stills & Nash. The song part is fairly short, and it's the kind of track this listener wishes could go on a lot longer. As Warren and Davis sing about reflecting on the joys of being human, it's a touching moment, and following the 'Drifting aimless, climbing spirals' line, the music does just that. The rhythm turns to triple time and resembles a spinning musical box; acoustic guitar and celeste arpeggios create a tone poem with Warren's wordless, ethereal vocal in the distance. Parts of this coda evoke a similar atmosphere to 'Neptune, the Mystic' from Gustav Holst's *The Planets'* – not the first time echoes of Holst had coloured the band's music (see 'Purple Spaceships'). This section runs through some interesting mood shifts before resolving on a major key as the musical box recedes into the distance and the track fades. During the 2007 Stackridge reunion, 'Friendliness (Part One)' was performed together as a unified song for the first time with 'Friendliness (Part Two)' and was also mixed as such on the *Purple Spaceships Over Yatton – Best Of Stackridge* CD that later-Stackridge-member Glenn Tommey compiled around that time.

'Anyone For Tennis' (Warren)

Continuing the brilliant opening salvo, the third track highlights the other side of James Warren's musical character and is a glorious pastiche of the Charleston rhythm so popular in the early 20th century. With style reference perfectly observed, Evans' performs a slow violin prelude, backed by Andy Davis' piano chords, with saxophone, played by Andy Leggett (of the Pigsty Hill Light Orchestra) doubling the violin on the second half of the prelude. With a large dose of whimsy, this leads into the song's brisk palm-court rhythm, with Warren piping at the higher end of his register whilst comping away on guitar, accompanied by Andy Davis on piano and a surprisingly nimble bass line from the rough builder's-digits of Crun Walter. Mutter Slater swaps his flute for a woodblock, cymbal and whoopee whistle on this number, and displays a penchant for percussion that would resurface from time to time in his Stackridge career. Evans' shows a Stephane Grappelli influence in his jazz violin interjections, and the whole concoction is highly contagious: no doubt one of the reasons it sneaked out as a single a week before the album. Needless to say, airplay was practically non-existent again, and this third Stackridge single failed to trouble the charts.

Warren's highly-whimsical lyric contains many amusing couplets and rhymes, and the line 'Now cramp has stopped me mining for uranium' has always made me smile. The fact that he rhymes the final word of this line with 'cranium' and then invents an entirely new word – 'insanium' – only increases the amusement quotient for this listener. Levity abounds, and conceptual continuity makes an unexpected appearance in the middle eight when 'Marzo's mother' is invoked – thus perpetuating the private universe Stackridge had created that so delighted the legions of fans and equally perplexed the hordes of disbelievers.

'There Is No Refuge' (Warren)

This is the third Warren composition in a row on side one, and he swaps back to his philosophical hat. Sporting a truly gorgeous melody of hymnal proportions, the simple arrangement of just piano and violin supporting the vocal, only highlights the tune's inherent loveliness. Accused by some of being an example of 'sixth-form poetry', the lyrics may be a tad self-conscious, but the sincerity shines through, and the profundity of the final line is beyond question. Andy Davis chips in to harmonise beautifully with Warren on the last three words of the line 'When understanding comes, there is love', with a deliciously protracted melisma on the word 'love', extending over three bars before giving way to a heartbreakingly beautiful violin solo from Mike Evans, underpinned by Davis' piano chords. For me, 'There Is No Refuge' remains one of the most genuinely moving moments in the Stackridge canon, with not a whiff of whimsy in sight.

'Syracuse The Elephant' (Walter, Davis)

Although he penned tunes of the complexity and perfection of 'Lummy Days', many of Andy Davis' melodies could be of almost nursery-rhyme simplicity, and 'Syracuse The Elephant' is a case in point. It was always more a clever arrangement than a great song, with lyrics again by Crun Walter. The song part of 'Syracuse' – which makes up the introduction and a repeated verse and chorus – employs less than a handful of chords, with a blindingly obvious melody line across the major triad: spanning an octave. It's given interest courtesy of an arrangement blown up to grandiose proportions in progressive rock style. The Mellotron blazes, Mutter Slater adds some onomatopoeic elephant trumpeting with his flute, and Billy Sparkle thrashes enthusiastically around his kit, creating a *big* sound. Stripped of this arrangement, the song wouldn't work half as well, but because of the performance's undeniable charm, it holds up.

Sung by Davis with assistance on the chorus harmonies from James Warren, the sad tale of the misplaced elephant unfolds, and another animalistic character is added to the Stackridge cosmology. Domiciled in Bristol Zoo, poor 'Syracuse' dreams about the 'herbal niceties' he discovered back in the veldt, lamenting that he 'Wants to go home'. Although – somewhat confusingly – verse two states he was 'Born and bred in Bristol Zoo', so his pining for the wild must be purely instinctive! The song's main point of interest is its extended arrangement, which obviously evolved through the band kicking it around in the live set for a good while – judging by the significantly different arrangement on the John Peel session take from six months before the album version was mixed. This is also proof that this track belongs firmly in the Sound Techniques sessions of August, rather than those earlier Rockfield/De Lane Lea sessions of late 1971, and therefore is pretty much guaranteed to feature a Walter bass line, which I'm certain it does.

After the initial song verses, the key switches to minor for a long, sad violin solo over a two-chord piano part and guitar arpeggio, which perhaps represents the elephant's longing for his ancestral homeland. After this poignant interlude, a delightful modulation illustrated by Evans' sweetly-trilled violin springs us into an unexpected waltz version of the melody, performed with typical Stackridge whimsy, and irresistibly bringing to mind the bizarre vision of a waltzing elephant! Swinging through some impressive key changes with ease, we then crash through the undergrowth into the next section of this programmatic travelogue through our elephant's beloved jungle, as Sparkle beats his drums with mallets, and a Mellotron sitar sample from Davis and some Eastern-sounding flute from Slater confuse us further as to whether our elephantine buddy is of the Indian or African variety, and the jungle's steamy atmosphere consumes us. A loud sitar twang brings us back to reality and a reprise of the song section, in which 'Syracuse' heads west to become a Hollywood star, but despite this fame and fortune, still pines for his rightful place in nature: a sad tale indeed.

Undoubtedly a fine arrangement, 'Syracuse The Elephant' closes side one in epic style. Clocking in at 8:45 in length, it is the album's longest track.

'Amazingly Agnes' (Warren)

Side two opens with the cod-reggae of 'Amazingly Agnes' – a song Andy Davis claims the band tried using many different arrangements in various styles before they settled on this final reggae-influenced groove. With its wordy witticisms sitting slightly uncomfortably atop the rolling rhythm, the final result still sounds something of a compromise with no clear chorus or middle eight to break up the longish two-part verses.

The clever lyric, though, is pure James Warren, as yet more animalistic characters are introduced – this time an unnamed mule who has fallen in love with a cow called Agnes; the latter displaying an unusual passion for the works of Renoir and imbibing Spanish wine. This tale of unrequited interspecies love is touchingly rendered by Warren as the band skank away behind him, with authentic timbale fills from Sparkle, some rolling organ from Davis, and another touch of Slater's whoopee-whistle and percussion to drive things along. Initially suffering from 'mild schizophrenia', our equine hero progresses to 'wild bibliomania' by the second verse and makes an ass of himself by attempting to swallow three encyclopaedia volumes, bringing a whole new meaning to the term 'reader's digest'! Not that this appears to have any effect at all on diverting Agnes' attentions towards our lovelorn mule, who ends the song in a pigsty, sitting on a stool, feeling a fool. The band describe this scenario in a delightful *a cappella* harmony break before playing out with the repeated 'la la' chant, adding a catchy coda to another slightly daffy Warren ditty.

'Father Frankenstein Is Behind Your Pillow' (Warren)

Something of an odd-track-out on the album, 'Father Frankenstein' was almost certainly recorded at De Lane Lea on 2 December 1971, and rumours persisted at the time that it was originally slated for a maxi-single along with both sides of the previous single. As it happens, the track was kept in the can to provide one of the high spots on side two of *Friendliness*.

Yet another James Warren composition – but very different in structure and feel from the preceding track – the rich sonic texture marks this out from the tracks recorded at Sound Techniques. The introduction is led by an unknown clarinet player, and as its gently winding melody sets the mood nicely, it leads into a James Warren vocal backed by guitar and rich, creamy chords from Andy Davis, possibly on harmonium. There are occasional interjections from some percussion instrument low in the mix (which sounds like a fishing reel being cast), and an elaborate walking bass line of great subtlety enters the fray, almost certainly performed by Warren. This illustrates some delicious chord changes in the second half of the verse. Several discreet synthesizer notes decorate the last three lines of the first verse: a sound rare on an early Stackridge recording but employed with the utmost taste.

Lyrically 'Father Frankenstein' appears to be an oblique love song, heavily impressionistic in its imagery, perhaps attempting to articulate the darker patterns that swirl within the human psyche. The contrast of comparing a fair face to a Damask rose, combined with the notion of a dark icon such as Dracula caressing the subject's windpipe, underlines this, adding a slightly unsettling feel to the first two verses: completely at odds with the music's reassuring and lush romanticism. This darker strand is emphasised by the music momentarily moving away from the major key in the first middle eight, where the rhythm becomes a march and the lyrical landscape broadens into a historical perspective, taking in several mythical West Country landmarks in the shape of Glastonbury and Batheaston Villa. Between the repeated middle eights, the key reverts back to the major for a richly-textured passage that positively drips opulence and features an ornate orchestral swirl – firstly behind an unexpected Hawaiian guitar solo (most likely played by Davis), and then led by the sweetest high-register violin-playing from Mike Evans. Billy Sparkle adds some impressive brushwork to this middle section, and the whole ensemble turn in a magnificent performance. The mysterious clarinet player imparts a distinctive flavour to the second marching middle eight, in which the lyrical emphasis turns back to the personal. The laid-back final verse features some sublime flute lines from Mutter Slater, weaving around behind Warren's final lyric exhortations in which he invokes Bathsheba, the Glades of Adyar and English theosophist Annie Besant – just to make sure that the sweeping imagery of this extraordinary song hasn't left any bases untouched. As the final chord is heard, the very Beatlesque effect of guitar lines recorded backwards add an experimental edge, bringing to a close one of the album's finest tracks.

'Keep On Clucking' (Walter, Davis)

Rock – in the traditional understanding of the term – was never Stackridge's strong suit in the early days. But they did occasionally get down and boogie

– as on this little routine cooked up by Crun Walter and Andy Davis, and the result comes across as obvious parody rather than authentic boogie-rock. Walter famously takes over lead guitar and serves up a batch of cliché rock riffs over the reunited Warren/Sparkle rhythm section that powered the debut album, as Warren attempts to return to his bass instincts.

The lyric introduces another slightly shady character into the Stackridge lexicon, in the shape of Sam McGurkey: a farmer who traded in his wife and seven kids for a thousand battery hens. A lyric with a clear vegetarian manifesto, it shows more concern for the plight of the chickens than for McGurkey's recently retailed family! By Stackridge standards, the music is somewhat uninspired and reinforces the impression that the band are attempting something in what is, for them, less-familiar territory, and it's a track that is, in truth, something of a filler in the company of so many high-calibre compositions. As a change of pace and a bit of knockabout fun, it works fine, but its unremarkable nature elicits a less characterful performance from Warren on his usually fluent bass, as he sticks to the basics here. It does at least boast a solidly catchy, sing-along chorus, marking it out as potential single material – a status it surprisingly never attained, as the follow-up to 'Anyone For Tennis' was to be a brand new non-album track, so no second single was taken from the album.

'Story Of My Heart' (Slater)

As the second side of *Friendliness* points towards a conclusion, we're taken into more impressionistic territory by the first Mutter Slater composition to be featured on a Stackridge record. The first in an occasional series of ambient pieces from Slater, 'Story Of My Heart' is based around the piano rather than his more familiar flute. Apart from his plaintive piano melody – doubled with a harmony when repeated – the gentle sound of wind chimes is the only accompaniment to this evocative little tune. Viewed as a filler track by many Thrashers, I really love this peaceful piece that highlights Slater's ongoing interest in ambient style and also with triple-time rhythm, both of which he would return to again on several notable occasions over the coming years. The coda is marked by several stabbing piano chords that break the trance-like atmosphere set up by the previous two verses, and it ends unsettlingly on an unresolved suspension, as the wind chimes tinkle into the distance.

'Friendliness (Part Two)' (Warren)

The ambient feel continues as the previous track's wind chimes fade, and Andy Davis' harmonium announces the arrival of the second half of the song 'Friendliness', sounding as if it has engine trouble, as each wave of deep, dark sound fades out again until it seems to catch on the eighth time around, then holds on a sustained chord under a slow, cantering piano riff that recalls the wild west – a tune also used by The Who on 'A Quick One, While He's Away': the mini-opera title track of their 1966 LP. Very different in feel from the more guitar-oriented first part, the concluding part of 'Friendliness' features the same wonderful vocal harmonising from Warren and Davis, but this time over piano and harmonium accompaniment. As with the first part, it feels far too short for such a gorgeous song, and the well-crafted lyric cements the sentiment of kindness over greed, contrasting the striving for worldly gain with what we would be better off concentrating on as a race – empathy and compassion – concluding with a statement that this sometimes volatile band would've been well-advised to heed more often at certain points in their turbulent career: 'Have no fear/I only need your friendliness'. The atmosphere of experiment with tone and timbre carried over from 'Story Of My Heart', continues, as Davis' piano dissolves into cascading arpeggios, then ends with a free-form sequence that perfectly primes the listener's ear for the entrance of the final track from this wonderfully well-rounded album.

'Teatime' (Walter, Davis)

Sometimes, simplicity is beauty. Such is the case with this final track from *Friendliness*, on which Walter and Davis combine their words and music respectively to create a perfect whole. A song that sits at the very heart of Stackridge mythology, 'Teatime' was a cornerstone of the live set throughout their classic period and a showpiece for Mutter Slater's flute and Mike Evans' violin-playing. As well as flute, Slater also provides percussion in the shape of a set of bells on elastic placed around his ankle, showing the influence of English Morris, as he stomps on the second and third beats of each bar in a triple-time arrangement of great ingenuity.

The opening verses are taken at a peaceful and relaxed tempo, as James Warren sings the evocative lyrics that appear to bid adieu to a number of things, each alternate line commencing with 'Goodbye'. An ideal closing track, 'Teatime' carries an endearing pathos for many Thrashers, with a bittersweet twist that tugs at the heartstrings, most tellingly on the line 'Goodbye, the dream has stopped growing'. The sense of loss that permeates this lyric is partially ameliorated by the resigned comfort offered by the final line in each verse, in which Warren and Davis sing, in very English style, that the answer is to 'Go home and have tea'. The simplicity of both the melody and the two-chord sequence that accompanies it, contrasts gloriously with the flute and violin curlicues that decorate the verses, imparting an almost medieval flavour to the music. The descending instrumental interlude that follows the verses is one of great beauty – a gorgeous combination of Slater's flute and Evans' violin, creating a passage of classic pastoral loveliness. The final few bars of this melody have been used on later occasions by several artists, the most familiar perhaps being on the 1994 hit single 'Kiss From A Rose' by Seal. Whether this was a Stackridge influence or just the coincidental logic of this sequence in triple-time is open to debate.

Falling back to just Warren's guitar arpeggios for the middle section, Slater states an elegant melody on his flute and then proceeds to improvise as only he can, bringing in jazzy phrasing as he builds. Those with a musical inclination may notice a fascinating trick of the ear in this section. It can be heard either as a slower 3/4 rhythm or if the ear counts each guitar note across the arpeggios, on a faster 6/8 rhythm, then the entrance of Walter's bass anticipating movement to a faster tempo can be slightly disorienting. This is the aural equivalent of one of those optical illusions where the brain can view an image one way or another, but not at the same time! The suggested tempo change arrives with the clattering entry of Billy Sparkle's drums, as the band vamp on two chords and Mike Evans improvises wildly on his violin: something he has always excelled at. As the violin heads for the stratosphere, he reprises the elegant melody from the middle section, as Slater's flute joins in with it, and this sweeping violin/flute duet over the mad gallop of the rhythm section evokes a grandiose splendour. Why the band chose to fade this out rather than go for the magnificent, decelerating live ending that featured Slater's wheeling flute figures is something of a mystery and a great pity.

1972 Radio Broadcast

Personnel:
Andy Davis: guitar, electric piano, Mellotron, vocals
James Warren: guitar, vocals
Mutter Slater: flute, vocals, percussion, bird whistles
Mike Evans: violin, vocals
James Crunberry Walter: bass
Billy Sparkle: drums, percussion
Recorded: Paris Theatre, Regent Street, London, 15 June 1972
Broadcast: Radio One In Concert, 24 June 1972
Label: BBC Windsong
Release date: 1992 (Included on the BBC Radio 1 Live in Concert compilation CD)

There has been some debate over the correct recording and broadcast dates of this *In Concert* programme, as the BBC had it listed as 21 July, and Stackridge's erstwhile manager Mike Tobin had a cassette copy of the recording dated 15 June with a broadcast date of 24 June. Research has tended to bear out Tobin's claims, as this writer remembers listening to the *In Concert* broadcast on a transistor radio whilst queuing for the Status Quo/Malaka gig at Dagenham Roundhouse, which did indeed take place on 24 June. The BBC is somewhat notorious for temporal confusion, so all evidence indicates that we now have the correct recording and broadcast dates.

'Teatime' (Walter, Davis)

A slight feedback problem is in evidence on this recording of 'Teatime', and the flute is very high in the mix, with Mutter Slater over-blowing slightly in places. James Warren's vocalising is also wayward, and his obvious pitching difficulties are another indicator that perhaps the band encountered monitoring problems at this gig. The occasional overblow aside, Slater's flute is as moving as ever, and this remains the best-recorded example of his classic wheeling flute over the decelerating closing sequence: sadly omitted from the studio version. Mike Evans throws in some wonderful violin solo improvisation in the coda section too, including an exquisite high trill.

'Lummy Days' (Davis)

Taken at a galloping pace, the band's theme tune is a lot faster than the studio recording, and really bounces along during the marching sections. It differs from the *Friendliness* version on the seesawing parts that link into the middle movement and occur again before the final few bars – on the album, these were played on piano then cello, but here are performed solely on Andy Davis' Mellotron. The flawlessly executed violin solo on the gentler central tract is ample illustration of what a high calibre and reliable musician Mike Evans could be: hardly ever less than perfect and a priceless asset to any band. Slater's flute cartwheels on the half-speed section are way up front in the mix, and the tuba-like parp on the final exclamation mark accentuates the irrepressible humour that was the hallmark of early Stackridge.

'Amazingly Agnes' (Warren)

As 'Amazingly Agnes' starts, James Warren informs us that the words are 'very important' but we 'probably won't be able to hear them': a common-enough occurrence with early 1970s PA systems. The piping flute on the intro of this lazy reggae shuffle is a major difference from the studio version, but Mutter Slater soon puts it down to concentrate on his whoopee whistle, woodblock and cymbal contributions, also throwing in some scat rhythm vocalising behind Warren's lead on the second half of the verses. By the time of my first Stackridge gig a few weeks later, 'Agnes' was bidding farewell to the live setlist, and I only witnessed this number performed once, and have a memory of Mike Evans also joining in the percussive mayhem along with Slater. More suspect pitching is in evidence from James Warren, but this improves a tad when Andy Davis joins him on the later verses for some solid vocal harmonies. There is no *a cappella* break on the last couplet as on the studio take, with the band skanking through behind the vocals instead. After a shout of 'One more time', the chanting coda comes to an end, and Davis adds an electric piano chord as an afterthought.

'32 West Mall' (Davis, Warren)

Andy Davis' guitar accompaniment on '32 West Mall' ushers in a gentler interlude, with lush three-part harmonies from Davis, Warren and Slater: very much a feature of that first Stackridge album. After his initial harmony verse, Slater gives a slight cough, then brings out his various bird whistles, tootling behind Davis' vocal. On the final chorus, he throws in some rhythmic vocal interjections, along with Davis' guitar parts.

'She Taught Me How To Yodel' (Roberts, Emerson, Sciver)

Mutter Slater next announces the 'Michael Evans vocal talent spot' to the audience with the mispronunciation 'Opportunity Knacks', and we are treated to Evans' unique rendition of 'She Taught Me How to Yodel', in which he eschews the 1962 Frank Ifield reading of this tune (which was originally written in 1941) for an impromptu one of his own. Frank does get a nod, though, in a snatch from his big hit 'I Remember You'. Slater chips in along with Evans on the first yodel but wisely gives up, leaving him to go on and scale the heights, utilising his impressive yodelling skills, including an unbelievably high final note as his performance is swiftly followed by mass hysteria from the audience! I saw the band perform this number live just once – on my first Stackridge gig in July 1972, before the Mike Evans' vocal feature was changed to a cover of 'Twist and Shout', performed Beatles-style of course.

The Man in the Bowler Hat (1974)

Personnel:
Andy Davis: guitars, keyboards, percussion, vocals
Mutter Slater: flute, keyboards, percussion, vocals
James Warren: guitar, vocals
Mike Evans: violin, vocals
Crun Walter: bass
Billy Sparkle: drums
George Martin: piano ('Humiliation') and orchestration
Derek Taylor: horn
Jack Emblow: accordion
Ray Davies: trumpet, cornet
B. Lamb: trombone
M. Fry: tuba
R. Chamberlain: clarinet, saxophones
Andy Mackay: saxophone ('Dangerous Bacon')
String quartet on 'Humiliation' – Reg Leopold: violin, William Reid: violin, Graeme Scott: viola, Vivian Joseph: cello
Recorded: AIR Studios, London, July to September 1973
Producer: George Martin
Engineers: Bill Price, Denny Bridges
Label: MCA
Release dates: 24 January 1974 (MCA), 1996 (Edsel/Demon CD), 2007 (Angel Air CD)

The classic lineup of Stackridge were in full flow as 1973 dawned, and much new material was emerging in the live set alongside the established favourites. The year started with the return of Crun Walter on 10 January after his appendix operation, when Stackridge supported Wishbone Ash at the Rainbow Theatre in Finsbury Park, London. The Newham Thrashers were there, and we unfurled our 'Welcome Back Crun' banner halfway back in the stalls as Stackridge took the stage.

There were many great and crazy gigs throughout 1973 as the band continued to expand their horizons, introducing seven new numbers into the set as the year progressed. The gig at the Marquee on 6 February saw the first set change when a trio of new songs appeared: 'The Lyder Loo', 'The Galloping Gaucho' and 'The Road To Venezuela', played in sequence mid-set. Later that week, at the Cooks Ferry Inn gig in Edmonton, we were treated to the glorious new instrumental 'God Speed The Plough', which saw Billy Sparkle making full use of his tympanis. It wasn't until the gig at The Greyhound, Croydon, on 17 June that the final trio of new tunes were unveiled: 'Fundamentally Yours', 'The Last Plimsoll' and 'Dolores'. In traditional Stackridge fashion, this material evolved as it went along, and five of these tunes ended up on the album. Another was eventually released from a BBC session ('The Lyder Loo') and one was never officially released, although it featured on a Radio One session that summer ('Dolores').

Before all this, back in January, the initial sessions for the 'Do The Stanley' b/w 'C'est La Vie' single took place with Bill Price as their new sound engineer, assisted by Denny Bridges: indicating that these were the band's first recording sessions at AIR London Studios. These two engineers were then domiciled there, and both later worked with the band alongside producer George Martin on *The Man in the Bowler Hat*. Exactly when George Martin became involved with the band is something of a grey area, but the sessions for the two single cuts were produced by the group themselves, and by the summer, Stackridge were rumoured to be recording a concept album planned to be called *The Road to Venezuela* and were presumably self-producing as they went. These sessions eventually collapsed, and by July, the band were ensconced in AIR London Studios with George Martin at the helm and well under way with what we all hoped would be their magnum opus and big commercial breakthrough album.

History, however, had different ideas, and even before the album was completed, it had been announced that Mutter Slater and Billy Sparkle would be leaving the band, and the classic lineup looked as if it was coming to an end. The first I heard of this devastating news was at the Reading Festival when Stackridge performed in the middle of a bill topped by Genesis on 26 August 1973. Billy Sparkle left first and was replaced by John White for a short period, with Mutter Slater still intact as the band fulfilled their date sheet and left a memento of this short-lived lineup variation in the form of a September 1973 performance for HTV: an ITV franchise for Wales and the West Country. This live session was eventually made available via a freebie CD with *The Rhubarbarian* fanzine and shows the band sounding incredibly tight but also somewhat uptight, running through some of their usual set selections. The CD includes an interesting rehearsal snippet of the band practising a new Andy Davis tune as he plays it to them on piano while shouting out the chords, which evolved into 'The Volunteer' – more about this song later in this chapter. The rehearsal version provides a fascinating insight into the band's working methods in learning new pieces. John White's tenure behind the kit was brief. By October, he was out of the picture, claiming that his legs had turned to wood after dabbling in the occult! By the time *The Man in the Bowler Hat* was finally released on 24 January 1974, the classic lineup had ceased to exist, and a new transitional lineup hit the road to promote the third Stackridge album, more of which later.

The cover artwork for the album was prepared by John Kosh, and consists of a front cover photograph by John Swannell of a Julie Andrews-type female figure wearing a bowler hat and clad in a pink pinafore as she approaches across a grassy meadow, backed with a golden tinted horizon and dark clouds glowering overhead. The band name is in black, written across this darkling sky, and slashed across the bottom right-hand corner of the sleeve is a red diagonal stripe with 'Inside: The Man in the Bowler Hat' written across it in black. The rumours at the time were that the female figure in the photo was actually one of the band's male road managers in drag: namely Alistair Rainsford. The rear of the gatefold sleeve is plain white with printed credits and song lyrics all over it. Opening up the gatefold, there are portraits of the six band members, separated by rectangles of a raffia basketwork design. Dave Borthwick's colour-tinted photos of Mutter Slater (pale yellow), Mike Evans (pink) and Crun Walter (blue) work best, while the photos of Andy Davis, Billy Sparkle and James Warren are in full colour. In Warren's photo, there's a mysterious chap in a bowler hat in the foreground: possibly the one advertised by the red slash on the front cover. For me, as a piece of artwork, the *Bowler Hat* cover lacks the warmth and charm of the *Friendliness* sleeve. A much larger budget had been thrown at this third Stackridge album than had been available for the first two though, mainly due to George Martin's involvement, I would guess, as MCA had hoped this would be the band's breakthrough album. Sparkle's exit and Slater's defection scuppered that possibility, but it still contains many fine examples of the band's very best music.

'Fundamentally Yours' (Davis, Smegmakovitch)

Preceding the album release by several months, 'Fundamentally Yours' had already seen action as the B-side of the 'The Galloping Gaucho' single and opens *The Man in the Bowler Hat* in some style. Beginning life as an Andy Davis knock-around on piano, its genesis was witnessed by various Newham Thrashers (including myself) in the dressing room at Cooks Ferry Inn, Edmonton, after the band's February-1973 gig there. Sporting a Beatlesque swagger, this George Martin-produced version motors along smartly, propelled by a sterling performance from the Walter/Sparkle rhythm section, on which the bass swoops and punches with consummate ease while Sparkle turns in one of his finest percussive displays on record. Atop this secure foundation, Andy Davis rocks the track along on his piano – further solidifying the bedrock for James Warren's rhythmic guitar punctuations and Mike Evans' filigree violin swirls, to decorate the sonic landscape. A fetching harpsichord part completes the picture, and the effect on the listener is akin to rummaging in an aural jewelry box with finely-detailed musical gemstones being uncovered at every turn of Martin's delicate-yet-brittle arrangement. The distinctive intro, with its repeated double clap-along piano chords, leads into a heartfelt Warren vocal on this breathlessly wordy song. The mysterious Smegmakovitch writing credit was explained by Warren in a radio interview at the time as an attempt at a joint lyrical effort between himself, Mutter Slater and Crun Walter. But it later emerged that the truth of the matter appeared to be that Smegmakovitch was in fact, more likely just Walter himself. Warren's endorsement of the Smegmakovitch name as a joint writing credit may possibly have been a cosmetic agreement between the band members for a more democratic share of royalties, than being the bald truth. Essentially a song about writing a letter,

'Fundamentally Yours' is perhaps an attempt to articulate the inadequacies of words and the limitations of language when it comes to expressing complex emotions, often leading to miscommunication of ideas.

'Pinafore Days' (Slater, Smegmakovitch)

The Man in the Bowler Hat saw the rise of Mutter Slater as a main writer for the band. His compositional contributions to the first two albums had been negligible, but here he blossoms into a writer of some promise. Three of the tunes are solely his, and he's also part of the group credit: the anagrammatic Wabadaw Sleeve on the album's final track 'God Speed The Plough'.

'Pinafore Days' is a glorious little tune, owing a debt to the waltzing Strauss dynasty in its triple-time construction. George Martin's regard for this particular recording was demonstrated a quarter of a century down the line when he selected it as the Stackridge contribution to his career-spanning retrospective box set *Fifty Years in Recording*. Given the full Martin orchestral treatment, 'Pinafore Days' is yet another collection of sonic delights, as the tuba, horns, glockenspiel and Slater's flute, eddy and flow beneath a somewhat deadpan but nevertheless charming vocal by Mike Evans. Various features of the lyric are illustrated by onomatopoeic sound effects, such as bouncing dickey birds and a bell striking one o'clock, adding to the charm quotient. The endearing lyric appears to be a pining for a lost innocence as a parade of very English imagery passes before our ears, recalling mugs, buttercups, spats, dancing crinoline and the like. High on whimsy, 'Pinafore Days' also scores in the poignancy stakes, courtesy of its affecting chorus with its evocation of 'Sketching phantoms drawn from the years', as we look sadly back at lost youth and happier, more-carefree days.

'The Last Plimsoll' (Davis, Smegmakovitch)

This Andy Davis tune lends credence to the statement by Mike Evans in the HTV interviews recorded at the time that the writing bias in 1973 was more on upbeat piano-led songs, rather than the guitar-oriented compositions of earlier years. A real stomper, 'The Last Plimsoll' allegedly emerged from a comment made by Crun Walter at a particular gig when he expressed a desire to 'Massacre the audience down to the last plimsoll', and there were also early indications from James Warren that the lyric for this number originally concerned vegetarianism: a fad favoured by Walter at the time. All that changed as the tune developed, and the final lyric is a somewhat flippant skit on gangsters.

There's nothing lightweight about the arrangement, though, and the gravitas of 'The Last Plimsoll' lies almost entirely within the music. Another effective George Martin production nicely highlights the strengths of this segmented tune, beginning with an archetypal Stackridge riff on Andy Davis' piano, leading into a dynamic guitar-heavy hook line and a verse sung in his patent downbeat style, underpinned by a walking bass line from Walter. Some tick-tock clock effects seem to indicate that time is running out for someone in gangster land in the second half of the verses, before Warren chips in on the chorus harmonies, along with some handclaps, raising the aural temperature a few degrees.

The more complex middle section building up towards Mutter Slater's flute solo, is pure delight, as the intro riff returns then develops and modulates through a skilful arrangement, eventually morphing into a stalking bass line from Walter, along with some heavy breathing from Davis as the gangsters presumably pursue him down some back alley until a scream signals the arrival of the flute solo. Not as explosive as its live variants and perhaps slightly under-represented in the mix, it is nevertheless a peerless example of Slater's talent as a flautist. After the harmonised coda, Slater continues to improvise, and Mike Evans' violin contributions – while subtle – are beautifully judged, and add to the unique atmosphere of this track: especially his Grapelli-like quote towards the end of this section. A return to the intro riff – this time cleverly lifted from a minor to a major key – makes a perfect denouement to the track. The whistle blown on the very last note signifies that the forces of law and order have arrived at last but possibly too late.

'To The Sun And Moon' (Slater, Denman)

Originally sporting James Warren lyrics and known as 'There Is No Moon', these were subsequently discarded and this Slater tune ended up being welded to a poem by Peter Denman. Sung in a ridiculously high register by Warren (to the detriment of his diction), the marriage of music and words is rather less than effective. The tune is certainly pleasant enough, and George Martin adds some keening strings and a French horn: the solo from the latter being the high point of the track. In a Rhubarb Thrashers newsletter at the time of release, Warren credits Walter with 'intergalactic wah-wah bass' on this track, though little evidence of its cosmic import can be discerned among the rather claustrophobic strings running like syrup over the arrangement. The first slight disappointment of the album – although a nice tune – the finished recording is something of a filler track in such illustrious company.

'The Road to Venezuela' (Davis, Smegmakovitch)

Originally to be the title track to the third album, 'The Road To Venezuela' is undoubtedly a Stackridge classic. The fade-out of the strings on the previous track leads into some fine Andy Davis fingerpicking on acoustic guitar, foreshadowing the chords before the intro to the song begins. This segue was sadly split with a gap when the album was mastered for CD in the 1990s, which was a pity.

Something of an exception on this album, this is very much a guitar song and was obviously written on this instrument by Davis. Crun Walter's salty lyric is watered down slightly for public consumption, as the reference to 'consorting with a whore' in the final verse becomes a more innocuous 'walk along the shore'. Strongly recalling The Beatles again, the acoustic bias of this arrangement is underscored by Walter's athletic bass, as Billy Sparkle lays back on the beat in economical style, giving the track a nice sense of space, leaving ample room for *Marvellous Mutt* on castanets and tambourine to display his percussive skills. Davis' slightly doleful vocal is lifted a notch – as always – when James Warren joins him on the later choruses to harmonise, and Mike Evans' violin is a major feature of this track, especially the Latinate punctuations that follow the verses. Opting for a double-tracked violin solo on the energised middle section – rather than the more-tuneful live variant – Evans' manic sawing leads into a dramatic drop in dynamics, as the arrangement falls back to a sequence of harmonics played by Davis on his acoustic, with sweet violin leading back into the spirit-lifting sequence of the last verse and the even higher liftoff of that oh-so-sing-a-long chorus.

Inspired by the *Road to...* series of films featuring Bob Hope, Bing Crosby and Dorothy Lamour, 'The Road To Venezuela' was originally intended to be the springboard for a South American-slanted concept album – presumably chronicling the adventures of 'The Galloping Gaucho' – until the band ran out of conceptual imagination on said project, leaving the songs to fend for themselves as separate entities. Whether the protagonist of 'The Road To Venezuela' is the gaucho himself or not, is best left to the listener's imagination, as the 40,000-mile journey in search of the millionairess unfolds, and characters such as magician Chan Canasta and comic-strip character Jungle Jim make an appearance amongst the flora and fauna of the Pampas and the rarified air of the Andes: where llamas will forever 'fly above the blue lagoon'.

'The Galloping Gaucho' (Slater, Smegmakovitch)

The sparkling single that preceded the album by several months, to my mind 'The Galloping Gaucho' is the ultimate neglected pop classic of the 1970s. Unsurprisingly though, it failed to ignite the charts, but maybe it would've stood a better chance had it received the airplay its quality merited. Reviewed by *Sounds* as 'Outsider of the week', and championed by Stuart Henry on Radio One at the time, it was a slightly crazy single release, as Mutter Slater – the singer of said song – had just quit the band. Whether he would've been tempted back if the single had galloped up the charts is a moot question.

A wonderful start to side two of the album, 'Gaucho' is one of Slater's cleverest tunes, opening as it does with the melody perched atop a diminished chord. This unusual compositional device lends the track a distinctive, lurching gait. The melodic and harmonic structure is shown off to perfection by George Martin's delicious arrangement, taking in organ, horn, trumpet, cornet, tuba and accordion, in addition to a tighter-than-tight group performance, and all wrapped up in a matrix of swirling fairground Wurlitzer. All the fun of the fair indeed! There are some lovely touches to Martin's arrangement as it wends its way through this marvellous tune, executing a perfectly weighted buildup with exquisite attention to dynamics *en route*.

Of particular note are session player Jack Emblow's cascading accordion runs on the left side of the stereo mix on the second verse, and a peerless brass arrangement on the final verse, highlighting a glorious melody: counterpoint to the main tune. As Slater's flute leads the band into a perfect classical cadence to wrap up the track, all you can do is stand and applaud really. Praise should also be apportioned for the band performances here – the Walter/Sparkle rhythm section has rarely been recorded as well as on this album, with 'Gaucho' being a particularly shining example of their watertight rhythmic combination as they meld to lay the most secure of foundations for this tricky tune. Walter's chromatic rise under the final stanza of the last verse is an absolute masterstroke, and he has seldom sounded as ruthlessly efficient on the bass as he does here. Sparkle also has a chance to get his triangle into action during the piping intro, being an instrument favoured by him in the early years, and had actually featured in the credits on the band's eponymous debut album a few years earlier. Andy Davis' piano again drives the forward momentum of the track, while Slater's fluttering flute rides atop the grand orchestral flow and Mike Evans' violin curlicues add to the cantering effect of the tumbling carnival-flavoured instrumental interludes. A further interesting rhythmic quirk is the inspired five-beat bar that leads into the instrumental breaks, enhancing the freewheeling feel of these passages. James Warren's guitar contributions are understated on this more piano-led track, but he can also be heard along with Davis on backing vocals. The music hall influence is obvious, as is the joy that flows from this tune: a shaft of pure sunlight in a world oft-plunged in self-absorbed misery. This slightly daffy tale is light of heart and fleet of foot: undoubtedly like the gaucho himself.

'Humiliation' (Warren)

Having been the dominant writer on the first two Stackridge albums, James Warren's contributions to this third album had been strangely curtailed to just two tracks, aside from whatever input he had on the group composition 'God Speed The Plough'. Here we find him in ballad mode, offering a typically-convoluted melody over an impressive, somewhat sprawling but ultimately logical chord sequence. Compared to other tracks on the album, the arrangement is stripped down to just Warren's vocal, George Martin's piano, and a string quartet recalling Martin's work on Paul McCartney's 'Yesterday'. The only other musical feature is a horn solo in place of a middle verse.

The lyrics comment on the human condition and come over as well-meaning, if slightly earnest, and when combined with the arrangement, evince a slightly mournful feel, all the more so for following the ebullient 'Gaucho'. Warren's vocal performance is characteristically stratospheric in his best choirboy style, and for the most part is seamlessly imparted, aside from a touch of suspect pitching on the last line of the second repeat of the middle eight. Although a pretty-enough melody, I admit to never having found 'Humiliation' too endearing – its confessional style being at odds with the bulk of the band's more traditional storytelling bias. But as a change of pace and mood in the context of the album, it has its place.

'Dangerous Bacon' (Warren, Smegmakovitch)

As simple as the previous track was intricate, 'Dangerous Bacon' comes over as something of an early-Beatles tribute, and actually name-checks the fab four in the lyric. As opposed to the last Warren tune, this one rocks along, and is recorded as a straight-down-the-line group performance, complete with a four-beat hi-hat count in, then straight into the lyrics. The whole track has a somewhat blatant four-square feel, and the sax solo – played by Andy Mackay from Roxy Music – is similarly unsubtle and reminds me of an old 1970s TV advert for a company called International ('Nice people and nice places, Inter-nat-ion-al'), although I have no recollection of what was being advertised: possibly furniture.

The best musical feature is a surprisingly muscular guitar solo on the coda that – although uncharacteristic of Warren at the time – is probably played by him. The lyric – in the first two verses at least – alludes to growing up in the 1960s and contains some entertaining couplets. The last verse appears to expand to a more global ecological view, and shows traces of Crun Walter's vegetarian manifesto of the time, with some fabulous lines. With an excellent last verse supported by some creamy Beach Boys-style backing vocals and that tough guitar coda, 'Dangerous Bacon' is a track that gets better as it goes along. It certainly livens up side two of the album, and proves to be the perfect antidote after the slightly lugubrious effect of 'Humiliation'.

'The Indifferent Hedgehog' (Davis, Smith)

A surprise inclusion on the album, this Andy Davis tune of childlike simplicity appeared from nowhere, never having featured in the Stackridge live set up to that point. Vying with 'To The Sun And Moon' for being the album's weakest track, 'Hedgehog' features a somewhat croaky Davis vocal over a piano track akin to finger exercises, and a picked acoustic guitar. James Warren's enlightening, tongue-in-cheek comment in a contemporary Rhubarb Thrashers newsletter explained that the band obtained the vocal effect by 'jamming Andrew's head in a combine harvester'. I bet they had a job getting that into AIR London studios! Whatever, the results are certainly less than enthralling, and well below the standards we'd come to expect from the band. The placement of 'Hedgehog' immediately prior to the majestic 'God Speed The Plough' is the only error of judgement in the album's track programming by George Martin, opening as it does with a brace of piano chords with a similar feel to the superior 'Plough'. The only delightful moment comes in the coda, where the guitar imitates a dulcimer with an ear-pleasing rolling effect that really suits the tune. It's just a pity this didn't happen earlier, to lift the spirit of the track, and unfortunately, the poor old 'Indifferent Hedgehog' remains one of the least celebrated of the animalistic inhabitants of the Stackridge universe.

'God Speed The Plough' (Wabadaw Sleeve)

The grand finale of the third album is credited as a band composition under the pseudonym Wabadaw Sleeve: a group-composition moniker previously used in the credits of the single 'Do The Stanley'. However, the two Wabadaw Sleeve compositions couldn't have been more different from each other.

The main theme is a tune that Mutter Slater came up with that was developed by Andy Davis, presumably with some arrangement ideas thrown in from the rest of the band. 'God Speed The Plough' had been a feature of the live set for most of 1973, and had developed as a showcase for Slater's flute and Mike Evans' violin. Another of the band's bold orchestral statements, the descending chord sequence from the second half of the theme that opens and closes the piece, sports a few bars that recall Beethoven's 'Piano Sonata No.8 – Pathetique (2nd movement)'. This is especially evident on the intro as Slater joins in on glockenspiel alongside Davis' piano on the first section, before the sweetest of violin passages over a two-chord modulation links the gentle opening statements to the energised middle section. On this storming passage, Slater shines as never before, with some octave-dipping flute over a brash, tympani-laden backing, his flute keening and wheeling like a flock of starlings breaking over a brooding English landscape as the storm clouds ominously build. Then, as the tempest breaks, Evans' violin saws a savage furrow through the proceedings, with a Mellotron choir stoking up the tension in the background. Martin's superb orchestration ensures that the track swells to a magnificent climax, and as the ascending choir head for the heavens, the storm subsides into a gentle triple-time restatement of the opening theme. Then, the tympani rolls once more as a full orchestra takes up the main theme in all its grandiosity. With progressive rock written all over it, 'God Speed The Plough' is a fabulous reflection of its time, combining a classical influence with the adventurous spirit then abroad in rock, creating a timeless recording of great beauty.

Although disarmingly simple in construction, 'God Speed The Plough' wins out on the atmosphere it generates in conjuring up mental pictures of the English countryside: 'reminiscent of Hardy's Dorset' as a *Melody Maker* reviewer put it. In a contemporary Rhubarb Thrashers newsletter, it was referred to by James Warren under the less evocative title 'God Speed The Launderette'.

In many ways signalling the end of the first Stackridge era, this marvellous tone poem closes their third album in some style.

Related Songs

'Do The Stanley' (Wabadaw Sleeve)

First appearing in the live set towards the end of 1972, 'Do The Stanley' was the ultimate easy-to-do dance-craze number that slotted seamlessly into the Stackridge mythology. The idea for the song started on a road journey in the group van on the way to one of their many gigs in 1972, when Mutter Slater commented that there didn't appear to be many dance-craze songs written these days. This soon solidified into someone saying, 'Why don't we write one for a single then?'. So Slater had a think and soon set to work on this task. Although credited under the Wabadaw Sleeve moniker, it was indeed a Slater composition that the rest of the band chipped in on.

The live version would feature Mike Evans' reeling violin jigging around the melody, but when it came to recording 'Stanley' as a single, the live arrangement was dropped in favour of a brass band feel, which suited the tune admirably. With a big, brash sound, 'Do the Stanley' was presumably tailored with the hope of airplay, but apart from hearing it on *The Jimmy Young Show* on Radio One once, it was noticeable by its absence as far as national radio went. A rumour went around at the time that a mention of the Queen in the lyrics had instigated a radio ban, although how much truth there was to this story is debatable. With its bright, blaring brass and throaty up-front Slater vocal, 'Do The Stanley' is certainly hard to ignore and has had its detractors, even among Thrashers. But with its bold, slow march rhythm and baton-twirling demeanour, its lineage is clearly that of the marching band. In my view, it's actually one of the great brass band tunes of its era, and with better exposure would probably be in the repertoire of brass bands up and down the country, along with 'The Floral Dance' and the like.

'C'est La Vie' (Warren, Davis)

Under its original title, 'Tealeaf In The Snow' – a line extracted from the Warren lyric – this number was demoed sometime during the winter of 1972/1973. Evolving from that early, heavier version, it gained a chorus, ended up as 'C'est La Vie' and was released as the B-side of the 'Do The Stanley' single on 23 February 1973. A delightfully delicate recording, the first verses of this tender ballad consist of a Warren vocal supported solely by Andy Davis' classical-flavoured, finger-picked guitar. The lovelorn lyrics stay just the right side of mushy, and suit this very pretty tune to a tee; the phrasing of the triple-time melody giving the lyric a personal, conversational feel that draws the listener into the story. The stark verse opens up into a gorgeous spread of three-part harmony backing vocals on the first chorus, accompanied by tambourine. Warren's vocal is harmonised on the verse following this chorus, the higher line skimming the very top of his range with some of the most vertiginous vocals he's ever recorded, while a casual harpsichord-style line shadows the vocal melody. Mike Evans' violin weaves counterpoint around the main tune in this verse. The final chorus sees Crun Walter exposing his softer side as he plays some piping recorder along with the backing vocal lines. On the second half of this chorus, there is a bouncing, shimmering effect on the left-hand side of the stereo picture, where the track seems to go slightly hazy – the reason for this remains a mystery. 'C'est La Vie' is another of those overlooked Stackridge gems that will repay your attention – Davis' feather-light Flamenco guitar finale being of particular note: proof if it were needed of his brilliance on this instrument.

This track was later included on the *Do the Stanley* compilation LP released in 1976, as well as appearing on the Edsel/Demon CD re-release of *Bowler Hat* in 1996 and the Angel Air CD re-release of *Friendliness* in 2007.

'Let There Be Lids' (Trad arr. Evans)

The band's live dustbin lid extravaganza 'Let There Be Lids' is a medley of the traditional Celtic reel 'Four Poster Bed' and the ever-accelerating train ride of Ervin T. Rouse' 1938 fiddle tune 'Orange Blossom Special'. Mike Evans' frantic violin-playing is accompanied by Mutter Slater, Crun Walter and the band's roadie Pete Donovan bashing metal dustbin lids together as percussion. The studio version was recorded during the summer of 1973 at AIR London during sessions for the aborted concept-album project *The Road to Venezuela*. At the time, it was rumoured that a new single called 'The Lyder Loo' was planned, with 'Let There Be Lids' as its B-side, but this never emerged. 'Let There Be Lids' however was eventually released as a bonus track on the *Do the Stanley* compilation album in 1976 as well as the 1997 Edsel/Demon CD re-release of *Bowler Hat* and, as a bonus track on the 2006 Angel Air re-release of the *Stackridge* album. A band-produced recording and the only surviving artefact from those summer sessions, it is something of a disappointment and definitely lacks the fluidity of feel displayed so often live and on various bootleg versions. The band sound rather tired on this rendition, despite Mutter Slater and Crun Walter's attempts at livening it up with some yokel banter. Unusually, even Evans' violin intonation sounds less than perfect and Billy Sparkle doesn't sound his usual self either as they strive to replicate the electricity generated in front of an audience. Matters are not helped by the inclusion of that so-called instrument, the whistle (the kind referees use, not the pennywhistle), blown at indiscriminate points.

1973 Radio Broadcast

Personnel:
Andy Davis: banjo, piano, Mellotron, guitar, vocals
James Warren: guitar, vocals
Mutter Slater: flageolet, flute, percussion, vocals
Mike Evans: violin
Crun Walter: bass
Billy Sparkle: drums, percussion
Recorded: BBC Langham, Studio 1, London, 7 February 1973
Producer: Pete Ritzema
Broadcast: Bob Harris Show, Radio One
Label: BBC Worldwide/Strange Fruit
Release date: 1997 (Included on The Radio One Sessions compilation CD)

A good measure of what a forward-thinking band Stackridge were in the early-1970s can be gained by a study of the material they put forward for their various radio sessions at the time. For their Radio One session four months prior to this one, they'd performed four tracks from the then-unreleased new album *Friendliness,* and for their session in January 1973, had chosen another two as-yet-unavailable songs amongst the four they performed. For this Bob Harris session, they offered four more freshly-minted tunes. As a gauge of just how new these numbers were at the time is the fact that the first hearing most Thrashers had of them in the Stackridge live set was at the Marquee gig on the day before this session was recorded.

'The Lyder Loo' (Davis, Warren)

The first of this quartet of new material is 'The Lyder Loo' – a song title that had been mentioned by Mutter Slater in an earlier *Melody Maker* interview, when he described the lyrics as evocative of a place 'like Shangri-La', postulating it as a serious song pondering the concept of Utopia, the title then being spelt 'Lida Loo'. Somewhere along the line, this concept underwent a drastic change and the final lyrics concerned the foolhardiness of smoking. They are allied to an unabashed jaunty tune, and a dark humour shines through in the extremely catchy chorus of 'Lyder Loo, it's killing you'. This version of 'The Lyder Loo' is extremely well-recorded, with Andy Davis' banjo panned to the left-hand side, and Slater's flageolet introduction to the right. The dynamics of the arrangement are spot on, as Crun Walter's bass enters at the first chorus along with Mike Evans' dancing violin figures on the left-hand side, giving the track a great build.

The amusing lyrics lay it on the line for the unfortunate smokers among us, and that killer chorus just makes you want to join in and sing along. It sounds like Slater harmonising along with Davis on the choruses, between his bouts of 'flageo-lation' where he blows on his pennywhistles for all he's worth! Billy Sparkle's restrained contribution of just bass drum and tambourine is noteworthy and is quite perfect in its simplicity. After the final chorus, Slater gives a trill, and his slight overblow on the last flageolet phrase just adds to the live feel of this fun-filled performance.

One of the questions that surround this particular song is the authorship of it. The credits on the BBC release list it as a Davis/Warren composition, but I strongly recall James Warren telling us at the time that the lyrics were by Crun Walter, and they certainly sound like they come from the bearded bass player himself. The fact that Andy Davis sings it, suggests to me that it may be a tune he knocked out on his banjo, then paired it with the lyric of his usual writing partner Walter's. The band themselves don't seem to be able to agree on who created this number. There have even been suggestions that Slater may have been involved, but the debate rages on, and the mystery surrounding authorship of this enigmatic tune remains.

'God Speed The Plough' (Wabadaw Sleeve)

The band's second new offering was their first major new instrumental since 'Lummy Days' initially graced their live repertoire many moons before. This performance most closely resembles the live version so loved by Thrashers during 1973, before George Martin's heavily orchestrated arrangement for the third album was conceived. The Beethoven-influenced opening passage on Andy Davis' piano is here accompanied by Mutter Slater playing a repeating two-note glockenspiel motif on the first beat of each bar, and the tempo is taken at a deathly-slow pace in this section. As the energised middle part takes flight, Slater's flute can be heard on the left and Mike Evans' violin to the right of the stereo picture, session producer Pete Ritzema doing a grand job on the engineering front. As the violin solo arrives, the tempo accelerates into it, and Evans impresses with some fluent and very high-octave improvisation. When the tune dips into the gentler triple-time restatement of the opening theme, Billy Sparkle adds some three-beat tympani rolls before his last protracted roll sounding like thunder and merging into the grand reprise of this theme, led by Davis' Mellotron, along with the flute and violin. A triangle from Sparkle on the final chord closes this early version of 'God Speed The Plough', which serves as a reminder of how the live version sounded back in early 1973.

'The Road To Venezuela' (Davis, Smegmakovitch)

With their full eclecticism on display during these sessions, Stackridge switch to a new Andy Davis tune with a distinctly Beatlesque feel. This differs from later versions in that Davis is clearly on electric rhythm guitar rather than the softer feel of later acoustic variants. James Warren appears to add some harmony guitar riffs on his electric, along with Mike Evans' Latin-flavoured violin punctuations, and Warren also lends his harmony vocals to the later choruses, hitting some extremely high notes on the wordless coda harmonies. An indication of how early a version this is can be heard by the fact that Evans' violin solo is entirely absent – presumably not having yet evolved – and the central tract here consists of Davis' guitar harmonics, Evans' descending violin lines and Mutter Slater's understated percussion.

'The Galloping Gaucho' (Slater, Smegmakovitch)

Another song yet to evolve into its final form was 'The Galloping Gaucho', this being the earliest available version. With a much longer piano introduction that runs through the entire verse chord sequence, and with Crun Walter's bass sliding seductively around underneath, it's topped off by some comical, almost hornpipe-like electric guitar from James Warren. Billy Sparkle's cymbal punctuations are more-pronounced on this early performance, and it gives the track an odd loping feel. Andy Davis' descending piano glissandi lend a forward momentum as the track progresses, and Mike Evans' sawing violin parts complete the picture. The linking jig parts are played in unison by violin, flute and electric guitar, with Evans throwing in a very high-octave slide indeed after the second instrumental interlude. The full tale of the dashing gaucho has not yet fully matured, and the final verse is just a straight repeat of the first one. No classical cadence from the flute is evident on this early version either, and what sounds like a harmonium can be heard on the closing chords of the song.

1973 Radio Broadcast

Recorded: Paris Theatre, Regent Street, London
Date: January 1973
Producer: Jeff Griffin
Broadcast: BBC In Concert, Radio One
Date: 15 February 1973
Record Label: BBC Windsong
Released: 1992 (included on the BBC Radio 1 Live In Concert compilation CD)

'Anyone For Tennis' (Warren)

Only two recordings from this concert are included on the BBC Windsong release, and 'Anyone For Tennis' is the first. Andy Davis hits a real clunker on the piano introduction, to howls from members of the audience. James Warren's pitching is all over the place, too, as he struggles with the key on this tune, losing it completely on the word 'mining' when his voice cracks. Mutter Slater, though, turns in a fine performance on his woodblock, cymbal and whistle, and as the number ends, he yells out 'Wakey, Wakey!' in best Billy Cotton-style, followed by the usual thrash through the 1918 Leo Wood tune 'Somebody Stole My Gal', where he beats the hell out of his cymbal while scatting the vocal along with Mike Evans' violin. This amiable piece of nonsense ends with an impressive snare press-roll from Billy Sparkle and a bounce around the kit: cue mass hysteria from the assembled Thrashers!

'Syracuse The Elephant' (Walter, Davis)

Before Stackridge commence 'Syracuse The Elephant', Bob Harris announces a dedication to the Kingston, Guildford and Bathampton mobs to the great delight of various members of these aggregations. The first of the BBC's savage edits see the intro ripped apart as the opening chords cut crudely into the last of Mutter Slater's intro flute flurries and Andy Davis' vocal. The Mellotron sounds slightly out of tune with the guitar, but there's a perfect violin solo from Mike Evans as always on the middle section, and as this leads into the modulation, there's a prominent dodgy bass note from a slightly distracted Crun Walter.

As it goes quiet – anticipating the entry of the waltz passage – Slater approaches the mic, and someone in the audience yells 'Wait for it!', anticipating Slater's usual stage comment in this quiet dip, and he replies, 'You've spoilt it all now' with a crowd response of a collective 'Ah!'. Some loose piano chords in the waltz section indicate that Andy Davis is definitely having one of those days, and as the jungle arrangement commences, he temporarily swaps his piano for some hand-held bells to add to that jungle-fresh flavour. With full Mellotron chords under the final verse, the progressive rock feel is very much in evidence, and as the song ends, the boom-mic that swings out over the audience is just over my head and I let out the loudest yell of appreciation possible: to later boom out of radios across the land!

Unfortunately, when the BBC took these tracks for inclusion on the Windsong compilation CD, they completely cut out my passionate bellow, annoyingly replacing nearly all the applause between tracks with the same edit taken from a later 1975 concert. Spoilsports!

The Transitional Lineup: October 1973 to April 1974

With Mutter Slater and Billy Sparkle departing in September 1973, the band had to rejig the lineup. The seismic shock of Slater's defection made it hard for most observers to imagine the band carrying on without him. To a large proportion of Thrashers, he was the heart and soul of the band, as well as their undisputed frontman, and his absence was bound to leave a void that would be hard to fill. That the band not only soldiered on but thrived and produced some of the most adventurous music of their career, speaks volumes about their resilience and depth of talent.

Although Slater had been the more public face of Stackridge, it was Andy Davis who had always been the unspoken leader of the band and prime mover behind nearly every reinvention they went through over the years. His solution here was to take the unexpected step of placing himself at the back of the band, occupying the recently-departed Billy Sparkle's seat at the drum kit. He then drafted in two new members – session player Rod Bowkett: to compensate for his own abdication from keyboards, and ex-Audience reed and woodwind man Keith Gemmell, who not only replaced Mutter Slater on flute but also included clarinet and saxophone in his armoury. James Warren and Crun Walter remained on guitar and bass, respectively. This expanded palette of sound – combined with the additional composing talents of Rod Bowkett – meant the whole dynamic and direction of the band underwent a subtle transformation.

However, there was still the thorny question of a new album to promote, as *The Man in the Bowler Hat* was due to be released in the New Year, featuring the classic lineup rather than the transitional one. Stackridge were subsequently booked for their first big promotional gig at the Rainbow Theatre in Finsbury Park, London, on 19 December 1973. It proved to be quite an evening, and while I was mooching in the foyer with the other Thrashers pre-gig, producer George Martin turned up with his new chauffer in tow: none other than ex-Stackridge percussionist Billy Sparkle in his new job role! Mutter Slater was also there with them to check out his former band's new lineup. Since leaving Stackridge, he had taken gainful employment as a petrol pump attendant but was also studying music theory after encouragement from George Martin during the sessions for *Bowler Hat*. The big tragedy of this short-lived transitional lineup was the fact that they never got around to adding any official studio recordings to the Stackridge canon, and the only mementoes left to posterity are two Radio One sessions, a live Capital Radio broadcast (but what a broadcast!) and some live tracks from a gig at Sheffield Polytechnic. All these artefacts are only available via unofficial releases, although it must be stressed that Stackridge as a band were always accepting of fans exchanging unofficial recordings, and it is refreshing that Thrashers virtually always exchanged any bootleg recordings between each other for free. Thankfully there are a lot of these recordings of rare and unreleased tracks available, as there was much incredible music created by this transitional lineup.

Here then, to understand how the bigger picture of the Stackridge canon of music links up, I need to divert and discuss some of these more-neglected pieces from this transitional era, as many of the themes created were recycled into future album tracks. In the seven months that the transitional lineup operated, they packed in around 80 gigs: not a bad tally.

1973 Radio Broadcast

Personnel:
James Warren: guitar, vocals
Mike Evans: violin, vocals
Keith Gemmell: clarinet, saxophone, flute
Rod Bowkett: keyboards
Crun Walter: bass, vocals
Andy Davis: drums, vocals
Recorded: BBC Langham, Studio 1, London, November 1973
Producer: John Walters
Broadcast: John Peel Show, Radio One, 19 November 1973
Session remains unreleased by the BBC, but is preserved on the Un- series of unofficial releases.

'McGregor'/'Zorgan's Daughter' (Bowkett, Paint)

Symbolically chosen as the new set opener, 'McGregor' displays a whole new direction for Stackridge after the loss of Slater and Sparkle. Presented in two contrasting parts – the first a jazz-tinged instrumental, the closing section a hymnal ode – these disparate approaches hang together to make a surprisingly coherent whole in this adventurous composition. The four-bar opening phrase alone is an impressive piece of writing – a kind of skewed take on 'Westminster Chimes', bringing to mind the ticking of a clock and the passing of time. Cunningly constructed with three repeated four-note phrases played on guitar and keyboards – running in different and unusual directions, the whole thing underpinned by a resounding pedal E from Crun Walter's bass – it creates the somewhat unsettling feeling that time is slowly and inexorably slipping away, as we hang poised on the brink of some approaching uncertainty. It's an inspired way to open a new chapter in the Stackridge story, and perhaps a subconscious influence on the band's choice of 'McGregor' as the new set opener, a gateway to pastures-new for the band and its fans to explore. Its resolution into a finger-twisting, elastic bass riff – sounding like simplicity itself but devilishly hard to play and requiring strong digits to pull off convincingly on a bass guitar – is as brilliant as the opening phrase.

The new Walter/Davis rhythm section does a sterling job, as Andy Davis really swings on the drums; his use of the ride cymbal and the tom-tom fills in particular accentuate the jazz swing on this track. His drum style reminds me a lot of Paul McCartney's distinctive forays behind the kit: a similarly great all-around musician to Davis. The jazzy twists of 'McGregor' are wholly new territory for Stackridge, and are in no small part influenced by the versatility of their new keyboard player Rod Bowkett. The memorable clarinet part provided by new recruit Keith Gemmell sits atop Walter's twisting bass line and bears a strong Frank Zappa influence. A series of sharp punctuations, followed by furtively darting piano runs, dissect this passage and bring to mind the cartoon-like image of a character – perhaps the titular 'McGregor' himself – surreptitiously glancing around one corner, then another, before tiptoeing to safety from some imaginary pursuer. This is followed by a spread of syncopated linking chords that explore a jazz fusion landscape in the same vein that Weather Report simultaneously mined. These chords have the effect of changing the key up a semitone once it rejoins the bass riff again for an improvised clarinet passage of some distinction from Gemmell.

After another clutch of syncopated chords and a further key change, an ascending six-note arpeggio – like the spreading rays of the rising sun – leads us into the vocal section of the piece. With a cushion of big church-like organ chords, the hymnal feel is tangible, but in true Stackridge fashion, the most incongruous words are juxtaposed against this dreamy soundscape. Lyrically related to 'Fundamentally Yours' by dint of being another letter song, the first verse and chorus are a missive sent from a Miss Crooks to resident agony columnist Mike Evans, here referred to under his *nom de plume* 'Big E'. Our young lady ('Zorgan's Daughter' perchance?) seems to have a post-hockey compulsion to eat radioactive monks whilst in the showers. From whence these monks came, and indeed why they became radioactive is not revealed, and neither is the reason for Miss C's cannibalistic tendencies. The second verse and chorus is Big E's reply to this conundrum, and contains some startling references to digestive processes. It's all very surreal stuff and rendered in a fetching two-part harmony 'twixt Warren and Davis.

The authorship of this number is traditionally credited to Miroslav Paint: a pseudonym for the combined writing talents of Walter and Warren. The idiosyncratic nature of the second half of 'McGregor' bears this out, but I would also argue that the jazzy first section is somewhat atypical for these writers and is most likely a contribution from the muse of Rod Bowkett, therefore making it more likely that this is a Bowkett/Paint composition. The bass riff of the opening part of 'McGregor' would find a new lease of life when it was recycled into 'Benjamin's Giant Onion' on the next Stackridge album.

'The Laughing Policeman' (Penrose)

The very English tradition of music hall had always exerted a strong influence on the band, borne out by this cover of the old Charles Penrose chestnut. Taking over from 'Twist And Shout' as Mike Evans' live vocal feature, the Big E makes 'The Laughing Policeman' his own with a typically boisterous performance, including a knock-knock joke in the spoken interlude ('Irish stew in the name of the law'), where I think Keith Gemmell plays the straight man to Evans' joker. Musically, the track is pumped along at a rate of knots by Bowkett's piano and Walter's bass as Davis adds some extra push on cowbell. Great fun it is, too, prompting John Peel to comment, 'Ah, they don't write them like that anymore'.

'February In Shropshire' (Davis)

If further evidence were needed of Andy Davis' composing genius, you would need look no further than this startlingly-joyous instrumental. 'February In Shropshire' is simply his best instrumental composition for the band after the glorious 'Lummy Days'. A hugely accomplished piece of writing, this durable tune would later find a revival when the millennium lineup reinstated it into the Stackridge live set, and despite it never having had an official studio recording, they included a version on their live album *Pick of the Crop* released in 2000: more of which later.

From the off, Mike Evans' quicksilver flurry of notes on the violin intro sets the pace, as the band romp headlong into the memorable main theme, bouncing gaily along with an irresistible forward motion on this triple-time tune. The tight violin-led initial theme emphasising the 7th of the chord, alternates with a slightly looser section where Keith Gemmell gets his saxophone into action. The two contrasting parts give the track a perfectly weighted, almost organically-breathing tension and release as it progresses.

As an example of getting maximum development out of an initial melodic idea, 'February In Shropshire' takes some beating. Much as Beethoven did with his 'Symphony No. 5' – where he derived much of the melodic material from just the two-note, four-beat opening motif – Davis returns to his main theme here in several different guises. The first of these is with a brilliant, purposeful use of discord on the comical middle section, where the guitar, piano and violin play simultaneously but in unusual intervals on every note of the triple-time rhythm. The effect is zany, and brings to my mind the image of tiny woodland creatures scurrying about their business as they emerge from hibernation!

The resolution from this mad section into a series of furious descending violin triplets pushes the picture back to widescreen again, and the band charge through an ensemble passage that displays an impeccable logic and a supreme melodic sense of imagination. The relentless forward-motion of the track then comes to a halt, and in another compositional masterstroke, the emphasis of the main theme is changed once more, this time from the 7th to the major. This passage evokes morning mists rising from the Shropshire meadows as the cows chew their cud. Then Bowkett's lightly-tripping harpsichord appears to lead us up to higher ground, as we look out over a very English landscape. A quick blast of gypsy violin from Mike Evans gives us pause for thought before Bowkett's sweeping downward glissando on piano has us romping back down into the valley with the return of the main theme in all its glory. The coda is a brief exercise in the art of canon, as each instrument states the theme, overlapping with the previous one. And just to make sure all bases are covered, the band drift into a free-form improvisation as the sax squeals, the violin slides and the landscape appears to melt and twist before us. As this cacophony ends, you can just hear Andy Davis utter, 'Alright, alright and goodnight' from behind his drum kit before the band hammer out four staccato notes from the theme to close this masterpiece.

'The Volunteer' (Davis, Smegmakovitch)

Continuing the grand tradition of eclecticism displayed by the previous lineup, this new version of Stackridge unveil the completed version of this Andy Davis tune first aired as a brief rehearsal snippet two months previously on the HTV sessions. Now replete with Walter's Crimean War-inspired lyrics, 'The Volunteer' comes on like a Victorian parlour ballad, telling the tale of an unfortunate conscript and his run-ins with the dubious likes of Sergeant Major Busby and the even-more-unsavoury Colonel Upshot-Bagley.

The first verse is sung by Davis, accompanied by Bowkett's piano and punctuated by Keith Gemmell, giving his best impression of an army bugler on his clarinet. James Warren takes over lead vocals on the second verse, and it features a slight lyrical difference from the later studio version sung by Mutter Slater in that it sports the line 'Though it seems unthinkable, my legs are insiberial'. Whether this last word is meant to represent the condition his legs are in or is a whimsical variation of 'in Siberia', I'm not certain! Andy Davis joins Warren to sing a brief last verse before Mike Evans turns in a wonderful violin solo over three lots of repeated verse chords on the coda, the last of these supported by some high Warren backing vocals.

Another very strong Andy Davis composition, 'The Volunteer' is one of the few from this Slater-less lineup that found a productive life in the years following the dissolution of this short-lived but fascinating shuffle of the Stackridge personnel pack.

Broadcast: Capital Radio Live Night Out, Global Village, London

Date: 16 February 1974
Host DJ: Tommy Vance
Later available as a 2CD set given as a 'freebie' with fanzine The Rhubarbarian in 2010

Saturday 16 February 1974 marked one of the great moments in Stackridge folklore, as the transitional lineup collided with Capital Radio DJ Tommy Vance, resulting in an evening of mayhem, broadcast across the capital's airwaves live and unexpurgated. Unfortunately, I missed out on attending this event due to a previously-arranged liaison with a long-forgotten female at a Nektar gig at Dagenham Roundhouse. I'd seen Stackridge perform the previous evening at Hendon Polytechnic and indeed saw them a few days later at the Marquee, but thankfully this legendary gig is enshrined for posterity on the excellent *Complete Global Village* two-CD set – a freebie with *The Rhubarbarian*, which is an excellent Stackridge/Rhubarb Thrashers fanzine published by superfan and later 21st-century Stackridge merchandising stall stalwart: the inimitable Ade Macrow. The rehearsals for this concert are also available on this set, giving an enlightening glimpse into the backstage world of the band. As well as featuring many roughshod and partially-completed performances – including snatches of 'Georgia On My Mind' and Grieg's 'In The Hall Of The Mountain King' – it also highlights some extended Mike Evans violin improvisations in the form of 'Evans' Violin Concerto' and 'The Star And Cheeseburger Suite'. The gig itself is the epitome of chaos, and as well as some great music, we are treated to Tommy Vance making a complete fool of himself, muddling titles, missing cues, asking daft questions and getting even dafter answers. Add to this a sound engineer that appears to be on some kind of medication, and the outcome is one of the oddest live radio broadcasts of the 1970s!

'McGregor'/'Zorgan's Daughter' makes a great opener with its eccentric, jazzy first section, and on this occasion, Andy Davis' vocal mic seems to be mixed twice as loud as James Warren's for most of the gig, with the effect of making this number sound vocal-harmony heavy. An extraordinary reading of 'Purple Spaceships Over Yatton' sees Mike Evans' sliding violin so far upfront in the mix that the band sound psychedelic in the extreme, and it's always good to hear Keith Gemmell stretch out on flute on a number that previously seemed unthinkable without Mutter Slater's contribution. Tommy Vance's attempt to get a sensible interview out of James Warren preceding the linked duo of 'Every Living Hole' and 'Spin 'Round the Room' is hilarious. When he comments on Warren's 'posh' accent, the diminutive one replies, 'It's all affected, I suspect'.

These two songs appear to have little in common thematically but were always paired in performance throughout the transitional period. 'Every Living Hole' proved to be a complex, bizarre track and is discussed in more detail in the section on other unreleased material below. 'Spin 'Round The Room' displayed strong traditional jazz influences, and would find an active life with the succeeding *Extravaganza* lineup, so will be more fully discussed in that chapter.

A trio of tracks from the then-current album *The Man in the Bowler Hat,* are featured – 'Pinafore Days' with Warren's cowbell striking one o'clock, 'God Speed The Plough' and 'Dangerous Bacon': likened by Tommy Vance to 'an exploding breakfast'. More chaos ensues when Mike Evans performs 'The Laughing Policeman' with an enthusiastic vocal, broadcast so loud that the distorted manic laughter is almost scary in its intensity, and heaven knows what the unsuspecting listener made of it all!

Tommy Vance's attempts to interview band members amongst the bedlam become ever more farcical, and in a memorable sequence towards the close of the set, he finds himself one tune ahead of the band in his introductions and he never quite recovers himself.

'The Volunteer' finds Davis' backing vocals crazily out of proportion in the radio mix, and as the jigs fire off between that number and the glorious 'February In Shropshire', our host is completely at sea, although he appears to be enjoying the spectacle nevertheless. At one point, DJ Nicky Horne can be heard yelling to an oblivious Tommy Vance, 'Tommy, your mic's not working, man!'. Dragged back for an encore of 'Lummy Days' and referred to by T.V. as 'a bunch of absolute monarchs!' this wonderfully unique incarnation of the band sign off an unforgettable broadcast in classic style: a night to remember indeed.

Additional Material

'Every Living Hole' (Bowkett, Paint)

This curious song is one of the band's oddest creations with its convoluted structure and post-holocaust-scenario lyrics, as well as a mind-bendingly fractured arrangement taking the listener on a trip from a verse/chorus structure, through a neoclassical interlude and into a Gregorian chant mantra. It also name-checks the enigmatic 'Zorgan' character that appeared in the Stackridge lexicon on occasion around this time. Compositionally, it appears to be a further Bowkett/Paint collaboration. Unfortunately, this adventurous piece failed to make it onto record, and mysteriously vanished when this short-lived lineup dissolved in the spring of 1974. Luckily, a live version was included in the Capital Radio broadcast.

'After The Tetracycline' (Bowkett, Paint)

A notable addition to the Stackridge set occurred at Middlesex Polytechnic in Hendon on 15 February, where this writer observed Crun Walter pre-gig, scribbling lyrics onto a scrap of paper as James Warren chipped in with suggestions: which, of course, made it another 'Miroslav Paint' lyric. It turned out to be the final touches to a new song the band had been cooking up, that entered the set that very evening and featured a rare vocal spot for Mike Evans, with a little help from Crun Walter. This song never received an official release but was thankfully preserved for posterity on a good quality bootleg of the performance at Sheffield Polytechnic a few days after the Hendon gig.

With its convoluted structure and jazz-like modulations, the music had Rod Bowkett's fingerprints all over it and proved to be the most bizarre cross between Zappa, The Goons and The Bonzo Dog Band, with an odd mutated march parading lyrics that James Warren reckoned concerned acne. But with refrains such as 'Let no man surprise your behind' and 'I demand that everybody copulate', it certainly raised a few listeners' eyebrows! Another in the long series of West Country landmarks mentioned in Stackridge songs also appears in the final stanza in the shape of Monkton Combe.

Musically, it was one of the band's most complex creations, and some of its themes were later recycled into future tracks by both the *Extravaganza* and *Mr. Mick* lineups: more of which in later chapters.

Extravaganza (1975)

Personnel:
Andy Davis: guitar, vocals
Mutter Slater: flute, Mellotron, vocals
Keith Gemmell: clarinet, saxophone, flute
Rod Bowkett: keyboards
Paul Karas: bass, vocals
Roy Morgan: drums
Mike Evans: violin ('The Volunteer'), scat vocals ('Who's That Up There With Bill Stokes?')
Recorded: AIR Studios, London, July to September 1974
Producers: Tony Ashton, Stackridge
Engineers: Geoff Emerick, Pete Swettenham, Gary Edwards
Tape Op: Pete Henderson
Label: Rocket
Release date: January 1975

By April 1974, the ever-restless Andy Davis initiated a further change of line-up for Stackridge when he asked James Warren and Crun Walter to leave the band. This came as a big shock for many fans and possibly an even bigger surprise for the duo involved. Walter is said to have taken it philosophically, but apparently, Warren took it harder and wouldn't reconcile his fractious relationship with Andy Davis until the pair worked together again as The Korgis four years later. The first many Thrashers knew of this latest reshuffle was at the Marquee gig on 7 May when the new lineup made its live debut. Ex-Rare Bird bassist Paul Karas essentially took both Warren and Walter's place, providing vocals and bass, and session player Roy Morgan arrived to occupy Andy Davis' vacant drum stool, leaving Stackridge's main shaker-and-mover to step upfront once more on guitar and vocals. The retention of Keith Gemmell, Rod Bowkett and Mike Evans from the previous lineup ensured some degree of continuity, but the biggest softener for the blow of losing the ever-popular Warren and Walter, was the return of the fans' beloved Mutter Slater, once more providing vocals and flute, and becoming Stackridge's resident Mellotron player.

Much of the transitional lineup's new material was jettisoned in tandem with these latest changes, although a few numbers were retained and reshaped, including 'Spin 'Round The Room' and 'The Volunteer'. The saddest casualties were the excellent 'February In Shropshire', 'Every Living Hole' and the eccentric 'After The Tetracycline'. Several of these tunes would at least enjoy a live revival when they were adopted by the millennium lineup in 1999.

Within a few months, the new 1974 lineup could be seen dashing off sessions at AIR London Studios amongst a plethora of live dates on their busy schedule as they crisscrossed the country. On stage, much swapping of instruments took place, ensuring an engaging evening's entertainment and some hot playing, as the new personnel built up a rapport with each other and the fans, getting better and better as they progressed. Mike Evans' last gig with this lineup was at London's Chalk Farm Roundhouse on 18 August, although he'd already contributed to the new album. By the time of its release, all that remained of these contributions were some violin on the coda of 'The Volunteer', and his vocal scat on the otherwise instrumental 'Who's That Up There With Bill Stokes?'. In hindsight, the band jumped in a bit too soon to record a new album, as by the time the amazing Extravaganza tour arrived in February/March 1975, their live performances were a blazing inferno of creativity, and some excellent new material had expanded the set out alongside the *Extravaganza* tracks and a selection of old favourites.

Extravaganza was released in January 1975, just as Stackridge were gearing up for their big promotional push. This was launched by an invitation-only gig put on by Rocket Records at the Shaw Theatre, Euston, on 2 February. It was a swish affair and an amazing evening as the band unveiled their expanded set, playing six tracks from the new album, four of their older tunes and four brand new numbers. Sitting among the Thrashers in the audience watching the set were Elton John, Kiki Dee and Neil Sedaka. After an extraordinary performance where the band played out of their skins, Elton must've thought he'd signed a winner to his record label.

I managed to catch the band three times on the Extravaganza tour, which wound up at The Greyhound, Croydon, on 23 March, and every performance sounded and looked incredible. However, the album failed to chart, despite decent sales to the faithful. But it's a disc that has stood the test of time and is generally well-regarded by many Thrashers.

The album cover design this time was by a company called Cream and is once again a gatefold sleeve. It's based on a poster design by Alain Weill, which depicts what looks like a Victorian circus troupe chatting and relaxing, set against a beige background with the band name above them and the album title below. The poster picture of the circus folk is spread over the front and half the back of the sleeve, with the track titles listed down the left side of the picture. Inside the gatefold, the lyrics and credits are displayed with head and shoulder portraits of the six band members and a female from the circus troupe along the bottom of the inside cover. In many ways, it's a sleeve that sums up the image of much of the music within, as there are elements of the ambience of the 'Big Top' alive in the eclectic musical mix that's presented.

'Spin 'Round the Room' (Bowkett, Vernon)

A survivor from the Slater-less lineup, 'Spin 'Round The Room' previously featured a James Warren vocal during that era but was now sung by Paul Karas. It makes a bright and breezy start to the album, and the crisp production by ex-Ashton, Gardner and Dyke pianist and vocalist Tony Ashton is one of the first things that strike the listener. Released as a single, it suffered the same fate as all Stackridge singles before or since, with not even a sniff of chart action.

Newly signed to Elton John's flagship Rocket Records, this release lacked the promotional clout afforded to Stackridge labelmates such as Kiki Dee.

A Rod Bowkett tune – as many on *Extravaganza* were – the lyrics were provided by Lucy Vernon. Still retaining its trad-jazz elements, 'Spin 'Round the Room' is driven by Bowkett's piano and features a fine Karas vocal performance; his sonorous voice way out front in the mix. The requisite clarinet clichés from Gemmell conjure up the atmosphere of this somewhat hidebound subgenre of jazz as the new dynamite Karas/Morgan rhythm section swings impressively. An authentic crackly-vinyl sound is added to the jiving coda, and completes the illusion of times past, with a run-out groove click sound effect as the track fades.

'Grease Paint Smiles' (Bowkett, Bathos)

A further Stackridge mystery emerges in the 'Grease Paint Smiles' credits in the form of Rod Bowkett's writing partner Bathos. Formerly known as 'Fancy Meeting You Here' and sporting different lyrics, this song was originally an engagingly boozy little drinking song when it graced the set in the summer of 1974. I'm fairly certain it was sung by Mutter Slater in this incarnation, but by the time the band tackled the tune in the studio, the mysterious Bathos had evidently restructured the lyric along the lines of the rather tired *sad clown* premise – a well-trodden path, having peaked some years earlier with Smokey Robinson's infinitely more sublime 'Tears Of A Clown'.

Andy Davis takes the vocal here, but doesn't turn in the best performance of his career, attempting to sound world-weary but ending up having a few pitching difficulties. The backing track is a superb taut construction, with the rhythm section tight as ever.

'The Volunteer' (Davis, Smegmakovitch)

One of the last songs to spring from the muse of the classic lineup back in September 1973, the version performed by the Slater-less band had featured a split Warren/Davis lead vocal, but this had evolved into a Slater vocal by the time the *Extravaganza* lineup recorded it. The highlight of side one of the album, 'The Volunteer' is a Stackridge classic all the way, as Slater's vocal ranges from fragile to boisterous and he brings to life this Crimean War saga. The Mellotron strings buoy the gentler verses, and the snap and crackle of that inimitable rhythm section add an extra pop to the jaunty, raucous choruses. The half-verse preceding the coda is harmonised by Andy Davis and Paul Karas, and as the instrumental playout piles in, one of the few remaining Mike Evans contributions to the album can be heard in the form of a wonderfully melodic violin solo, though somewhat truncated compared with his extended foray on the previous lineup's Radio One version. Davis puts the track to bed with a down-home country-flavoured electric guitar solo, leading into an elegantly constructed end-piece, which ties up a superb arrangement of a great song.

'Highbury Incident (Rainy July Morning)' (Davis, Bowkett, Slater)

A song with two titles, this was referred to as 'Rainy July Morning' when released on the hybrid compilation album *Pinafore Days* issued by Sire Records in the US in 1974. That featured eight tracks from *The Man in the Bowler Hat* and two from *Extravaganza* – recalling the treatment some of The Beatles' early albums received in the States when tracks were chopped and changed from the proper UK releases.

Unusually, this is a three-way composition, and being Mutter Slater's only writing credit on the album, it seeks to imitate some of the pace and atmosphere previously generated by 'The Last Plimsoll', but it definitely lacks the pizzazz of that famous track. A sax-driven mid-tempo pop/rock confection, the lyrics are fairly anonymous compared with some of the past flights of fancy cooked up by the band, although the track itself is a pleasant-enough toe-tapper.

'Benjamin's Giant Onion' (Bowkett, Bathos)

This track appears to be an attempt to return to the storytelling tradition so redolent of classic Stackridge. Only this time, a combination of lack of inspiration and poorly thought-out production contributes to a minor *faux pas*, as the tale of an onion grower on a 'funny farm' in Beeding-on-Wold, falls a bit flat. The lyrics are at best hopeful, and the tune is hummable enough, but the arrangement and production are the worst on the album, with wan vocals, trebly guitars and uninspired sax doodling colluding to provide a less than satisfying listening experience. A mild surprise occurs on the coda, though, when a mutated version of the priceless 'McGregor' riff makes an unexpected appearance to add a hint of menace and act as a musical illustration of the final lyrical twist of giant onions sprouting feet and marching on a hapless human race: no doubt intent on creating the perfect onion-centric world. This concept of mutant vegetation had been previously explored with spectacular results by Genesis a few years earlier on their epic 'The Return Of The Giant Hogweed': inspired by science fiction works such as John Wyndham's *The Day of the Triffids*.

Of note is the fact that the nod to 'McGregor' on the coda, adds credence to my theory that Rod Bowkett was indeed likely to have been the principal musical architect of that former-neglected Stackridge song. This tall tale of a demented onion grower proved to be much more effective when it was showcased in the live set during the Extravaganza tour in 1975, with a great mime on the menacing coda by the ever-theatrical Mutter Slater, stunning audiences throughout the land.

'Happy in the Lord' (Welton)

Side one closes with an inspired cover version of this Phil Welton song also recorded by his own band Fat Grapple. Guaranteed to lift the spirits again just when such a boost was needed, it opens with some atmospheric church organ, the clearing of throats and the rustling of hymn books before the band take flight, along with a Spitfire flying from speaker to speaker to illustrate the opening lines. Andy Davis' guitar shimmers and shines, and the ever-impressive rhythm section of Karas and Morgan drive the track along behind Mutter Slater as he sings his song of praise with tongue firmly in check.

The lyrics are witty, if slightly cynical, as the narrator admits that his next appearance in church will probably be 'When Granny snuffs it eight years later'. The track boasts a killer chorus that's hard to resist singing along with, as many Thrashers eventually did when Slater made yet another return to the Stackridge lineup for the spectacular series of gigs from 2007 onwards, and this thoroughly engaging slice of pop/rock enjoyed a welcome live revival. With one of the strangest endings of any track the band ever recorded, I always imagined it was Paul Karas reciting the bizarre sermon over the coda, finally dissolving into a fit of stifled giggling. But it was apparently producer Tony Ashton whose mock-sanctimonious tones close side one.

'Rufus T. Firefly' (Bowkett)

As we flip the album, the hearty laugh that opens side two seems like a continuation of the mirth that closed side one, although this time it sounds like a Slater laugh. This particular side of vinyl illustrates a dichotomy in the approach of this lineup, and you get the feeling that the four tracks are the real meat-and-potatoes of this band's manifesto. Like the more song-oriented first side, Rod Bowkett is again the dominant writer, but here the band get down to some serious playing.

'Rufus T. Firefly' was previously known as 'Chasing The Ladies', then 'The Biggest Spotty Dog You Ever Did See', before settling on its final Marx Brothers-inspired moniker. It was – somewhat oddly, given its anticlimactic nature – the set closer throughout the summer gigs of 1974 before it was shunted into mid-set to make way for the more dramatic 'Who's That Up There With Bill Stokes?' during the autumn.

With its chugging rhythm and super-smooth flute and guitar riffs, 'Rufus T. Firefly' is perfect soundtrack music, and has indeed been employed in this capacity for television on occasion. The influence of Frank Zappa is felt – not for the first time in Stackridge music, but never as strongly as on this album. A study of the truly marvellous rhythm section playing on this track will repay your close attention, as Paul Karas' bass and Roy Morgan's drums lock into a beguiling embrace to punctuate every twist and turn of this disciplined ensemble performance, demonstrating the sheer professionalism and musicianship of this remarkable Stackridge lineup, as they negotiate the cleverly-interlocking themes of this streamlined instrumental.

'No-One's More Important Than The Earthworm' (Haskell)

This is possibly the most straightforward rock number released under the Stackridge name up to that time, and probably stood out in the 1974 set for that reason. Best experienced on the visual *Old Grey Whistle Test* footage of this lineup from February 1975 – where the Mellotron-soaked intro can be heard to maximum effect – Rod Bowkett opted for added organ on the curtailed opening of the album cut, giving the track a slightly different flavour. This also cut short Andy Davis' abrasive *rock god* introductory guitar parts, and was a slight disappointment at the time.

Paul Karas gives a great vocal performance on this re-named cover of Gordon Haskell's 'Worms': a song that originally appeared on the composer's 1971 album *It Is and It Isn't*. The lyric is an animal allegory of cosmic perspective, displaying all the sweeping grandeur of the best 1970s progressive rock. In combination with Mutter Slater's Mellotron, Andy Davis' treated guitar riffs and Keith Gemmell's soaring saxophone; the song is evocative of vast cliffs, misty vistas and boundless horizons. And despite its sad, resigned reflection, I find it a strangely uplifting experience. Taken at a slow pace, 'Earthworm' exudes a subtle controlled power, and the band's performance here is once again top-notch. It is a pity they chose to fade out the guitar arpeggios at the end instead of employing the more-effective juddering halt of the live version, though.

'Pocket Billiards' (Bowkett)

From the cover downward, this fourth Stackridge album leans towards the imagery of the big top, and never more so than in this third track on side two and set opener throughout 1974. Of the three instrumentals on the album, this is my favourite by far. Excellently arranged with not a semiquaver out of place, its triple-time construction conjures up the razzamatazz of the circus, and is perhaps the perfect aural illustration of the album cover artwork. Displaying immaculate Karas/Morgan rhythm section work, Mutter Slater's flute and glockenspiel combine sweetly with Keith Gemmell's clarinet, and Rod Bowkett plays some delicious piano with reverb added in all the right places. It must've been something of a coup to have the engineering services of ex-Beatles engineer Geoff Emerick on the team too. Of course, the circus wouldn't be complete without the Stackridge ringmaster Andy Davis lending his inimitable guitar presence to the proceedings, with some ear-munching wah-wah riffs providing a welcome bite to the tastiest treat on side two.

'Who's That Up There With Bill Stokes?' (Bowkett, Davis)

Here Stackridge go for the big closer, with all guns blazing. The third in the series of Zappa-inspired instrumental pieces, this is perhaps the most Zappa-esque of all, recalling the atmosphere of 'Peaches En Regalia' from his 1969 album *Hot Rats*. Playing-wise, the band really kick up a storm, as Keith Gemmell's sax and Mutter Slater's glockenspiel play the main theme in unison over a cooking rhythm section, and Slater swaps to tympani for the Morse code-like percussive bridge parts. Mike Evans' scat vocal lines introduce a dose of eccentricity into the mix, and it was to be the last we heard from him in a Stackridge capacity until the millennium lineup convened in 1998. There follows a four-bar bridge of five beats to the bar before we settle into a cyclic middle section. This gives Gemmell a chance to cut loose for a sax solo over a modulating riff in 7/4 time – extruded from the main melody and played by Rod Bowkett on piano and Paul Karas on bass, although this solo appears to take us from A to B without passing any spectacular scenery *en route* before depositing us into a tense tympani-pounding buildup that's all blood and thunder. The release back into the main melody again is almost anticlimactic after such a sweat-drenched, tension-building exercise, but at least the band build up to a blockbuster ending, complete with Slater's crashing tympani and Gemmell's squealing sax.

Despite the fact that the band are undoubtedly playing their socks off on 'Bill Stokes', I've always felt the track was somewhat half-arranged and suspicious that so much more could've been done with this material. These musings were confirmed on the band's outstanding Extravaganza tour, as during the gig at The Greyhound, Croydon on 23 March 1975, they unveiled a short-lived much-loosened-up version of 'Bill Stokes', which can only be described as one of the best Stackridge performances I have ever witnessed.

Additional Material

As with most incarnations of Stackridge, there were those compositions and covers played live that had no official release. Fortunately, some of these have been captured on various unofficial recordings exchanged between Thrashers, but sadly, some still haven't emerged from the mists of time. The most obscure of these songs is probably the mysterious 'Tex Ritter', which Mutter Slater introduced (and I think sang) at the Marquee gig on 7 May 1974. It's a pity I have no accurate recall of the tune, as this was the only time I heard it and quite possibly the sole time the band performed it. Unless a recording of this gig turns up, it looks like we'll never get to hear 'Tex Ritter'. The next mysterious title was 'Mango Tango', which the band allegedly performed at the Ugly Bug Ball at Bedford College in Regent's Park, London, on 28 June 1974. Although I was at this gig, I cannot confirm this as I had passed out on the loo after too much Newcastle Brown Ale and missed the Stackridge set completely (I was still a teenager!). Whether this was a new number or not, is debatable, as the instrumental 'Rufus T. Firefly' had various titles before settling on that name. So maybe it was yet another moniker for that song, or maybe not: who knows?

There was another new development in the set when at Queen Mary College in Mile End, London, on 8 November 1974, Stackridge played a new arrangement of 'Do The Stanley' as the encore. What made this new configuration of the song so interesting, was the fact that it had a minute or so of instrumental music on the opening section that had an exciting familiarity to long-term Thrashers. Those who'd studied Stackridge music through the years, soon sussed that it was an adaption from the instrumental middle section of the *lost* track from February 1974: 'After The Tetracycline'. It wouldn't be the last recycling job from this most obscure of Stackridge tunes: of which more in the next chapter.

Yet another neglected composition was premiered at The Winning Post in Twickenham on 8 December 1974 when Paul Karas introduced a new number called 'Cox Of The Cambridge Crew', though thereafter it became known as 'Tuscalusa Races'. Happily, this was captured on Ian Nicholson's recording of the gig, along with the new arrangement of 'Do The Stanley'. Soon taking pride of place as the 1975 Extravaganza tour set opener, 'Tuscalusa Races' was performed as an extended song but fits in more snugly with the great Stackridge instrumentals, as the bulk of this number was the band getting into some serious playing. With many memorable themes linked together in a driving arrangement with the usual tighter-than-tight playing, space was also left for some looser improvisation, making for a superb opening number, and it was another composition that sounded very much like Rod Bowkett's work. The fact that this number never had an official studio version, was a big loss, but at least Thrashers had the unofficial live Winning Post version to remind them what an excellent tune it was.

With lyrics describing a race of some kind with a machine that was a 'steam-powered wonder', the music matched this feel with an inexorable forward motion that felt like the listener was riding along to the memorable themes, many of which carried that special Stackridge whimsy in their free-flowing passage, occasionally sounding like the music for some crazy cartoon race!

The 1975 Extravaganza tour brought forth another brace of escapees in the shape of 'The Virgin And The Blind Man' and 'Don't Forget The Beer, Dear'. The former was an acoustic comedy song performed solo by Paul Karas on guitar and vocals; the latter a music-hall interlude and another Gordon Haskell song performed by Mutter Slater to Rod Bowkett's piano accompaniment. No recorded Stackridge versions of these have so far surfaced, but I took the liberty of covering both these songs on the Stackridge rarities cover-version album *Prescription* that I recorded for charity in 2007 to raise cash for the Macmillan Nurses Fund. This was following the sad loss to cancer of longtime dedicated Thrasher Jim Timothy earlier that year.

A final pair of new tunes entered the Stackridge set on the *Extravaganza* lineup's ill-fated final tour that summer – 'Bad News': an excellent new Andy Davis tune, plus another instrumental 'Pictures Of The Queen', which on the one hearing I had of it at The Greyhound, Croydon gig on 6 July 1975, didn't really come up to the high standard of this lineup's earlier instrumentals. 'Bad News' would go on to a further lease of life during 1975/1976 when added to the set of the *Mr. Mick* lineup and was nicely captured on a band-sanctioned live soundboard recording at King's College, London on 2 October 1975, and so will be discussed in more detail in the next chapter.

1975 Radio Broadcast

Recorded: Paris Theatre, Regent Street, London
Date: 7 January 1975
Broadcast: BBC In Concert, Radio One
Record Label: BBC Windsong
Released: 1992 (included on the BBC Radio 1 Live In Concert compilation CD)

With the new album now released and in the stores, the band lined up for a BBC Radio One *In Concert* performance on 7 January 1975. Featuring five tracks from the freshly-available *Extravaganza* album, plus three older numbers, six of these performances were eventually released on the *BBC In Concert* CD in 1992, the missing casualties being 'Pocket Billiards' and 'Spin 'Round the Room'. This broadcast was a prelude to the *Extravaganza* tour, that saw this variant of Stackridge at their absolute live peak.

'God Speed The Plough' (Wabadaw Sleeve)

Mutter Slater has a lot more space for his flute on this version of the classic instrumental, as he takes the melodic lead lines through much of the whole first half instead of splitting it with piano and violin as of old. His tone is exceptionally pure on the opening sections – especially on the first two moving melodic statements – and he delivers his usual quicksilver variations on the first half of the upbeat section.

The baton is passed to Keith Gemmell's clarinet for the second half of the energised middle segment, and it's a slightly less effective reading than Mike Evans' passionate violin-playing was on previous versions, although it is perfectly performed by the ex-Audience reed man. The conclusion of this glorious instrumental is buoyed by Mellotron and provides a grand finale to a fine performance.

'The Volunteer' (Davis, Smegmakovitch)

The band's irrepressible humour surfaces on Mutter Slater's take on 'The Volunteer'. He gives a performance that veers from moving to amusing as the various components of this well constructed Andy Davis tune move from minor to major keys, and the tale of the unfortunate conscript unfolds. There is a wholly-unnecessary edit by a BBC technician, that chops out Slater's bellow of 'Hands off cocks and on with socks' on the second chorus towards the conclusion of the piece and several bars of music thereafter: censorship in action, I fear!

'Who's That Up There With Bill Stokes?' (Davis, Bowkett)

This new instrumental shows off the band's chops and is dispatched with aplomb, despite Rod Bowkett hitting a rare clunker on piano in a moment of distraction. Keith Gemmell's sax solo is slightly more passionate here than on the album cut, and it's another good performance.

'No-One's More Important Than The Earthworm' (Haskell)
'Earthworm' displays the full live arrangement, as Mutter Slater's surging Mellotron backs up some fine Andy Davis guitar on the emotive intro. Another sparkling performance of this moving song, Paul Karas gives his all on bass and vocals, while Keith Gemmell rips into some great sax soloing towards the close of the number.

'The Galloping Gaucho' (Slater, Smegmakovitch)
An efficient and tight version of the more lighthearted-but-evergreen 'The Galloping Gaucho' brings a raucous audience response, with much joining in to the tall tales of the 'six foot drip with a plastic whip'. The bass bubbles along impressively in a tight embrace with the drum kit as Slater encourages the studio audience to let go and have some fun.

'Dora The Female Explorer' (Stackridge)
'Dora' chugs along beautifully, powered as ever by Mutter Slater's puffing harmonica, and this version sports some added entertaining stop-time breaks on the coda that give Rod Bowkett's piano a chance to throw in some interesting variations among much whooping and hollering from band members: bringing this fun-filled version to a close.

Mr. Mick (1976)

Personnel:
Andy Davis: guitar, keyboards, vocals
Mutter Slater: flute, keyboards, vocals, narration
Keith Gemmell: clarinet, saxophone
Crun Walter: bass
Pete Van Hooke: drums
Joanna Karlin: vocals ('The Slater's Waltz')
Pete Gage: Bed track ('The Dump', 'Steam Radio Song')
Recorded: Ramport Studios and Studios, London (Mixing), November 1975 to March 1976
Producer: Andy Davis
Engineer: Denny Bridges
Label: Rocket/Stallion/Dap/Angel Air
Release dates: March 1976 (Rocket), 2000 (Stallion CD), 2000 (Dap CD), 2007 (Angel Air 2CD)

The summer of 1975 turned out to be a depressing one for Stackridge fans. After the brilliance of the *Extravaganza* tour the previous spring, a further summer tour saw the stability of the band in peril as the lineup imploded after Andy Davis decided to shake things up once more. Following a few months in flux – during which various characters came and went, including Mutter Slater's brother Peter 'Slipper' Slater and ex-King Crimson violinist David Cross – the new lineup was announced in October 1975. Andy Davis, Mutter Slater and Keith Gemmell went forward together and welcomed bassist Crun Walter back into the fold, also adding session player Pete Van Hooke on drums. Generally regarded as the least popular of the Stackridge variants by a large proportion of Thrashers, the *Mr. Mick* lineup was also possibly the boldest aggregation, striking out fearlessly and perhaps foolishly with a raft of new material and an apparent dismissal of the band's recent past. Support for the band was visibly wilting during this era, as, in live performance, fans were fed a diet of unfamiliar and largely sombre new music, and old favourites were completely abandoned.

The subsequent LP *Mr. Mick* was recorded as a concept album, and to get the full picture, it needed to be listened to from start to finish in one sitting. Rocket Records then scuppered this possibility by chopping the original running order to bits, making an abstruse work even more confusing. On its release in March 1976, it received a lukewarm welcome from the media and Thrashers alike. In a contemporary review in *Melody Maker*, Colin Irwin called it 'a grey allegory', and it didn't help that it emerged in the cultural heat-death of the progressive-rock concept album and the advent of the punk revolution. Never has an album felt so out of time – a largely joyless work on the subject of old age, cast adrift in a music scene about to be turned upside down by an energetic youth explosion. That having been said, *Mr. Mick* is not as bad an album as some of its detractors would have you believe. It boasts a handful of fine tunes and a brace of undisputed Stackridge classics in 'Can Inspiration Save The Nation?' and 'Fish In A Glass': both of which found an active musical life again during the band's glorious 2007 resurgence.

The album artwork – directed by David Costa – features a black-and-white front cover photograph taken by John Swannell, who'd previously provided the cover shot for *The Man in the Bowler Hat* – this time showing a head-and-shoulders shot of a beautiful young nurse and a grizzled old man, side by side. This is set against a grey background, with the band name and album title above in black, giving the sleeve a rather doleful ambience. This time the budget didn't run to a gatefold, and the rear of the sleeve shows the lyrics and credits printed in black against a white background, and in the top left-hand corner is a small black-and-white photo of the five band members strolling towards the camera. It all makes for a dour and rather low-budget-looking sleeve. Although something of a curate's egg, *Mr. Mick* has proven over time to have some superbly durable tunes. To my ears, it has redeemed itself to a large degree, and in many ways, is actually one of the band's most uncompromising statements.

Hitting the road again after an eight-week break in which the album was completed, the promotional tour saw Stackridge augment their lineup with the addition of ex-Greenslade keyboardist Dave Lawson and session guitarist Ray Russell. This gave Andy Davis a chance to get back to playing some guitar, as the late-1975 gigs had him pretty much exclusively stationed behind his keyboards. An appearance on *The Old Grey Whistle Test* on 9 March showed off the new lineup with Mutter Slater clad in overcoat, scarf and cloth cap, Andy Davis back on guitar and vocals, while Crun Walter's imposing figure dominated stage-left, complete with voluminous beard and big overcoat. Behind the keyboards, Dave Lawson looked like a contemporary shampoo advert with his shiny black barnet, and extra guitarist Ray Russell sported a Flying V guitar. It all started to feel like a band running out of time by now, though, and so it would prove to be on the Mr. Mick tour when the band jiggled the set and even seconded The Wurzels' 'Twice Daily' into the set: such was the dearth of inspiration around. As Mutter Slater has since commented, 'We were getting tired by then'.

After the butchered *Mr. Mick* album limped out, Slater and Davis did the usual round of promotional interviews. Davis mentioned in one such grilling that he had an idea for a piece based on the dance band on the Titanic – who allegedly played on as the ship went down. But, ironically, the good ship Stackridge was heading for its own metaphorical iceberg. On returning from a trip to America to negotiate with Seymour Stein of Sire Records on a possible release for a live album of the *Mr. Mick* saga, the band found their management offices gone, and the band finally dissolved in June 1976 with substantial debts. Many observers at the time thought the Stackridge story was over. But they would be proven wrong in the fullness of time.

'Hold Me Tight' (Lennon, McCartney)
After Rocket Records carved up the ***Mr. Mick*** tapes, the current single was added as the opening track. A cover version of the McCartney potboiler from the 1963 LP *With the Beatles*, Stackridge at least manage to make it their own with this reggae-tinged arrangement, although it remains the least distinguished of the band's singles. The original is something of a glorified filler track by The Beatles' high standards, but Stackridge slow it down and tag on a catchy clarinet hook line, giving it a pleasant, if somewhat innocuous lilt. Andy Davis handles the vocal in his usual inimitable fashion, Mutter Slater is conspicuous by his absence, and Crun Walter anchors the track with an economical bass line. As a single, it achieved airplay as Simon Bates' Record of the Week on Radio One, and it even seemed that there may be a hit for the band at this late stage, but in retrospect, I don't think the record was really up to it.

'Breakfast With Werner Von Braun' (Davis)
With a Beatles influence still lingering, this is an atmospheric track with a very basic piano hook, played over Crun Walter's somnambulistic bass line, and given character by Keith Gemmell's clarinet arabesques recalling the eastern feel of The Beatles' *Magical Mystery Tour* era. As an instrumental, it doesn't really add up to much and bears no comparison to the previous highs of Andy Davis' composing career in this sphere. Incidentally, a slightly longer version was released as the B-side of the 'Hold Me Tight' single.

Slater used to introduce this one as 'Bobby Crush meets the Pink Floyd'. which pretty much sums it up, I guess.

'Steam Radio Song' (Davis, Augarde)
Steve Augarde is the author of the children's book that the album is based on. 'Steam Radio Song' gives us a glimpse of the old Stackridge magic, as Andy Davis bends a note on his guitar and Crun Walter crunches in on bass to anchor the 6/8 swing of this track underpinned by a dancing, syncopated piano riff generating atmosphere-plus. The strong verse melody is let down slightly by an almost monotone middle eight, but this doesn't detract too much from an emotive song. Mutter Slater makes it his own with a powerful vocal, and drives home the point – or should I say pointlessness – that many unfortunately experience as old age creeps upon them. This bleak comparison between the fate of old people and unwanted articles cast out onto a rubbish dump, makes for harrowing and somewhat uncomfortable listening, as the grey landscapes of this sepulchral album unfold.

'The Dump' (Davis)
This is something of a sound experiment by Andy Davis, using his Mellotron and various synthesizers, acting as a descriptive backdrop to Mutter Slater's narration as he brings to life a vision of the stinking dump that pensioner Mr.

Mick has wandered onto in his search for a meaning to his miserable existence at the Yatton Home for the Elderly. To his disintegrating senses, the whole rubbish dump appears to be coming alive, and after the steam radio had regaled its tale in the previous track, this short instrumental interlude links into 'The Cotton Reel Song'.

'Save A Red Face' (Slater, Augarde)

Also known as 'The Cotton Reel Song', this is Mutter Slater's first composing contribution to the album, and sports a rollicking tune with a wide plodding gait like a giant out on a stroll, and is accompanied by an extremely catchy clarinet riff played by Keith Gemmell. Comical and tragic all at one time, the cotton reel recalls a time of glory, riding on tapestries fit for a king, before being cast out on the rubbish tip just like Mr. Mick. With another fine vocal performance by Slater, this track is engaging, and really came to life in 2007 when it was revamped as a great live number, featuring some fat trombone riffs in place of the clarinet of the original.

'The Slater's Waltz' (Slater, Augarde)

Side two opens with Mr. Mick's next encounter on the dump, this time with a pair of worn-out old ballet shoes, and before Mick knows it, he's performing a *pas de deux* with them atop the dump, accompanied by a rather lovely Mutter Slater melody. An elegant waltz, the track begins with only piano backing, as Slater takes the part of Mick, and guest vocalist Joanna Karlin stars as the singing ballet shoes. It could only happen on a Stackridge album! After the brief song section, the band swing full-tilt into the waltz, as Slater plays piano and harpsichord, Crun Walter's bass pirouettes on the fulcrum of the music, and Keith Gemmell's clarinet performs a ballet of swirling runs around this matrix. A synthetic string pad is in evidence on the middle eight – not an instrument featured much before in Stackridge music, but the *Mr. Mick* album occasionally displays a reliance on synthesizer pads. The band usually generate a good deal more magic with their inspired use of more organic instrumental choices, but the synthesizer was at the time creeping more and more into use with their contemporaries too, and apart from a brief eclipse by the buzz-saw guitars of the punk movement, went on to dominate – and at times stagnate – popular music in the 1980s. But that's another story.

'Coniston Water' (Slater)

Although Andy Davis is the dominant writer on *Mr. Mick*, Mutter Slater's trio of compositions more than hold their own, and his final offering is in the form of an instrumental, which originally rejoiced under the name 'Bagley Reservoir' before changing to the more poetic but less amusing 'Coniston Water'. Where this fits in with the convoluted tale of our intrepid pensioner is in the form of a daydream, as memories drift back to a romantic encounter with the pub landlord's daughter at this location.

The composition is a return to Slater's occasional ambient style, with a languid, drifting melody of long soprano sax lines over a string-pad backing, fostering a pensive atmosphere. This is broken by a triple-time interlude of fast, dissonant up-and-down piano runs, recalling the neglected but brilliant 'February In Shropshire' from 1973. Perhaps this passage represents a temporary tumble back into Mick's dark psychosis before coherence returns for a reprise of the floating first section – whatever, the effect is slightly unsettling. All in all, 'Coniston Water' seems to lack a solid arrangement, and its brooding, intense atmosphere does become a touch oppressive by the close of the track.

'Hey! Good Looking' (Davis, Walter)

Not to be confused with the 1951 Hank Williams country standard of the same name, this is a welcome return by the classic writing team of the two original Stackridge founders. Earlier compositions by this pair were credited the other way around as Walter/Davis, but a more sensible alphabetical system seems to have emerged by the time *Mr. Mick* came along.

The reggae influence that informed 'Hold Me Tight' is brought into sharper focus here, with some wonderful bass-playing from Crun Walter on this lilting Caribbean-influenced number. Keith Gemmell employs his soprano sax to decorate the arrangement, and combines with session player Pete Van Hooke's tightly-efficient drumming and some added percussion: most noticeably the 'fish'. The verses evince a warm, sunny feel, with a bridge that casts slight tonal shadows as a girl's voice suggestively chants, 'You can stay here if you're nice to me', followed by some heavy breathing. Andy Davis renders the vocal in a downcast tone, giving the track a slightly lugubrious feel, but this was reversed when the millennium lineup adopted the song in 2000 and featured some gloriously sunny harmonies to highlight its best aspects. Although this song was placed in the penultimate position on the 1976 Rocket release, its rightful place is at the beginning of the album – a position to which it was restored when Walter found the original master tapes in his attic in 2000 and the correctly sequenced version of the album was finally made public. As the opener for the restored album, this track represents a dream that Mick is having prior to being rudely awakened for breakfast (with Werner Von Braun, of course!) by a nurse in the care home at which he is domiciled. As Mutter Slater's Mellotron swells under a poignant soprano sax coda, the tune is brought to rest.

'Fish In A Glass' (Davis, Walter)

A beating bass drum introduces the finest track on *Mr. Mick,* as the album closes on a high point with another Davis/Walter classic. Frank Zappa's influence once again hovers over the music as the instrumental first half of this epic, builds in intensity. Powered along by some of Crun Walter's best-recorded bass-playing, he sounds like an absolute giant, and the watertight Walter/Van Hooke rhythm section shows what it's capable of. Mutter Slater flicks piano chords with aplomb as Keith Gemmell rasps into his saxophone over the driving rhythm, recalling the glory days of the *Extravaganza* lineup: such is the track's powerhouse feel. Halfway through, the tempo abruptly changes to a slow thud as the string pads build and the music slowly rises before the entry of Andy Davis' vocal: the thick raucousness of which really suits this number.

With a melody recalling 'If Everyone Was Listening' from Supertramp's 1974 album *Crime Of The Century*, Davis relates the dilemma of Mr. Mick trapped in his metaphorical jar like a fish in a glass. The lyrics betray a different concept, though – that of the seen-it-all rock star with nowhere left to go but down, and other versions of this song feature alternate lyrics along these lines: more of which later. The double-time chorus again evokes The Beatles, as Davis sings of 'Revolution, spinning 'round and 'round your head', and concludes there is no solution, so, 'I think you'd better sing instead' – perhaps suggesting that Mick was once a rock star, before old age and senility overtook *him*. With a biting guitar solo from Davis, using the stomping chorus chords, the track points to its conclusion with a call-and-response chant where 'They started to laugh, at a fish in a glass', before fading away on a towering two-chord modulation with rising string pads supporting it, making a glorious end indeed to the final Stackridge studio album of the 1970s.

The Original Mr. Mick

When the tapes of the original *Mr. Mick* album were unearthed, it came to light that there had been quite a bit of music completely cut out of the Rocket master. *The Original Mr. Mick* was released on Dap Records in 2000 and features the intended running order with all the narration present and correct. The album still opens with a sample of Alan 'Fluff' Freeman doing a radio dedication over some synthesizer doodling, but instead of going into 'Hold Me Tight', the opening salvo is 'Hey! Good Looking'. Some of the mixes differ slightly from the Rocket Records version. For example, there is tons more reverb on Keith Gemmell's clarinet parts on 'The Slater's Waltz', and the sound quality varies too, being generally inferior to the Rocket release. However, on the 2000 release, we regain some of the lost music, so it's a case of swings and roundabouts really, and the true Stackridge fan will of course want both – a situation remedied when Angel Air released the two variants in one package in 2007. The additional *Mr. Mick* material not featured on the Rocket release, is discussed below.

'Mr. Mick's Walk' (Davis)

As Mick wakes from his dreamy slumber, it's time for 'Breakfast with Werner Von Braun' – or at least a fellow inmate who believes he's the German rocket scientist – before Mick decides to go for a walk, spins his walking stick, and where it points, he heads off to. Mick's wanderings are accompanied by Andy Davis' blues-based 'Walking Music' – mainly a somewhat-repetitive piano riff, as

Mutter Slater narrates the story in an occasionally uncertain tone which doesn't entirely convince, although there are some amusing couplets to enjoy along the way.

'Mr. Mick's Dream' (Davis)

Davis goes into some scalar piano runs to evoke a dreamier atmosphere as Mick begins to daydream, before the narration takes us back to a reprise of the 'Walking Music' as Mick heads further out of town, eventually reaching the local refuse tip where his adventures begin. 'The Dump' is here retitled 'Stinking, Sinking Music', after which Mick has his rendezvous with the steam radio, cotton reel and ballet shoes.

'Hazy Dazy Holiday' (Slater)

'Coniston Water' features an extended ambient coda with narration from Slater, evoking Mick's memory of a holiday in the Lake District in his dim and distant past – possibly around the time that Donald Campbell crashed his Bluebird craft attempting to break the water speed record on that stretch of water in 1968, judging by the allusions in the text.

'Can Inspiration Save The Nation?' (Davis, Walter)

A song that was featured with a much more convoluted arrangement in the live set of the time, this stripped-down and shortened version graces the 2000 release. Long neglected but rightfully restored – eventually to become a live highlight again from 2007 onwards – this is a masterful and moving piece of songwriting. Sounding a lot like the late great Alan Hull of Lindisfarne (one of Walter's favourites), Davis' voice suits this material like a glove, as the lyrics turn from a personal to a universal perspective, with a verse of great emotive power involving 'A mermaid plucking oil slicks from her hair'. The arrangement is a model of economy, with just guitar and voice from Davis with a particularly affecting middle eight supported by shimmering organ chords. This track proved to be a true rediscovered gem in the Stackridge coronet.

'Happy Ending Music' (Davis)

Extrapolated from the coda sequence of 'Steam Radio Song', this provides a glorious interlude linking into the swansong of 'Fish In A Glass'. It recalls the spirit of earlier incarnations of the band when it bursts in with a rolling burlesque swagger as the tympani rolls, the clarinet tootles, and Slater blows once more into his ancient flute. And for a couple of minutes, all seems right again with the world.

Mutter Slater 1976 Solo Sessions

'If You Were The Only Girl In The World' (Ayr, Grey)

There was a strange period in early-1976 when Rocket Records decided to try to promote Mutter Slater as a crooner. The sessions were produced by Geoffrey Haslam, who'd previously worked with artists as diverse as Ornette Coleman, Bette Midler and Jan Akkerman. The band arrangements were handled by Johnny Stirling, who was concurrently working with Peter Skellern. Two old standards were selected for recording along with the Stackridge original 'Dancing On Air'. The first cover was 'If You Were The Only Girl In The World': a hoary old chestnut penned by Nat D. Ayr (music) and Clifford Grey (lyrics) back in 1916.

The backing track is actually quite lovely in places, and begins with a delightful effect that sounds akin to a musical box over drifting strings (real ones!) playing the chorus melody, and this intro is quite touching in its tenderness. The orchestral arrangement is supported by some excellent guitar and bass-playing, which could well be session men, I suspect. Slater's crooning vocals are at best hopeful, and it feels odd to hear him attempting such a stratospheric vocal near the top of his range. It's amazing how his voice went from raucous and strident on early Stackridge tracks like 'Do The Stanley' and 'The Galloping Gaucho', to oh-so-fragile-sounding on these solo tracks.

Initially slated as a possible A-side, 'If You Were The Only Girl In The World' actually got as far as a having a fully-labelled demo single pressed, backed with 'Solitude' and allocated the catalogue number ROKN 504. A number of these survived, and I did manage to obtain one for my own personal collection.

'Solitude' (Mills, Delange, Ellington)

This cover of the Duke Ellington jazz standard – allegedly written in 20 minutes by Sir Duke while he was waiting for his band to turn up – is furnished with lyrics by Eddie DeLange and Irving Mills, and dates from 1934. By far the most artistically successful track from these sessions, it features a fragile but charming vocal by Slater. Best of all, he plays some distinctive flute backing frills before embarking on a gently meandering solo that twists and turns in an incredibly relaxed mode over the verse chords – like a gently rippling stream, before settling into a gorgeous brace of trills that evoke bluebirds fluttering around a flower. It proved to be his last-recorded classic flute solo of the 1970s.

'Dancing On Air' (Bowkett, Slater)

Not heard of since the *Extravaganza* lineup added it to their set in early 1975, this was exhumed and given a more brash, swinging big-band arrangement courtesy of Johnny Stirling. Considerably trimmed down from the more casual-sounding 1975 live Stackridge version, it features Slater whistling the melody on the intro and middle section and crooning on the verses. The repeated middle eight sees a slight strain on his voice as he pushes the higher octave, and these repeats are split with a guitar/brass call-and-response interlude with some nice guitar interjections (Whether this is Andy Davis or not is unknown, but it sounds as if it could be). Once in the can, it seems Rocket decided to go with this track rather than 'If You Were The Only Girl In The World' as Slater's debut solo single, backed with the excellent 'Solitude'. Guess what? It sank without a trace.

Additional Material

In the year 2000 – as part of the late Elessar Tetramariner's excellent unofficial series of archive Stackridge recordings made available free of charge to Thrashers – came a soundboard recording of one of the earliest gigs of the *Mr. Mick* lineup at King's College in London on 2 October 1975, engineered by Roger Rowe. This glimpse into the early days of the final 1970s Stackridge variant also hinted at the original concept the band envisaged for this project, containing much more material than what ended up on the Rocket release. Much of the music that ended up on the two variants of *Mr. Mick* was performed. The King's College set includes 'The Slater's Waltz', 'Hey! Good Looking', 'Bagley Reservoir' (later retitled 'Coniston Water'), a much longer version of 'Can Inspiration Save The Nation?' with an extremely odd repeated middle eight that was later excised, 'Fish in a Glass', 'Breakfast With Werner Von Braun', 'The Dump', 'Save A Red Face', 'Steam Radio Song' and 'Happy Ending Music'. The set for this tour also featured two songs unrelated to *Mr. Mick*: the set opener 'Bad News', and the encore: a cover of Lennon/McCartney's 'Your Mother Should Know'.

'Bad News' (Davis)

A lone survivor from the previous incarnation of Stackridge, 'Bad News' had been introduced into the set of the *Extravaganza* lineup for their summer 1975 tour, which proved to be that band's final outing. Detailing a day in the life of a downtrodden worker, it features a crotchet piano rhythm that strongly recalls classic mid-1960s pop, and it bears a passing resemblance to The Kinks' 1966 hit 'Dead End Street', both lyrically and musically. A mid-tempo ballad sung by Andy Davis and powered along by his stomping piano, it reduces to half-speed for the first half of the chorus, as the abused employee protests at 'Working to pay the rent, subsidizing the government', before Davis resumes the crotchet piano for the denouement of 'Forty years pretending I'm alive'. Mutter Slater wails along on harmonica on these choruses: an instrument I am a big fan of and would've liked to see him employ a lot more often. 'Bad News' is a fine song that deserved a band studio version, but this was not to be, although I did cover it on my 2007 charity album of Stackridge rarities, *Prescription*.

'Your Mother Should Know' (Lennon, McCartney)

The encore number more or less follows The Beatles' arrangement and was, in fact, the last song I ever saw a 1970s Stackridge lineup perform: at Imperial

College on 8 November 1975. Stackridge had a penchant for Beatles covers throughout their incarnations, but this one didn't measure up to their earlier efforts.

The Korgis (1979)

Personnel:
James Warren: bass, vocals
Andy Davis: keyboards, guitar, mandolin, drums, vocals
Phil Harrison: keyboards, percussion
Stuart Gordon: violin, percussion, mandolin
Glenn Tommey: keyboards
David Lord: keyboards
Bill Birks: drums, percussion
Al Powell: drums
Keith Warmington: harmonica
Kenny Lacey: percussion
Jo Mullett, Jo Pomeroy: backing vocals
Recorded: Crescent Studios, Bath, 1978-1979
Producer: The Korgis
Engineers: David Lord, Glenn Tommey
Label: Rialto, Edsel/Demon
Release dates: 1 July 1979 (Rialto), 1999 (Edsel/Demon CD)

In 1978, James Warren suggested to Andy Davis that they work together again. Whatever Warren suggested seems to have worked, as they made the decision to reunite on a new project, as writing and recording began again in earnest. The early demos secured them a deal with Rialto Records. Toying with various names, they were almost called The Venkas after Andy Davis overheard the waiter in a Russian restaurant using it as a swear word! They finally adopted the moniker of The Korgis, and one explanation for choosing this name was in deference to the Queen's dogs, but modified with a letter K, as Andy Davis was a fan of that letter's use in communist propaganda. The other explanation doing the rounds at the time was that their moniker was in deference to the synthesizer brand Korg.

Re-energised, the duo released their first single 'Young 'N' Russian' in 1979 to a blank reaction from the music business and public alike. However, the Andy Davis song 'If I Had You' followed hard on the heels of this first single, and amazingly it soared into the top 20: a feat Stackridge had never managed in all their years together.

The sleeve of their eponymous first album shows off their new image, consisting of suits, colourful kipper ties and enigmatic shades, with a garish pink background behind them on the cover. Another boxed photo on the rear of the sleeve is set on a tilt, making James Warren's tie look like it has a life of its own as it pokes out from his body at an impossible angle. Also included is an insert with the printed lyrics and amusing photos – mainly from the 1940s and 1950s – that relate to the subject of each song. This is a similar idea to the one employed on many 10cc sleeves and inserts in the early-1970s. The sleeve iconography evinces a colourful contemporary feel, and the duo soon found they were at the forefront of the more sophisticated form of power pop that evolved from the energy of punk, although, in truth their most popular tunes were the romantic ballads, and the harder-edged moments on display were rarer. With a synthesizer-heavy sound and a bunch of well-written commercial tunes, they had no trouble floating on the mainstream for a profitable couple of years.

'Young 'N' Russian' (Davis, Warren, Ridlington)

Starting with the sound of a striking match, this rather stiff-sounding track had already flopped as a single before the album was released. Andy Davis renders the vocal in a deep tone, attempting to match the lyric's seediness with his vocal texture, as a female chorus chips in on the title hook line. The rhythm is tight, processed, and quite unnatural, and apart from some trebly bass lines from James Warren, synthesizers dominate, and the track evinces a rather taut feel.

'I Just Can't Help It' (Davis)

After the band's chart hit with 'If I Had You', this was released as a follow-up but proved too similar in formula to make much of an impression on the public at large. Unrelieved by a middle eight, the verse and chorus have to carry this simple love song, and the slack is taken up by several Andy Davis guitar solos. The album version has a less-inspired guitar take, but the single boasts some incisive lead guitar from Davis and is the superior take for that reason. To paraphrase a contemporary review by the Canterbury-scene keyboard player Dave Stewart in *Musicians Only* magazine, it's the kind of record that sounds great when you're in love but overly slushy if you're not.

'Chinese Girl' (Davis)

Sporting some of the toughness that Davis had touted for The Korgis in press interviews of the time, some Oriental-style guitar motifs open this track, leading into an insistent thumping rhythm, driven by a simple riff. Some experimental sound effects, whir in the background, and abrasive, dissonant guitars give the track a hard edge that was right on the button in the new-wave times of 1979. The whole thing perhaps foreshadows the sound experiments to come on Davis' Slow Twitch Fibres project a few years hence.

'Art School Annexe' (Davis)

Dominating the writing on side one, Davis offers up this tune cribbed from The Doors' 'Hello, I Love You': a similarly simple pop tune to this one. 'Art School Annexe' displays a relentless chorus that wears a bit thin after several listens. The main point of note is the decelerated coda with a touch of psychedelia and some complex trebly bass runs from James Warren, whose bass playing throughout the album is exemplary.

'Boots And Shoes' (Davis, Warren)

This is undoubtedly the best song on side one, and this was proven when the reformed Stackridge revamped it for their live set in 2007 to magnificent effect. The original demo was closer to the hard-rocking Stackridge version if a bit more 1950s rock 'n' roll. But by the time it came around to recording this version, synthesizers had taken over completely and swamp much of this with claustrophobic string washes. Matters are not helped by a leaden rhythm, and the whole thing sounds a bit tired: a fate such a good song didn't really deserve. Some neat wordplay from James Warren attempts to rescue the situation, delivered in a somewhat nasal manner, and he almost growls the line 'But you're in chains' on the final verse. An overly long instrumental fade takes more shine yet off this recording, but thankfully, a better fate awaited this fine song.

'Dirty Postcards' (Warren)

Side two, and at last, we're firmly into James Warren territory, as it opens with the most Stackridge-like song on the album. With a welcome dose of lighthearted whimsy, Warren relates the tale of a friend who begins to perform eccentric acts after being hit on the head in a boating accident on the Norfolk Broads. These odd exploits include ironing the creases out of his face, and shocking the Pope with a less-than-savoury vision concerning St. Mark and an aardvark! Of course, in reality, brain damage is no laughing matter, and this lyric can safely be filed under black humour. Warren's suggestions on the matter are (as ever) to have a nice cup of tea and keep on sending the dirty postcards. The influence of Uncle Frank once again raises its head, as there's a direct reference to the 1970 Zappa album *Weasels Ripped My Flesh* in the second verse. Musically, the rhythm recalls 'Marzo Plod' from the first Stackridge album, carried by a swaying piano backing track and featuring a clever feint to a discord in the chorus, resolving on the final line. The inevitable synthesizer returns during the instrumental break following the jolly middle eight, and when you think the track has ended, an unnecessary reprise of this section fades back in for a coda. It's still one of the album's best tracks, though.

'O Maxine' (Warren)

The second of four Warren compositions on side two, 'O Maxine', is a jerky-sounding slow rock performance that isn't entirely convincing. Another late 1970s development, electronic drums are employed, and the string chords behind the chopping guitars play an ear-catching discord during parts of the verses. Andy Davis provides a somewhat embarrassing talking response to Warren's vocal on the middle eight and also throws in a smidgen of slide guitar for good measure.

'Mount Everest Sings The Blues' (Warren)

This Warren rocker is the highlight of the album and displays a genuine rock 'n' roll feel driven by his motoring bass, and I'm willing to bet that's Andy Davis on the drums. With a similar rhythmic feel to the Chuck Berry classic 'Memphis, Tennessee', the allusion to 1950s rock and roll is completed by some perfect period lead guitar fills by Davis and stoked by some cooking organ-playing. The lyrics are brilliant and pure James Warren – who else could imagine the woes of being the biggest mountain in the world? Full of wonderful, witty wordplay, this is one of the best tracks here, and more than worthy of following the Stackridge 1970s legacy. A fine band performance, Warren's superb bass flourish halfway through Davis' sizzling guitar solo is worth the price of entry alone, and the clever timing – dropping half a bar at the end of each verse – spurs on the tumbling forward momentum. This track is terrific fun, and the band sound like they're having a ball. It's completed by a change of tempo into a classic slow-blues ending.

'Cold Tea' (Warren)

The last Warren offering on the album sees him return to one of his favourite subjects: namely, tea. It's a parody of John Lennon's 1969 hit single 'Cold Turkey', only this time heroin is substituted with tea leaves, in a jokey lyric that wears a bit thin on repeated listening. But there are some of those words you rarely hear in pop songs: such as 'crapulous' and 'cadaverous', as you might expect from Warren's fertile lexicon. Andy Davis provides some authentic, cutting Lennon guitar chords, and the string washes keen away in the background as usual.

'If I Had You' (Davis)

The single that launched The Korgis' brief chart career employs a tune on the intro and chorus that is borrowed from Rachmaninoff, who in turn borrowed it from Paganini, so it's a fair cop. The melody from '18th Variation on a Theme of Paganini' makes for a great chorus and propelled this simple love song to number 13 in the UK in the summer of 1979. Andy Davis' and Stuart Gordon's mandolins ring out on the intro, immediately latching the ear onto the chorus tune, and by the time the record has ended, you're hooked and humming it. James Warren gives his best choirboy vocal performance, and Andy Davis provides the harmony on the choruses, and some delicious slide guitar, completing an irresistible sing-along summer hit that led to the unfamiliar sight of our two former Stackridge heroes miming on *Top Of The Pops* at last!

1978 Korgis Demos

Several demos of Korgis songs have emerged as bonus tracks on later CD releases. The three released on the 2005 compilation *The Korgis Kollection* give an interesting insight into the state of play in the band during 1978. At the time, vocalist Steve Lindsey was briefly in the formative lineup and contributed his song 'Lines' to the demo sessions. He eventually chose not to stay with The Korgis, and formed his own band called The Planets, who became labelmates on Rialto Records. A rocking version of the excellent Davis/Warren song 'Boots And Shoes' was also demoed at these sessions, as was 'Make A Fuss About Us', which later evolved into the instrumental 'Rover's Return': the closing track of The Korgis' 1980 album *Dumb Waiters*.

'Lines' (Lindsey)

It's immediately obvious that Steve Lindsey would've added more bite (excuse the pun) to The Korgis' sound. Displaying more edge than the later variants of the band, Lindsey's song 'Lines' features a choppy reggae feel but crossed with a pop/rock sensibility. It is catchy and clever pop writing, with lyrics contrasting different kinds of lines (washing lines, yellow lines, picket lines etc.) over a descending chromatic sequence and a melody that soon lodges in the brain. The chorus music sounds eerily like The Specials' number-1 hit 'Ghost Town', which was still three years in the future at this point.

'Boots And Shoes' (Davis, Warren)

When Stackridge revisited this song live in 2007, they wisely went back to the rocking feel of the arrangement on this kicking demo. With an almost aggressive edge and powered by some terrific rock 'n' roll piano histrionics (presumably from Glenn Tommey), 'Boots And Shoes' motors along at a rate of knots, making this one of the best versions. It's a shame it lost some of its grit by the time it was recorded for the debut Korgis album, but thankfully this was redressed by the Stackridge studio version appearing on *A Victory For Common Sense* in 2009.

'Make A Fuss About Us' (Davis)

Although this charges along at a high tempo, it's nowhere near as gritty as the other two 1978 demos. Musically it's essentially similar to the eventual instrumental version from *Dumb Waiters*, but with the addition of a chorus and a set of desultory lyrics. On balance, the instrumental version makes for a better listen.

Dumb Waiters – The Korgis (1980)

Personnel:
James Warren: bass, guitar, vocals
Andy Davis: keyboards, guitar, drums, percussion, backing vocals
Phil Harrison: keyboards, percussion
Stuart Gordon: violin, acoustic guitar
David Lord: keyboards, percussion
Jo Mullet, Ali Cohn: backing vocals
Stephen Paine: special synthesizer programming
Recorded: Crescent Studios, Bath, October 1979-March 1980
Producers: The Korgis, David Lord
Engineer: David Lord
Label: Rialto, Edsel/Demon
Release dates: 1 July 1980 (Rialto), 1999 (Edsel/Demon CD)

The band's next album *Dumb Waiters* spawned their biggest hit – the James Warren ballad 'Everybody's Got To Learn Sometime', which has since become a recognised pop classic and continues to gain cover versions into the 21st century. The single reached number 5 in the UK in summer 1980, and in May 1981 it spent three weeks at number 1 in Spain, also charting in France and the US. After a smaller third chart hit with 'If It's Alright With You Baby', also taken from *Dumb Waiters*, the hits inexplicably dried up. Though the debut LP had failed to chart, *Dumb Waiters* actually made it up to number 40 in the album listings that summer: in no small part due to the popularity of their biggest hit single.

With cartoon-like artwork, the front cover depicts a pointed dunce's cap with a large D on it that has been placed in a dumb waiter (the restaurant lift usually employed to send food between floors). This is a painting provided by artist Jeffery Edwards, while the overall art direction for the package is credited to the corporate-sounding Rowbottom and Balme. The reverse of the sleeve sports a large colour photo of the three musicians, who were then being promoted as the faces of The Korgis. The ever-photogenic James Warren is standing in the centre, with Stuart Gordon and Phil Harrison crouching down on either side of him. The background is cream with abstract splashes of primary colours across it in the style of artist Jackson Pollock and beneath the photo is the album tracklisting. Some copies of the album came replete with a Rialto Records promotional pack with a brace of black-and-white photos from the same session as the back sleeve picture, plus a press release giving the lowdown on the *new* lineup the label were pushing. Andy Davis was still well involved, despite not appearing in the press photos now, but he would back off with each successive album going forward.

'Silent Running' (Warren)

A click-clack intro leads into this attempt at futurism, painting a lyrical scene of a decaying future world and displaying a distinct green agenda that berates the 'madness no description can encapsulate'. An economical backdrop of piano pervades a track that ticks along like clockwork, perhaps indicating that time is running out. But musically, there's not a great deal to excite a listener in this number despite a farsighted lyric. Mind you, Joni Mitchell's 'Big Yellow Taxi' and The Beach Boys' 'Don't Go Near The Water' were highlighting these concerns ten years earlier.

'Love Ain't Too Far Away' (Davis)

Andy Davis serves up the next selection in the shape of this middling pop song. The vocal features an unusually deep-voiced James Warren as he forsakes his preferred falsetto, perhaps in an attempt to convey Davis' dour melody. A synthesizer adds some riffs with a Parisian accordion feel and the choruses are hung on an insistent guitar hook. But at an inordinate three and a half minutes, this track becomes a tad repetitive.

'Perfect Hostess' (Davis)

Although taking a more low-key role in the band, Andy Davis is still providing his fair share of material on this second album. James Warren remains in a lower register here, to articulate Davis' vision of the perfect hostess with her 'Carmen rollers'. The chorus is undeniably catchy, if a little overplayed, and side one of *Dumb Waiters* continues to await a real highlight.

'Drawn And Quartered' (Warren)

Driven by lumpy drumming and what sounds like a sequenced synthesizer, this track proves to be something of a lame disco duck and foreshadows nothing less than the sound adopted by 1980s duo Pet Shop Boys. Perhaps this means it was ahead of its time. The only musical point of interest is the key change in the verses, but unfortunately, this soon palls after several passes.

'Everybody's Got To Learn Sometime' (Warren)

In terms of side one of *Dumb Waiters,* the arrival of this simple but sublime pop classic is akin to the cavalry coming over the hill. At last, Warren demonstrates his unquestionable talent, in an atmospheric performance of what is fast becoming an evergreen British pop standard. With a score of cover versions following in its wake (including several live Stackridge versions), it's amazing that such a spartan song ended up providing him with financial security. Hugely atmospheric and buoyed by the usual cushion of string washes, a crystal-clear Warren vocal carries the subtle emotion of this lyric, heightened by the chord change from minor to augmented in the verses ('I need your loving') that releases into the chorus chant of the title. A simple figure played on what sounds like a koto, bridges the chorus back into the verse, and the killer punch is the plaintive violin solo from Stuart Gordon in place of a third pass at the verse.

Although the familiar version has only one repeated six-line verse, there's another version with an alternate second verse which replaced the original when Edsel Records issued the *Dumb Waiters* CD remaster in 1999. This alternate take is my favourite version, as the extra verse works really well and is as evocative as the first.

'Intimate' (Davis)

This atmospheric mid-tempo rocker is impelled by some great Davis guitar-playing, and he also drums up a storm behind the kit. James Warren hits the lower register again as he is wont to do when singing most of Davis' tunes. The drum fill leading into the hot guitar solo is particularly tight and tasty, and Davis' guitar brings to mind Pink Floyd's Dave Gilmour at his best, with some terrific bluesy licks.

'It's No Good Unless You Love Me' (Warren)

With its reedy organ, this up-tempo track comes on like a cross between early-1960s kitsch and skating rink music – particularly the instrumental break that recalls the feel of Del Shannon's 'Runaway', with its organ and imitation pizzicato strings, but without the charm of Shannon's 1960s pop classic. Be warned, though – if this tune lodges in your head, you'll find it hard to get it out again!

'Dumb Waiters' (Warren)

The title track is another great example of James Warren in rock 'n' roll mode, and though it's not quite as wonderful as 'Mount Everest Sings the Blues' from the debut album, it still manages to brighten up side two with its energy. Some fine Davis drumming drives it along, as Warren puns his way through the menu in the lyrics, and some added tambourine lifts the excitement in Andy Davis' guitar solo, treated with a liberal dose of reverb. All in all, this is an enjoyable bash, and deserved better luck as a single in the aftermath of the album's two other hits.

'If It's Alright With You Baby' (Warren)

Phil Spector-style bells and a wall-of-sound production confirm the 1960s influences at work here, with some added slide guitar from Andy Davis to decorate this archetypal Warren ballad. When released as a follow-up to their big hit, it charted but stalled just outside the top 40. Soaked in multitracked vocal harmonies, Warren even adds some girlie-type high-range vocals, and the middle eight sweeps the listener up into a warm wash of synthesized sound and harmony.

'Rovers Return' (Davis)

'Rovers Return' provides an instrumental end to the album but is in no way comparable to Andy Davis' previous brilliant instrumentals for Stackridge. Evoking the early-1960s again – in particular The Tornados' megahit 'Telstar', crossed with a Blackpool pier organ feel and propelled by Davis' drumming.

The title is not a tribute to the UK soap *Coronation Street*, but is a nod to the band's pet Jack Russell dog, who stars on a sample added to the then-new Fairlight sampler which represented the sharp end of musical technology in 1980. This device was borrowed from Peter Gabriel via shared producer David Lord, as there were precious few of them around at the time.

Oddly, this instrumental was released as a double A-side with The Korgis' 1980 Christmas offering 'Wish You A Merry Christmas' – a Warren attempt at a Yuletide classic – but it failed to chart.

Sticky George – The Korgis (1981)

Personnel:
James Warren: vocals, bass, piano ('All The Love In The World')
Phil Harrison: keyboards, spoons
Stuart Gordon: backing vocals, guitar, violin, banjo, percussion
Jerry Marotta: drums
Manny Elias: drums ('All the Love in the World')
David Lord: keyboards, wasp, spider, wind and string arrangements
Wind quintet on 'Contraband' – Steve Buck: flute, Stephanie Nunn: oboe, Dave Pegler: clarinet, Huw Pegler: horn, Chantelle Samuel: bassoon
Sheena Power, Jo Mullet (The Korgettes): backing vocals ('That Was My Big Mistake', 'Living On The Rocks')
Recorded: Crescent Studios, Bath, December 1980-February 1981
Producers: David Lord, James Warren
Engineer: David Lord
Label: Rialto, Edsel/Demon
Release dates: 10 July 1981(Rialto), 1999 (Edsel/Demon re-release CD)

Following the first few albums, Andy Davis receded further and further into the background as the friction that split the pair up in the early-1970s appeared to resurface, although Davis' writing and playing still continued to enhance The Korgis' output to varying degrees. By the time *Sticky George* hit the shops, the public face of the band was again James Warren, plus keyboard player Phil Harrison and violinist Stuart Gordon; the name *Sticky George* being inherited from one of Harrison and Gordon's earlier aggregations. James Warren had also had a brief dalliance with the pair in The Shortwaveband a few years after he left Stackridge. This combo had been described as sounding like 'Henry Cow meets Marlene Dietrich', and 'Stackridge with A-levels'. But their eponymous 1975 debut album was a patchy if eccentric affair. Meanwhile, despite more TV appearances ostensibly promoting the quality big ballad 'That Was My Big Mistake' in 1981, both that single and *Sticky George* made little impression on the early-1980s pop landscape, which was a shame, as it was by far the best of their first three albums.

The artwork is again a cartoon-like painting by Jeffrey Edwards, this time of a 40kg barbell dropped onto a wooden floor with the weights at one end breaking through the floorboards. The art direction was overseen by George Rowbottom. The reverse of the sleeve links with the front cover art, as it sports a photo of a running James Warren in a blue shirt with black vertical stripes and another of his crazy tie-at-a-silly-angle photos: this time one of a pinkish-orange hue and curling in an arc over his right shoulder as he runs into what appears to be the same cartoon room pictured in the front cover painting. The tracklist is at the bottom right-hand side of this picture. The inner dust jacket has the lyrics and credits printed on it, but in such garishly ridiculous colours (orange on grey) that it's nigh-on impossible to read.

'Sticky George' (Warren, Harrison)

In the late-1970s, mainstream popular music began to fundamentally change with the advent of digital technology and the rise of the synthesizer. Along with this came a big change in the way drums were recorded and mixed, and the album that kicked off this particular revolution was *Low* by David Bowie, released in 1977. Suddenly the drums were way up-front in the mix on an increasing number of pop records, and *Low* also introduced the sound of the gated snare: where the snare drum sound is fed through a noise gate that sucks away any reverb decay by essentially muting the sound at a chosen point. The legacy of these percussive experiments reverberated through pop, and *Sticky George* is infested with overly loud snare beats, although any experiments with noise gates are less extreme than on, say, Peter Gabriel's third album or some Phil Collins or Genesis records from the same era.

On the opening track, the downbeat rules with a rod of iron in this highly synthetic production. Less a song than a mood, this sounds somewhat unnatural and contrived. The lyrics seem to have been picked for their sound rather than any inherent meaning, and there's a paraphrase of a George Harrison line towards the end ('Better to travel than arrive'), which the quiet Beatle no doubt lifted from a translation of some Eastern scripture. Not an auspicious start to the album.

'Can't We Be Friends Now' (Warren)

Opening salvo aside, the songwriting quality in general on *Sticky George* proves to be a notch or two above the first two Korgis' albums, and the second track is a case in point. With an extremely relaxed tempo and some gorgeous lush harmonies, James Warren's plaintive plea to resolve a lover's tiff is easy on the ear and makes for pleasant listening. The stepped rising verse melody slowly ascends to the repeated chorus chant of the title. Some chorused lead guitar is interjected at various points, sounding like cushioned springing on a well-upholstered arrangement, and the track drifts off into a mellow fade-out, leaving this listener in a relaxed frame of mind.

'Foolishness Of Love' (Harrison)

With Andy Davis out of the picture in all but the occasional writing credit, one senses the former backing musicians Harrison and Gordon pushing for more of a share of band responsibility and recognition. The appearance of this Harrison composition is perhaps an example of James Warren relaxing the reins and giving in to band democracy. Heavily synthesized, it features verses with a floating feel and upbeat choruses bolstered by a cowbell. It's not a bad pop tune for all that, modulating up for the instrumental middle eight, falling back to the verse before a final round of choruses.

'Domestic Bliss' (Warren, Harrison, Gordon)

The democratic writing continues with this group composition. Loaded with ringing, burping and squeaking synthesisers, it sounds like a group performing

Above: Rhythm Festival 25 August 2008. L-R: Sarah Mitchell, Crun Walter, Andy Marsden (behind drums), James Warren, Mutter Slater and Andy Davis. (*Dave Baxter*).

Below: Bull Theatre, Barnet 6 May 2011. L-R: James Warren, Crun Walter, Clare Lindley, Eddie John, Andy Davis and Glenn Tommey. (*Dave Baxter*).

Left: Presenting new music that was not in their regular live set, the adventurous Stackridge debut album was released in 1971. (*MCA Records*)

Right: A selection of Stackridge radio sessions recorded between 1971 and 1973 was released on CD in 1997. (*BBC Worldwide*)

Left: The classic Stackridge line-up was captured in its full glory on the band's second album *Friendliness*. (*MCA Records*)

Right: The third album, with George Martin at the helm, almost catapulted Stackridge into the big league. (*MCA Records*)

Left: *Extravaganza* saw the return of Mutter Slater after a six-month absence as part of a brand-new line-up. (*Rocket Records*)

Right: The band's fifth album, 'Mr. Mick' saw the final Stackridge personnel change of the 1970s before they split. (*Rocket Records*)

Left: Andy Davis hailed from Yatton where, according to Stackridge legend, Purple Spaceships would land on the bowling green! (*Dave Baxter*)

Right: Distributed free at gigs in 1972, the 'Friendliness' comic was designed by Plastic Dog Graphics. (*Radiance McLaren-Draper*)

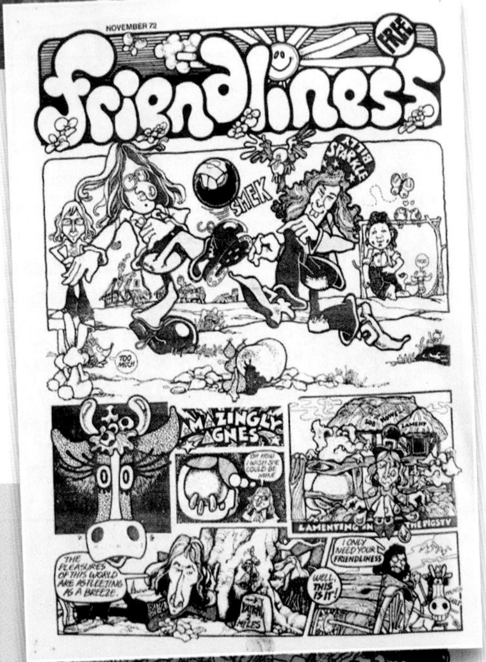

Below: The songs from *Friendliness* were brought to life via these amusing graphics from the 'Friendliness' comic. (*Radiance McLaren-Draper*)

Above: 'Almost The Greatest Show On Earth Tour' paired the band with Camel and ran through February/March 1973. (*Radiance McLaren-Draper*)

Right: Programme distributed at the Stackridge pantomime performances of *Treasure Island* in December 1972. (*Dave Baxter*)

Left: The Korgis' 1979 debut album found the two chief Stackridge songwriters Davis and Warren back together again. (*Rialto Records*)

Right: The second Korgis' album *Dumb Waiters* included James Warren's world-conquering hit 'Everybody's Got To Learn Sometime'. (*Rialto Records*)

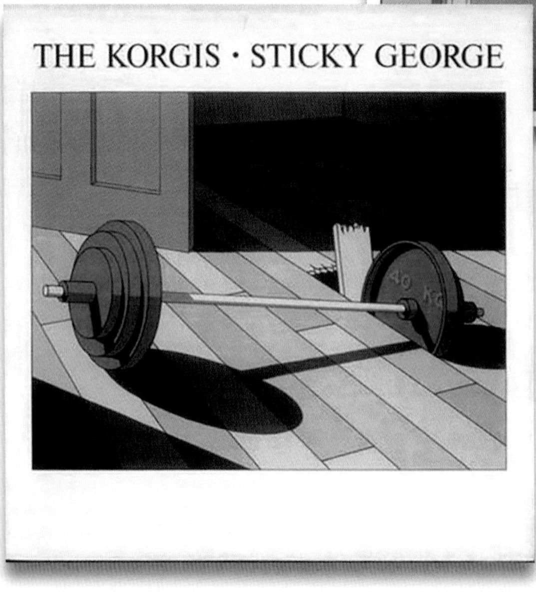

Left: *Sticky George* kept up the songwriting quality of the band's previous two releases and deserved a wider audience. (*Rialto Records*)

Right: Reuniting after 11 years, The Korgis' produced the glossy AOR-slanted album, *This World's For Everyone.* (*Angel Air Records*)

Left: Still going strong in 2001, the Korgis' added a handful of new tracks to *The Korgis Kollection.* (*Angel Air Records*)

Right: The new-look Korgis made a spectacular comeback in 2021 with the excellent pop album *Kartoon World*. (*Angel Air Records*)

Left: In 1999 Stackridge returned after 23 years with the release of *Something For The Weekend*. (*Dap Records*)

Right: The millennium line-up was captured live in 2000 with the release of *Pick Of The Crop*. (*Dap Records*)

Left: For the first time since 1973, the core four Stackridge songwriters all contributed to *Lemon 2002*. (*Stackridge Lemon*)

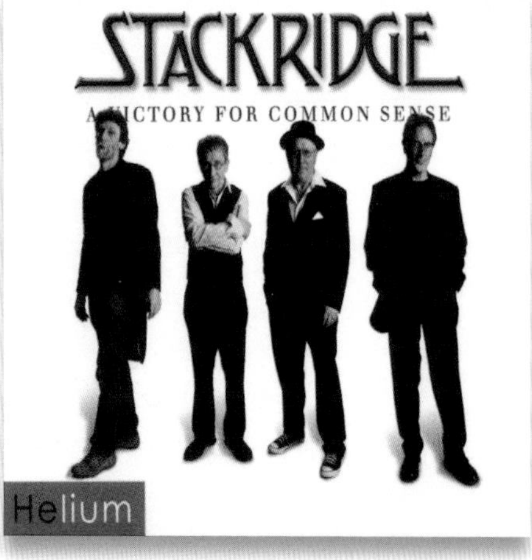

Right: Completing the band's 21st-century artistic renaissance, *A Victory For Common Sense* was released in 2009. (*Helium Records*)

Right: Recordings from three different concerts between 1972 and 1975 were compiled on the *1992 In Concert* CD. (*BBC Windsong*)

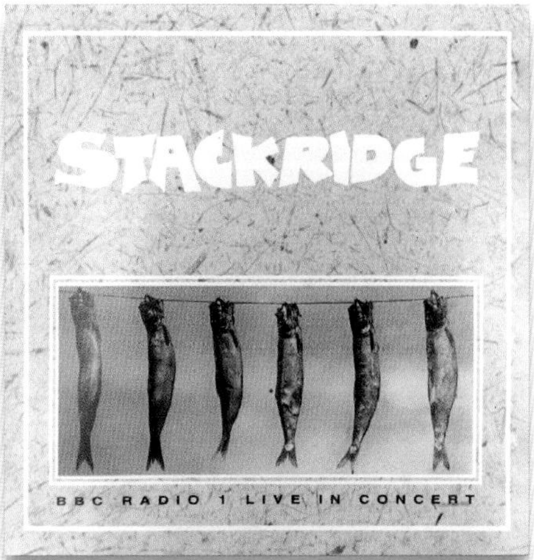

Below: The *4x4* DVD preserved live footage of the hot-sounding 2009 line-up, including the excellent 'Slow Train'.

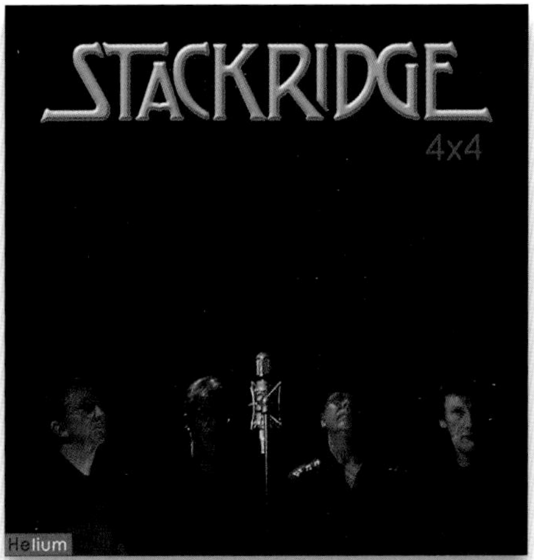

Right: The live Stackridge line-up of 2007 were captured on *The Forbidden City* DVD and 2CD set. (*Angel Air Records*)

Right: The last Stackridge concert in 2015, released as *The Final Bow*, with guest appearances by Mutter Slater. (*Angel Air Records*)

Above: Stackridge perform 'Lummy Days' at Rondo Theatre, Bath, 24 February 2007. L-R: Nigel Newton; Mutter Slater; Sarah Mitchell; James Warren. (*Dave Baxter*)

Right: Crun Walter and Andy Davis at the 100 Club, London, 16 March 2007. (*Dave Baxter*)

James Warren, Crun Walter and Andy Davis at the 100 Club, London, 16 March 2007. (*Dave Baxter*)

Right: Mutter Slater in declamatory mode at the 100 Club, London, 16 March 2007. (*Dave Baxter*)

Above: Glenn Tommey's trombone playing added another dimension to the Stackridge live sound between 2007 and 2015. (*Dave Baxter*).

Right: Stackridge at the Rondo Theatre, Bath, 1 April 2007: L-R Mutter Slater; James Warren; Crun Walter. (*Radiance McLaren-Draper*)

Above: Mutter Slater plays his trusty flute at the Astor Theatre, Deal, Kent, 13 October 2007. (*Dave Baxter*).

Right: Andy Davis gives his all on guitar and vocals at the Rhythm Festival, Bedfordshire, 25 August 2008. (*Dave Baxter*)

Mutter Slater strums his acoustic guitar at the Trinity Centre, Bristol, 6 December 2008. (*Dave Baxter*)

Right: James Warren, Crun Walter and drummer Eddie John at Bacon Theatre, Cheltenham, 3 April 2009. (*Dave Baxter*)

Left: Crun Walter on bass and Clare Lindley on violin at The Bull, Barnet, 6 May 2011. (*Dave Baxter*)

Right: Eddie John on drums and Andy Davis on guitar at The Bull, Barnet, 06/05/11. (*Dave Baxter*)

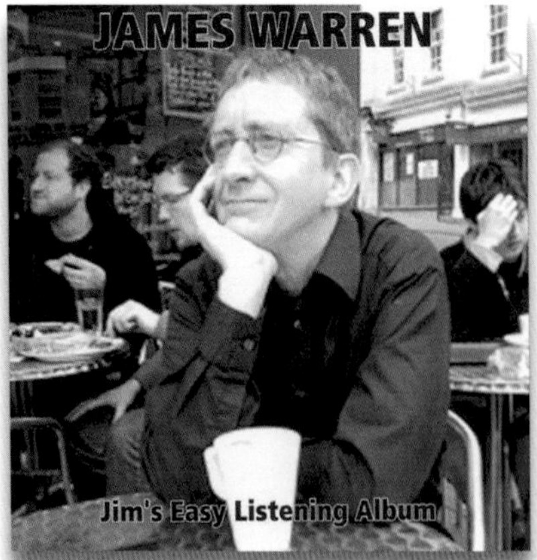

This page: Various solo and band albums by James Warren, Andy Davis and Mutter Slater. (*Sonet, MMC, Andy Davis, Dap, Angel Air, Thoroughbred*)

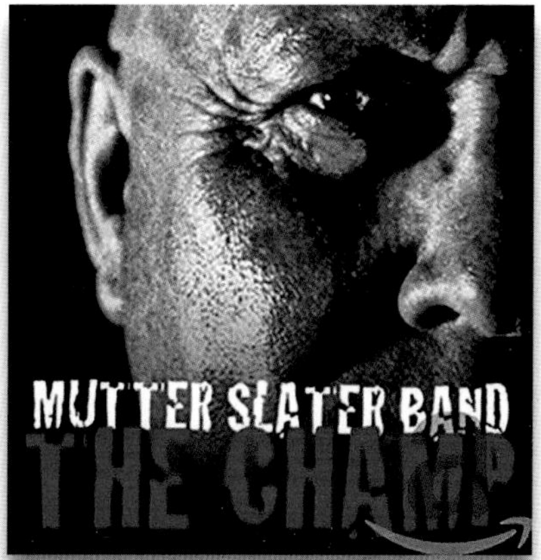

This page: More solo and band albums from James Warren, Andy Davis and Mutter Slater. (*MSB, Angel Air*)

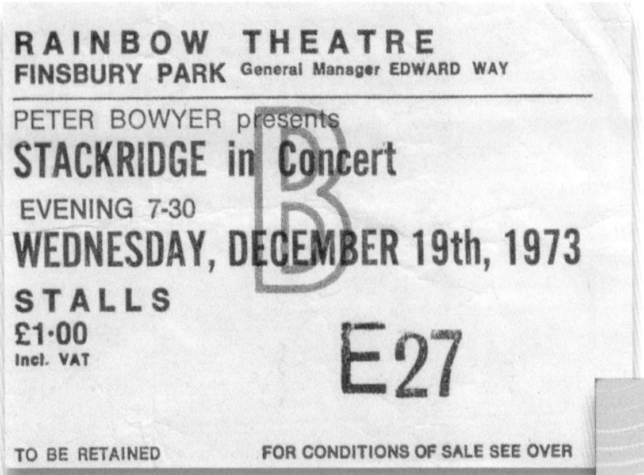

Left: The hottest ticket in town in December 1973: Stackridge performing at the Rainbow Theatre, Finsbury Park, London. (*Dave Baxter*)

Below: Stackridge played a short tour with Scottish band Cows during February/March 1974. (*Dave Baxter*)

Left: Poster for the millennium line-up's Christmas shows in 2000, showing the return of the 'Stackridge Gnome'. (*Radiance McLaren-Draper*)

Above: The author's 2007 covers album of Stackridge rarities, *Prescription*. (*Radiance McLaren-Draper*)

a catchy pop song in the middle of the testing chamber for Roland keyboard sound effects! It also feels like a song written by committee, and though eminently listenable, it's much less impressive than many of Warren's solo compositions for *Sticky George* or those written with his partner and equal Andy Davis.

'That Was My Big Mistake' (Davis, Warren)

When released as a single in 1981, this was billed as James Warren and The Korgis, and received some exposure, including a mimed TV performance on the *Marti Kane Show*. Despite this promotion, a place in the charts yet again eluded The Korgis.

This big ballad provides a grand end to side one and is a much more mature composition than the majority of tracks up to this point. It also has a thoughtful lyric from Warren, with some evocative couplets. The John Lennon influence looms large once more, especially on the second-verse line where he sings of being 'Shipwrecked in our sea of isolation'.

For once, the use of synthesizer is subtle too. These tasteful embellishments help to build the emotion on the verses towards the big chorus, and a more-guitar-oriented band could've easily transformed this into a power ballad, like The Carpenters' groundbreaking single 'Goodbye To Love' in 1973, which married a quality ballad to Tony Peluso's sustained fuzz lead guitar. As it is, Stuart Gordon has a fair crack at doing the same job for The Korgis as he lifts off into a wailing guitar solo on the build to the final choruses, backed by Phil Harrison's organ; the band sounding much improved by keeping things more organic for a change.

The only negative point I can find about this track is the occasionally overly loud snare drum downbeat that seems to have been purposeful as part of the production.

'Nowhere To Run' (Davis, Warren)

As a forgettable start to side two, this second collaboration with Andy Davis is not in the same league as the previous track. Setting the scene with some ambient synthesizer that attempts to create a creepy atmosphere, it soon morphs into a dirge of a song whose lyrics attempt to paint a post-nuclear portrait of doom and gloom, but it lacks the requisite atmosphere to carry such a heavy subject and has little of musical or lyrical interest to recommend it. For a more carefully-thought-out story set in the aftermath of a nuclear conflagration, check out the excellent 'Stagnation' from the 1970 Genesis album *Trespass*.

'Contraband' (Warren)

Now this is more like it! The best track on the album thus far, 'Contraband', is full of creativity and invention, harking back to the Stackridge glory days. With a definite oom-pah in its stride, this brisk romping march is greatly enhanced by its wind quintet arrangement courtesy of David Lord and some razor-sharp Warren wordplay. The quirky violin solo by Stuart Gordon amuses and delights and the clever, dropped beats of final verse are impressive. Sliding into an unexpected decelerating triple-time rhythm on the coda, the fade-out features a spoon solo played by Phil Harrison, accompanied by some manic laughter in the background.

'All The Love In The World' (Davis. Warren)

The highest quality ballad on the album, this is a sublime creation by the two great songwriters and was released as a single in 1981 to follow up 'That Was My Big Mistake'. It suffered a similar fate and failed to chart, but the unedited version presented here provides a shining peak for side two. With Warren unusually playing piano, he opens the track with slow chords before the band slide in seductively for the verse, with the synthesizer still displaying some taste as it subtly decorates proceedings. The arrival of the chorus soaked in rich vocal harmonies is akin to luxuriating in a warm bath, as a simple sentiment is perfectly expressed in this personal song of unabashed adoration. The synthesizer on the interlude following the second chorus recalls the instrumental side two of David Bowie's aforementioned *Low* album, and a four-bar guitar solo builds into the emotive middle eight, which rises to a consummate climax combining pathos and power. The dynamics of this recording are excellent, too and accentuate its artful structure. Although remade by The Korgis in the 1990s and beyond, this remains the superior version.

'Don't Say That It's Over' (Warren)

The other side of James Warren's muse is on display in this irrepressible slice of up-tempo pop, which provided a third single from the album and yet another flop. The Korgis singles output is consistently high, and it's a mystery why they never had a longer run of hit singles. With all the right pop clichés in place, this song puts them all together in such a way that the effect is an irresistibly beat-driven concoction which always makes me smile. Some of its best wordplay is inexplicably altered on the single (the more prosaic 'egg is on my face' becomes 'someone takes my place', for example), and the witty Moog solo was substituted for a more-cutting guitar solo on the Benelux mix, released on the continent.

'Living On The Rocks' (Warren)

The perfect album closer, this is a Warren ballad with a rich, yearning melody and boasts an opulent arrangement by David Lord, building to an orchestral climax of cinematic-overkill proportions. Skilfully written, it upholds the standard of ballad writing evident on this album. *Sticky George* is by far the band's most well-rounded album so far, with quality ballads ably supported by a couple of up-tempo winners by James Warren, and it certainly deserved to fare a lot better in the marketplace than it did at the time.

Additional Material

'Don't Look Back' (Warren)

When the ubiquitous Trevor Horn was on his hot run in the early-1980s, he managed to take time out to produce this little beauty. A one-off London Records single in 1982, 'Don't Look Back' finds James Warren in ballad mode with one of his most engaging melodies of the era, and Trevor Horn's lush production really brings out the best in this song.

Set in a sea of keyboard strings, the verse has some lovely chord changes which add poignancy to the 'no regrets, look to the future' thrust of the lyric. There are some nice lines to savour, including the very Warren-flavoured couplet 'I'm inclined to say I feel so sad/And I was the optimist, supposedly mad'. With its delicious melody, luxuriant production and well-judged modulations, the whole mélange is topped by a superb Mel Collins sax solo: surely the icing on a supremely well-cooked cake.

It was recorded at Trevor Horn's Sarm Studio and featured Ann Dudley from Art of Noise on keyboards and Warren himself on bass. At this point, The Korgis were being promoted as just James Warren and Maggie Stewart, although quite where the latter fitted into the picture is uncertain, though she did design some artwork for the band.

Despite a good push from London Records, the single barely managed to scrape into the top 75 but deserved much better.

'Xenophobia' (Warren)

The B-side of 'Don't Look Back', this quirky instrumental sounds like an outtake from the *Sticky George* sessions, with synthesized noises similar to that album's 'Domestic Bliss'. The brisk opening passage alternates with a more drifting ambient section with some pitch-bend synthesizer evoking a somewhat sleazy feel, crossed with a horror-movie vibe. The music moves back and forth between these two extremes before coming to a close. A very odd track indeed.

Burning Questions – James Warren (1986)

Personnel:
James Warren: vocals, guitars, percussion
Nick Magnus: keyboards, programming, drum sequencing
Andy Davis: pre-production sequencing, backing vocals
Glenn Tommey: percussion (Overdubbed in September 2006 for 20th-anniversary CD)
Recorded: Sonet Studios, London, January-October 1986
Producer: James Warren
Engineer: John Acock
Label: Sonet
Release date: December 1986

After the chart success of 1979 to 1981, Davis and Warren largely went their separate ways again for the next decade, though Davis did lend Warren a hand on his first solo outing *Burning Questions*. While Davis moved into session work and writing songs for other artists, Warren signed to Sonet Records, initially as a songwriter. But possibly due to the lack of uptake on his current oeuvre, he decided to record a new album. It proved to be something of an artistic nadir in comparison with his output before and after this era, not helped by the overbearing 1980s production values, as pop producers, in general, went mad over the new digital technology. The net result was to smother the life out of many records made in this era, *Burning Questions* providing an unfortunate example of this.

'Burning Questions' (Davis, Warren)

With a programmed drum rhythm and some electronic drum fills the title track of James Warren's debut solo album, clatters into life. Driven by a funky keyboard bass line and synth-brass stabs, there is also a sampled female opera voice added to the chorus as the track charges along, and this at least provides a catchy hook, but the song itself isn't really up there with the old Stackridge team's best previous work.

'Climate Of Treason' (Warren)

An even faster tempo ushers in the second track, whose main feature is Nick Magnus' 1980s-style keyboard and drum programming. There's an attempt at some unusual chord changes and minor-to-major key variations, but any trace of subtlety suffers badly due to the claustrophobic production. With Nick Magnus' track record (Steve Hackett, The Enid) you would maybe expect a more tasteful touch to proceedings, but perhaps Warren was pushing for that mid-1980s contemporary sound that was *de rigueur* for pop productions of that era.

'They Don't Believe In Magic' (Warren)

This was released as a single the following year, backed with the superior 'I'll Be Here', but it headed quickly for the bargain bins, where I picked it up. Announcing its entrance with some Disney sound effects, it does at least feature some guitar-playing which stands out among the more synthetic sounds on many of the other tracks. It also has one really nice upward chord change on the chorus that makes it memorable, but the song would've sounded more effective in a stripped-down arrangement to let it breathe a bit. This is a better effort, though.

'Possessed' (Warren)

Based on blatant synthesiser blocks, this track had already been released as a B-side credited to The Korgis. It has a glossy surface production that sits with the times it was made in, but doesn't travel at all well. The programmed drums drive it along, and it possesses a kind of stabbing, fast chorus, and it's a tad reminiscent of electro-poppers OMD in places.

'I Know Something' (Warren)

Warren offers yet another funk-derived keyboard-driven, upbeat concoction: it drives along relentlessly but fails to go anywhere very interesting, really. Like much of *Burning Questions*, it's a difficult track to analyse, as it's so of its time sonically speaking.

'True Life Confessions' (Davis, Warren)

Originally released as a single in 1985 under The Korgis' moniker, this track was backed with 'Possessed'. It's a simple pop song that predictably sunk without a trace, and sadly it was the first Korgis single that was just okay rather than fabulous. Sporting a rolling rhythm and a touch of calypso influence, the verses and repetitive choruses are a bit too similar, lending the track a slightly one-dimensional feel with a perfunctory middle eight thrown in. A synthesizer solo imitating steel drums strives to cook up a Caribbean vibe, and Andy Davis adds some Mariachi trumpet samples resulting in a track that is a pleasant-if-unessential listen.

'It Won't Be The Same Old Place' (Davis, Warren)

This ballad has a touch more quality and, in fact, went on to further life as a Korgis recording via a stripped-down acoustic version on their *Unplugged* release in 2005. This version sounds a tad tired, and though the production is toned down a bit, it audibly drags after a while. But the chorus is memorable and liable to get you humming once you've heard it a few times. All in all, this is a much better effort from the old Davis/Warren team than most of the album.

'Loneliness' (Warren)

A fast rhythm and more-synthetic pounding is in evidence on 'Loneliness', which doubles to a gallop on the choruses with a rhythm later used extensively and often to brilliant effect by The Divine Comedy in the 1990s. The lyrics again mention those *Burning Questions* of the title track, but we are still none the wiser about what said queries are or whether there are any burning answers in sight yet!

'Can You Hear The Spirit Dying?' (Warren)
Featuring a chromatic chord sequence and a kind of stop/start broken drum-box rhythm, this is an attempt at a bit more adventure in the melodic content. Again, it would be interesting to hear a more stripped-down version of this Warren song: allegedly one of his favourites of this collection.

'I Want To Remember' (Warren)
This is clearly an attempt at a John Lennon tribute but ends up sounding slightly creepy, as it deals with events on that dreadful night in December 1980 when Lennon was murdered. With a music box intro, car horns and a gunshot, it also has multitracked mumbled voices fading in and out as it proceeds, and it all feels a touch tasteless to me. It has a slow stalking rhythm and running for well over five minutes it definitely outstays its welcome.

Additional Material

'You Made Me Believe' (Warren)
The first of the bonus tracks on the 2006 Angel Air CD re-release, this starts off more promisingly with a real piano and vocals, and has an interesting stepped melody moving up the scale. Unfortunately, the 1980s-style production returns to rather sour the early mood it was building, which is a shame, as this is a decent track.

'How Did You Know?' (Siefert / Warren)
In the 2006 CD re-release booklet, Warren professes to be fond of this track which he co-wrote with his German buddy Matthias Siefert. It has a synthesizer riff and features Eddi Reader of Fairground Attraction on guest vocals. This was released as a single in 1987 but, not surprisingly, made no chart showing.

'I'll Be Here' (Warren)
Easily the best James Warren track from this era, 'I'll Be Here' was left off the original album and appeared as the B-side to the single 'They Don't Believe In Magic'. A conscious attempt by Warren to try and pen another standard that would be covered by other artists, it tapped back into his latent melodic/harmonic talent, although it's not in the same league as the more-finely-wrought creations of his earlier and later periods. However, it's a well-constructed tune that will get most listeners humming after several passes and displays some nice chord changes, too, with the production toned down for once, making this a worthwhile track.

Clevedon Pier – Andy Davis (1989)

Personnel:
Andy Davis: guitar, keyboards, vocals
Stuart Gordon: violin, hammer dulcimer, mandolin
Peter Allerhand: guitar
Will Gregory: saxophones
David Lord: keyboards
Jam Crisp: percussion
John Sheaffe: programming
Recorded: Crescent Studios, Moles Studio, Bath, 1989
Producers: Andy Davis, David Lord, Stuart Gordon
Engineers: David Lord (Crescent), Mike Long (Moles)
Label: MMC, Angel Air
Release dates: 1989 (MMC CD), 2005 (Angel Air CD)

Meanwhile, Andy Davis' path through the 1980s started with a spell on guitar in the band Slow Twitch Fibres, which marked the start of his relationship with longtime collaborator and bassist Pete Brandt. The lineup was completed by Dr. Dan Altman on keyboards and Roy Dodds on drums. They signed a deal with Rialto Records, and so were labelmates with The Korgis during the latter's successful chart run. Rialto had been set up by Nick and Tim Heath – sons of celebrated bandleader Ted Heath – and it proved to be a good home for both Davis and Warren over the turn of the decade.

Slow Twitch Fibres proved to be a less commercial proposition than The Korgis, and were somewhat quirky and left-field. They managed several singles on Rialto. The first in 1980 was a cover of the 1936 Irving Berlin standard 'Let's Face The Music And Dance', which Davis revisited again with his occasional aggregation, The 3 Cabelleros in the 1990s. The second single (in 1981) was the original 'This Is Your Lunch'. I checked them out in 1981 when they played a gig at Dingwalls in London's Camden Lock but was fairly underwhelmed.

After Slow Twitch Fibres, Davis concentrated on session work and writing for other artists, including Yazz, Manhattan Transfer and Tears for Fears: with whom he became resident keyboard player throughout their substantial string of hit singles and albums in the 1980s. Despite this busy schedule, he found time to record his first solo album and secured a deal for it with MMC Records. This was actually the first CD I ever purchased, back in 1990.

'Women Of Ireland' (O'Doirman, O'Riada, Maloney)

This Celtic-sounding instrumental was brought to prominence by traditional Irish folk outfit The Chieftains when Paddy Maloney arranged a tune composed by Sean O'Riada for the 1973 album *Chieftains 4*. With its sorrowful, expressive melody, this Irish air is tenderly performed by Stuart Gordon on violin and hammer dulcimer, with backup from Andy Davis' keyboards, making for a moving overture to the album.

'Jabe' (Davis)

Andy Davis, at his best, is a writer capable of expressing real emotional depth in his music. This track is a case in point, as he opens with a line that defines the difficulty of attempting to express deep emotion through the medium of song, as he sings 'I'm having trouble with my mother tongue'. He needn't have worried, as the emotion comes through loud and clear. Tinged with regret, the lyrics here hint at the most profound kind of loss we humans can suffer: 'When a voice is missing and a heart is stilled'. A slow song with a keening keyboard wash and synthesized bass, it's given extra poignancy by Will Gregory's atmospheric tenor sax lines that stoke the sadly reflective feel. Davis' heartfelt vocal sounds as if he's expressing a real personal loss as he sings regretfully, 'What kept me from loving you?'. It's all the sadder in that his tone fosters the impression that he really did harbour deep affection for the subject of the song. This is a beautiful piece of songwriting.

'5 Saxes' (Davis)

An experimental piece, with Davis' arrangement for five saxophones ranging from baritone to alto, multitracked by Will Gregory. Opening with a slow, sleazy theme sounding like lounge music for a night of seduction, it stops and starts a few times before being replaced by an odd popping and parping arrangement that's slightly bemusing with the bass end taken by the baritone sax, the middle by the tenor sax and the less attractive sound (to my ears anyway) of a slightly hysterical alto sax. Never mind, all is soon returned to a few more rounds of the sleazy theme to close out the piece, completing this slightly odd musical experiment.

'Hunger' (Davis, Brandt)

'Hunger' is an atmospheric song written for Slow Twitch Fibres. It was later revived by The Korgis, so it's a well-travelled and worthwhile effort. The chord sequence has an air of mystery and intrigue, and generates an undercurrent of unease which is exacerbated by an intermittent, slightly creepy marimba-like riff. The effect is almost filmic, bringing to mind a pair of eyes darting from side to side in trepidation. Davis' vocal carries a desperate-sounding desire for the object of his affections, as he asserts that 'Missing you gives me hunger'. It's a song of unfettered longing and keeps up the considerable quality level as this fine album progresses.

'Clevedon Pier' (Davis, Lord)

Along with the excellent 'Jabe', this is the album's other world-beating track. It's inspired by the Somerset landmark of the same name that's very close to Andy Davis' childhood home village of Yatton, and this spectral tone poem is a beautiful evocation of this local monument to a bygone age. With a timeless Celtic-sounding melody of impeccable musical logic, this instrumental floats majestically on a cloud of keyboard-driven sounds, akin to viewing the pier through an early morning mist that gradually clears as the track progresses. This collaboration with producer David Lord is a sublime creation, and after two verses, the heart-soaring rise into the glorious middle section is elating in the extreme. Returning for a reprise of the verse music, there then follows a long unresolved coda moving slowly and semitonally between keys, harbouring a feeling of uncertainty as the mist appears to descend again and we drift through this section as if in a dream state. The final resolution to the home key feels like finding a safe haven at last after a minute or so of disorientation. 'Clevedon Pier' is one of Andy Davis' most finely wrought creations, and is up there with his greatest artistic triumphs. It is simply beautiful.

'Basso Symphonie' (Davis)

Another instrumental, 'Basso Symphonie,' pales slightly after the spectral presence of the title track. It also sounds a lot more synthetic, despite the fact the previous track was also heavily synthesiser-based but somehow transcended that fact. This is listenable enough but feels more like an interlude of some kind.

'Over & Over' (Davis)

A synthesizer-driven bossa nova rhythm underlies this slightly repetitive song in which Davis sings 'Love calls my name, over and over'. It serves as a prelude to the next track, which it runs straight into.

'Changes' (Davis, Lord)

This synthetic-sounding instrumental opens with a sampled set of tubular bells playing a repetitive 14-beat phrase that launches us into a more regular 4/4 build-up. With synthesizers imitating orchestral instruments, it does have a slightly artificial feel, but the orchestration remains interesting as some marimba-like semiquavers bubble under-sampled tympani thumping over the bar lines, along with big, bold string stabs. The oddly irregular tubular bell riff returns a few times out of the blue, and there's a big orchestral key change prior to the ending sequence. This is an interesting enough track without being a clear highlight.

'Prelude' (Brennan)

Breaking the album up is a short guitar piece written by Pat Brennan: a composer/songwriter from Wicklow, Ireland. It's a gently reflective piece with a distinctly Celtic feel, beautifully performed by Davis. One of the hallmarks of this album is the Celtic influence on display.

'Clear Dawns' (Davis)

Closing the album, 'Clear Dawns' is an instrumental that returns us to the atmosphere of experimentation, with a changing series of piano chord clusters floating in an uncertain sea of string wash. It moves forward as if groping towards something intangible and slowly increases in intensity as it progresses. The music feels akin to climbing a mountain through a veil of mist, and as we eventually near the summit, Andy Davis, at last, unleashes a burst of emotional playing on his electric guitar: a rare appearance on this album for his usually-favoured instrument. After this peak, we descend again into the misty vista of the unresolved piano chords and string pad as the vision fades along with the track, bringing the album to a satisfying conclusion.

Additional Material

'Magic' (Davis)

Starting out sounding like an exercise in systems music – with repeated marimba-like patterns – this soon morphs into a slow ballad with a memorable melody. In a few years time, this would be re-titled 'Hold On' and re-recorded by a newly-convened Korgis lineup for their first new album in 11 years.

'Fred The Piano Man' (Davis)

The second bonus track on the Angel Air re-release of *Clevedon Pier* is a kind of ambient/symphonic drift performed on keyboards. Some string samples float slowly in an adagio mode, creating a pleasantly relaxing interlude. These are succeeded by a piano-playing some of the themes previously stated by the orchestral tones: presumably representing the mysterious Fred of the title. The strings resume for a short coda.

This World's For Everyone – The Korgis (1992)

Personnel:
Andy Davis: keyboards, guitar, drum programming, vocals
James Warren: guitar, vocals
John Baker: keyboards, guitar, vocals
Helen Turner: keyboards
John Griffiths: guitar
Debbie Howard, Samantha Howard: backing vocals
Recorded: Andy Davis' Studio, Bath Spa, 1990-1992
Producer: The Korgis
Engineer: Andy Davis
Label: Eurostar, Angel Air
Release dates: 1992 (Eurostar), 2006 (Angel Air CD)

'This World's For Everyone' (Davis, Warren)

The opening track on the first Korgis album since 1981 is another example of the stream of social conscience songs that proliferated in the wake of *Live Aid* and multiplied throughout the next decade or so. Generally well-meaning and occasionally released to actually raise funds for charities, the blunt earnestness of this style of songwriting can, on occasion, grate on the sensibilities. The track in question just about gets away with it, and sports a memorable melody and hooky chorus that lodges in the brain. Powered by digital percussion with a distinct world-music feel, it makes a pretty good opening salvo for The Korgis' comeback album. The demo was included in the bonus tracks on the 2006 Angel Air CD re-release.

'Hold On' (Davis)

A version of this was previously recorded by Andy Davis during the sessions for his solo album *Clevedon Pier* in 1989, under the title 'Magic'. A classic mid-tempo pop ballad performed in a typical early-1990s style, 'Hold On' is rendered here by the clear rich tones of vocalist John Baker (the new third Korgi). Firmly in the AOR ballad mode, this kind of generic but superior-quality pop was all the rage at the time. The tune is another real earworm, though, and after a few listens, it's the kind of melody that will start firing across your synapses when you least expect it. An alternate mix of this track was included on the Angel Air CD re-release in 2006.

'Work Together' (Davis, Warren)

John Baker's vocal adds an extra sheen to another glossy production on 'Work Together', which features another melody that gets in your head but still slots into the AOR template. The quirky humour and experimental edge that often surfaced on The Korgis' 1980s outings appear to be completely absent from this new incarnation of the band, and it's greatly missed. The new streamlined production displays huge professionalism but evinces a generally more-anonymous pop sheen to the material than the signature Korgis sound palette of old.

'Hunger' (Davis, Brandt)

Slightly edgier is 'Hunger' – minted by the old Slow Twitch Fibres team of Andy Davis and Pete Brandt. It also featured on Davis' 1989 solo album *Clevedon Pier* with a more-telling reading than this remake, but it remains a good song nevertheless. See the overview on the *Clevedon Pier* album.

'Show Me' (Davis, Turner)

This is not a cover of the classic Joe Tex soul stomper from the 1960s (shame, that would have been interesting!), but it does display some soul influences, especially in the slow funky riff in the verses that sounds like the bass-end of a clavinet. This riff was possibly influenced by the timeless Robert White guitar lick that graced The Temptations' 1965 hit 'My Girl'. The overall effect is of shiny mainstream pop – typical of the time and sounding remarkably like the Deptford band Squeeze in places.

'Who Are These Tears For Anyway' (Warren)

James Warren provides one of his patent sad Korgis love songs with this track. With the rhythm marked by chopping electric guitar, some bursts of Hammond organ drift beneath as Warren intones his tale of lost love. The chorus is typically catchy, and we are treated to a tidy Andy Davis guitar solo towards the end, along with more Hammond playing – the latter being an instrument that was specifically brought in for these sessions and featured on many tracks.

'No Love In the World' (Davis, Warren)

Another reasonable pop tune that fails to present anything special or very different, although it's melodic enough and features some staccato synthesizer stabs that sound like various interchangeable electro-pop bands of the decade leading up to this album. There is a refreshingly bluesy piano solo near the end, though, sounding very much like it could be Andy Davis.

'One Life' (Davis, Warren)

This is a return to the well-meaning save-the-world platitudes of the title track but does have a bit more life about it with electronically-simulated African percussion driving it along. Yes, we're back with the world music feel again and the fast-paced lyrics scan really well, with John Baker taking the lead vocal. The tune reminds me of Bobby Bloom's 1970 hit 'Montego Bay'. The verse leads into an all-join-in chant-like chorus of the title phrase, complete with punchy synth brass stabs *à la* Phil Collins' 1980s style (except Collins plumped for real brass, often courtesy of the EWF Horns). This is a decent track and a live winner when it was introduced into the James Warren and Friends set for their 2005 concerts.

'Love Turned Me Around' (Davis, Turner, Clarkson)
This intro is slightly reminiscent of 'In The Air Tonight'-era Phil Collins, with its drum machine toms and minor-key string wash. It sounds remarkably like a song written by committee, as a lot of pop was in the last decades of the 20th century, It is a less memorable track, although well sung by John Baker, as always.

'Wreckage Of A Broken Heart' (Davis, Warren)
With piano sequencing on the intro, this is another lovelorn lament from two guys who appear to be experts in that particular field. It sounds not unlike something Trevor Horn might've written for pop duo Dollar in the 1980s, but is not quite as sly. A Davis/Warren confection, it sports a rather breathless chorus that attempts to shoehorn the slightly unwieldy title into something catchy, but it all sounds a tad contrived in the end.

'All The Love In The World' (Davis, Warren)
Up next is a rather pointless remake of the fine ballad that originally provided a highlight on side two of The Korgis' 1981 album *Sticky George*. The original was well-put-together and full of feeling, but this remake is far less lush and sounds like the band are coasting on autopilot. My advice is to stick with the excellent original and give this one a miss. It is a great song, though. Yet another unnecessary alternate version of this song was added to the Angel Air CD release in 2006.

'Third Time Around' (Davis, Beacon)
As the title suggests, this is the third stab at the chanted world-music template that was beginning to be worked to death by the early-1990s. Showing a bit more vitality than most tracks on this collection, this is probably the album's least effective track in this vein, bested by the title track and the more-fully-realised 'One Life'. The electronic percussion thumps, the chanting chants, and yet more save-the-world proselytising falls on deaf ears. The 'Beacon' in the credits is Kim Beacon – former vocalist with String Driven Thing back in the early-1970s, who had also collaborated with Genesis' keyboardist Tony Banks on his 1979 release *A Curious Feeling*. Davis had co-written some songs with Kim Beacon at the tail end of the 1980s, and this is presumably one of those compositions.

'Everybody's Got To Learn Sometime' (Warren)
Yet another version of Warren's pension-plan song. Again, this remake is okay but still lacks the elusive magic of the 1980 single. This version was one of the first tracks recorded for this album, and came out as a single preceding the album, with all funds going to the International Hostage Release charity.

Additional Material
'The Way I Feel' (Baker, Warren)
A welcome addition to the Angel Air CD re-release, this is another track with a John Baker vocal performance, highlighting piano-led verses with some nice

lyrical touches, and a more-upbeat chorus evoking the title, and a sing-along melody. Though not a major track, it's still a pleasant listen.

'Mount Everest Sings The Blues' (Warren)

This is the treat of the CD re-release; a real gem recorded live at Trinity Hall, Bristol, on 12 April 1993 on a short spring tour undertaken by a five-piece Korgis lineup. Andy Davis had decided to stand down for the tour, so James Warren and John Baker recruited some local Bath/Bristol musicians to back them.

One of my all-time favourite Korgis songs, 'Mount Everest Sings The Blues' is the kicking rock-'n'-rolling ditty that was a highlight of the band's 1979 debut album. The atmosphere positively sizzles. Buoyed by an enthusiastic audience, the band really drive through a slightly extended reading of this Warren rocker. It's a fine performance with a superb Warren vocal, some hot and almost country rock guitar on a brace of solos, and a cooking organ solo to boot, complete with audience whoops and hollers. The cleverly dropped beat going back into the verses, propels the tune relentlessly forward, and it's a real joy to listen to. Did anyone record the rest of this hot-sounding gig? We need to know. If so, it should definitely be released as an album. What a scorcher of a track!

Andy Davis Band (1994)

Personnel:
Andy Davis: vocals, guitar, harmonica
Steve Robinson: acoustic guitar, mandolin, vocals
Alun Thomas: guitar, slide guitar, vocals
Richard Stubbings: accordion, vocals
Neil Deamer: bass
Clive Deamer: drums, vocals
Recorded live at The Hope Centre, Bristol, 29th July 1994
Producer: Andy Davis, David Lord
Engineer: David Lord
Label: Andy Davis
Release date: 1994

'The Chrysler Girl' (Davis, Ferguson)

By the 1990s, Andy Davis had formed his own band and fallen firmly under the spell of Americana. This album was recorded live but without an audience and displays his new outfit's country rock credentials. Kicking off with what would become one of his signature songs, this tribute to the feminine charms of New York's Chrysler Building is taken at a nippy pace, sounding akin to the earlier efforts of The Eagles. It's a great song that would not find its ideal arrangement until 2015 when Davis stripped it down to a slow acoustic treatment (more on that version later). Here it's dispatched with a fast country rock rhythm and some solo guitar from the man himself.

'Baby Good For You' (Davis, Ferguson)

Another Davis composition that would bounce back more than once, we're in a more relaxed mode, with a Jackson Browne vibe going down and tasty slide guitar from Bristol session man Alun Thomas. Davis had started laying the groundwork for his future solo direction with some soulful vocals on this considered, mature slice of songwriting.

'One Careless Night' (Davis, Ferguson)

The tempo is upped once more with Clive Deamer's cowbell and some tasty slide guitar from Alun Thomas, accompanied by Steve Robinson's mandolin. With his new writing partner Gus Ferguson, Andy Davis' latest durable batch of tunes show a much more genre-specific approach than he'd adopted in the past, and the sound throughout the album is consistent rather than adventurous, with every track displaying a country feel, whether up-tempo or laid-back.

'Confidential Heart' (Davis, Ferguson)

The chord sequence on the verse strongly recalls Ian Hunter's 1971 epic 'The Journey' from Mott the Hoople's seminal *Brain Capers* album. With its swelling organ chords and runs making it sound even more like Mott in their more country-influenced moments, you could be forgiven for thinking it's that band's Verden Allen on keys (no bad thing in my book!). Some weeping lap steel completes the illusion on another more-than-decent laid-back song from the Davis/Ferguson team.

'Rain, Rain, Rain' (Davis, Ferguson)

Yet another song that would run and run, Davis would revisit this slow burn of a song featuring a Ry Cooder-like funky riff on several more occasions after its debut here. It's a song that works on feel, as the main riff runs right through its verse and chorus. Once you get into the slow groove of this one, you kind of choogle along with it, as Davis sings about waking up in the fast lane. Perhaps he was lulled into a slumber-like state by the relentless slow riff of this number.

'The One Who Called You Sweetheart' (Davis, Ferguson)

The acoustic intro recalls Speedy Keene's 'Something In The Air': a number-1 hit for Thunderclap Newman in 1969. It evolves into a slow ballad with acoustic backing. There are some tight vocal harmonies on the later verses as the country feel dominates proceedings.

'That's What Friends Are For' (Davis, Ferguson)

Not to be confused with the Burt Bacharach/Carol Bayer-Sager song that was a hit for Dionne Warwick & Friends in 1985, this is another Davis/Ferguson original. Built on less than a handful of chords, it's a simple but plaintive tune that I often catch myself absentmindedly humming. Another one with legs, Davis revisited this one several times with a studio version by The Korgis recorded in 2001 and later released on *The Korgis Kollection*, and a live version on the band's *Unplugged* album in 2005. The version here is laid-back in the extreme and garnished with mandolin and harmonica.

'I Take It All Back' (Davis, Ferguson)

The tempo livens up for another dose of fast country rock, including yet more slide guitar. Andy Davis' shift to Americana extended to his other part-time outfit, The 3 Caballeros, who specialised in a kind of western swing but proved a lot more quirky and humorous than this outfit. Some of these influences would eventually filter back into the reformed Stackridge from 2007 onwards.

'Kings In Disguise' (Davis, Ferguson)

The closing track strongly recalls Dire Straits and is another up-tempo song. It even sports a similar story lyric to that band's 'Sultans Of Swing', this time concerning a 1950s band called The Kings In Disguise. Playing out with guitar and organ solos, it ends the album on a rousing note.

Jim's Special Edition Easy Listening Christmas Album (1999)

Personnel:
James Warren: guitar, bass, percussion, vocals
John Miller: electric piano ('The Frozen North'), bass ('We Didn't Get Along')
Richard Stubbings: piano ('Love, Death And Photographs')
Alun Thomas: guitar ('The Leaving Time')
Will Gregory: saxophone ('Can't Get Her Out Of My Head')
Stuart Gordon, Phil Harrison, David Lord: everything on 'Christmas In Japan'
Helena: backing vocals ('The Leaving Time')
David Lord: orchestration (Christmas In Japan', 'Love, Death and Photographs')
Recorded: James Warren's home, Glenn Tommey's garage and David Lord's flat, 1995
Producers/Engineers: James Warren, Glenn Tommey and David Lord
Label: Dap
Release date: 1999

'The Leaving Time' (Warren)

After his low point of inspiration in the mid to late 1980s, it was heartening to see James Warren getting back some of his former songwriting brilliance as the 1990s wore on. This track is a prime example of that. Some nice multitracked *a cappella* vocal harmonies open this song of murder and betrayal, juxtaposed with a jaunty tune and boasting a chorus that is eminently hummable. It became a live staple in the set of James Warren and Friends during their run of gigs from 2005 onwards, and the core of this aggregation would eventually provide the perfect backing band when the four main Stackridge writers returned to spectacular live performances in 2007.

'Can't Get Her Out Of My Head' (Warren)

Another laid-back example of Warren's shiny pop, this is a descendant of his patent Korgis style, but with a warm, organic feel thanks to the guitars, electric piano and a deliciously relaxing sax solo from Will Gregory. Warren is a past master at this kind of unpretentious, understated love song.

'Money Talks' (Warren)

The influence of Paul Simon shines through brightly on this sunny calypso, including a lyrical paraphrase from one of his songs at one point ('Diamonds on the Soles of his Shoes'). Brazen brass riffs enhance the salsa-like atmosphere as Warren ruminates on the pros and cons of filthy lucre.

'The Frozen North' (Warren, Miller)

One of Warren's collaborations with John Miller that didn't make it onto *Something for the Weekend*, this track swaps the balmy sunshine of the previous number for chillier climes, as Miller's electric piano forms the backdrop for this evocative love song taken at a very relaxed tempo. There are some typically-tangential lyric touches, and the track evinces a lot of feeling. This is fostered by a repeated chord shift from a major to a minor 6th during the verses, creating a slightly disconcerting air, and this is carried through to the fade-out, where Warren adds some vocal improvisation in his higher range.

'Everybody's Got To Learn Sometime' (Indie version) (Warren)
Yet another version of Warren's most famous and lucrative composition, it's not clear whether this is an indie-band cover or some mischief from Mr. Warren in the style of this genre of music. It swaps the pathos of the original for a less imaginative upbeat version of the song.

'Someday They'll Find Out' (Warren)
One of the songs that made it onto *Something for the Weekend* practically unchanged; this may even be exactly the same master tape used here that ended up masquerading as a Stackridge track on that 1999 comeback album. As such, I will defer discussion of this Warren pop confection until that release is reviewed later.

'If I Fell' (Lennon, McCartney)
A slice of knockabout fun recorded with Warren's occasional writing partner Sarah Menage, with some pre-track banter from the man himself, and very much in the homemade spirit of much of this album. One of the early examples of John Lennon's ballad style, this chord-intensive song is nicely sung by the duo during this enjoyable performance.

'We Didn't Get Along' (Warren)
Summing up the easy-listening moniker of this album, this is another of those easy-on-the-ear pop tunes that Warren seems capable of churning out in his sleep. This time there's a definite George Harrison influence in this pleasing chord sequence on a song dealing with romantic incompatibility. It's the kind of gentle quality pop that I find impossible to resist singing along with.

'Caroline No' (Wilson, Asher)
Beginning with some more Warren tomfoolery in which he recites a line from The Beach Boys' 1967 hit 'Heroes And Villains', it then launches into a straight cover of the closing track from that band's classic 1966 album *Pet Sounds*, as he respectfully replicates Brian Wilson's arrangement on this wistful ode to lost love – originally to be titled 'Carol, I Know' and representing Brian Wilson's feelings towards one of the first loves from his youth: Carol Mountain.

'The Crying Song' (Warren)

Almost too close in feel to John Lennon's solo hit '#9 Dream', to avoid the comparison, 'The Crying Song' was another of this collection transferred intact to *Something for the Weekend*, but was there retitled 'Have Faith In Love', after its chorus refrain.

'Christmas In Japan' (Warren)

A Korgis outtake from the 1980s, the only previous UK release of which was on the compilation album *The Best And The Rest of The Korgis,* although not credited on the cover at the time. Possibly an attempt to cash in the odd Japanese obsession with Christmas, it was probably released in that country at some point. A typically synthesized Korgis track of its era, it displays some clever Japanese-flavoured riffs and has the addition of a David Lord orchestration to accentuate its lush melody.

'Love, Death And Photographs' (Warren)

A surprisingly downbeat offering from Warren, this deathly slow ballad is accompanied by Richard Stubbings' first pre-Stackridge appearance on piano. It evinces a somewhat dirge-like quality with its minor-key music and funereal lyrics as Warren ponders human mortality, sounding quite unlike himself as his voice cracks and croaks. David Lord adds some keening strings to the middle eight before a return to the Spartan piano-and-voice arrangement that opened the song. As a change of pace on an otherwise lighthearted album, this track is a bit of a shock to the system.

'High On Love' (Warren, Menage)

The first of a brace of co-compositions with Sarah Menage (more of which would emerge on her solo album *Fool's Gold*), this track sounds positively euphoric after the mournfulness of the previous offering and is another example of the kind of breezy pop tune James Warren is so good at.

'It Must Be Time For Bed' (Warren, Menage)

One of Warren's most adventurous chord sequences and arrangements, this is another one that was lifted onto *Something for the Weekend*, there to be given a dose of Mike Evans' violin to add extra texture. It will thus be discussed in detail when I come to overview that album.

'Everybody's Got To Learn Sometime' (Warren)

Credited in the CD booklet as '?', the final track is the original 1978 demo of James Warren's song before the synthesizer textures were added. There is no evidence of the rumoured missing middle eight, which he is said to have cut out of the song after deeming it unnecessary. The demo retains the inherent charm of this simple but effective sequence as he shadows the changes with his bass.

Something for the Weekend (1999)

Personnel:
James Warren: guitar, vocals
Mike Evans: violin, backing vocals ('Fascinating World', 'Drinking And Driving'), vocals ('Vegan's Hatred Of Fish', 'Wildebeeste')
Crun Walter: bass
John Miller: keyboards
Richard Stubbings: keyboards, backing vocals, woodwind arrangement ('Sliding Down The Razorblade Of Love')
Tim Robinson: drums, percussion
Innes Sibun: fuzz guitar solo ('Fascinating World')
Hayward Slater: acoustic guitar ('Wildebeeste')
Terry Veale: guitar ('Five-Poster Bedlam')
Steve Robinson: backing vocals ('Drinking And Driving')
Graham Smith: harmonica ('Drinking And Driving')
Recorded: The Room At The Top, Terra Incognita, Bath, December 1997-1998
Producer: James Warren
Engineers: James Warren, David Lord
Label: Dap, Angel Air
Release dates: 12 October 1999 (Dap), 2007 (Angel Air CD re-release)

During the mid-1990s, the idea of a Stackridge reformation was floated again. This crystallized when James Warren got together with the eccentric composer/keyboard player John Miller for some songwriting sessions. The first fruits of this collaboration emerged on what was to become *Jim's Special Edition Easy Listening Christmas Album,* recorded in 1995 and finally given a public release by Dap Records in 1999 when the Stackridge comeback was in full swing. Three of the tracks featured on this collection were taken wholesale for the nascent Stackridge project, and added to other new tracks written especially for the new band album *Something For The Weekend*, also released by Dap in 1999. The original plan in 1997 was for the two main Stackridge writers – James Warren and Andy Davis – to team up with former bassist Crun Walter and violinist Mike Evans. But due to band management politics, Davis left before the rebirth had begun in earnest. This left James Warren as the central songwriter for this era of Stackridge, with minor writing contributions from Crun Walter and Mike Evans. The net effect was that the subsequent album displayed less balance than the Stackridge albums of old, although John Miller's involvement ensured that it had its share of eccentric moments. But the essential yin and yang of classic Stackridge was not as prominent.

When the album was re-released by Angel Air in 2006, featuring several bonus tracks that included a couple of Andy Davis' unfinished demos, it hinted at what this extra input could've led to had Davis stayed with the project from the start. A clearer picture of the kind of balance that he could've given the project can be gleaned by a study of the excellent *Sex and Flags* compilation (Angel Air, 2005), where Davis' contributions from the mini-album *Lemon 2002* – plus a track each from Warren, Walter and Mutter Slater – were combined with the best of *Something for the Weekend* and augmented by two further unreleased Andy Davis tracks, to create a wonderful album indeed.

Something For The Weekend was perhaps less a band album than a collection of solo tracks, enhanced to varying degrees by the other participants. Some of these contributors were eventually coerced into a live lineup, and at last, a new version of Stackridge was back on the road again, as John Miller (keyboards), Tim Robinson (drums) and multi-instrumentalist Richard Stubbings (guitar, flute, keyboards, vocals) joined Warren, Evans and Walter for a splendid couple of years of live concerts. John Miller made way on keyboards for the excellent Ian Towers, who also brought his guitar and vocal talents to the band in 2000. Tragically, this lineup imploded in early 2001, mainly due to the previously mentioned band politics and the promise of new material being worked on for a real band album from Stackridge – as evidenced by the new Warren/Towers song 'Happy Saffron' – was snuffed out prematurely. On a happier note, this cleared the way for the possibility of a reunion of the core four of Warren, Walter, Davis and Slater, which finally came to the most glorious fruition imaginable in 2007.

By the time *Something For The Weekend* hit the stores in 1999, CDs rather than vinyl had long been the order of the day and CD artwork had become inserts rather than 12" record sleeves, with the net result that by the 1990s, it was a truism that artwork as such had ceased to be as important as it was back in the 1970s, when it was often so much more part of the overall artistic statement for many bands and artists.

The front of the CD booklet for *Something for the Weekend* features a rather dark copy of the famous Beatlemania photo from 1963 showing a line of policemen – one pictured centrally with his helmet askew, holding back the hordes of young Beatles fans. This photo is tinted purple with 'Stackridge' emblazoned across centre-left in orange, the album title in smaller orange text below it. The booklet contains the lyrics and credits printed in white on a purple background with the track titles in orange. A page each in the booklet is given over to ruminations from Mike Evans, Crun Walter and James Warren. Evans' reflections on the early days of the band are amusing, while Walter and Warren's contributions are more arcane, the former presenting a surreal monologue on polyester sleeves, while the latter waxes loquacious on 'The Church Of The Eternal Haddock', with tongue firmly in cheek as usual! This CD was also notable for the first sighting of the 'Stackridge Gnome' since 1973, as his image appears on both sides of the back insert (The jewel case is clear plastic, so the gnome shows through when the disc is removed), and also on the CD itself. Interestingly, the gnome image has been reversed and is now facing the opposite way to its first appearance on the 1971 debut album: read into that what you will.

'It's A Fascinating World' (Warren)

With its neo-psychedelic feel, marvellously layered production and oddly lisping vocals from James Warren, this tongue-in-cheek paean to meditation makes a solid opening salvo to the first Stackridge studio album for 23 years. This trippy feel is continued into the coda, where eastern flavours permeate, and a frantic fuzz guitar solo from guest Innes Sibun turns into a cuckoo clock. The novice listener should expect the unexpected: as always in the bizarre universe inhabited by Stackridge music.

'Ruth, Did You Read My Mind?' (Miller, Warren)

A thigh-slapping hoedown of a track that really kicks up the sawdust, 'Ruth' is driven by James Warren's acoustic guitar and John Miller's piano, and features some witty, quick-fire lyric couplets detailing the plight of a heartbroken amputee! One wonders whether the lyrics are by Warren or Miller; perhaps they're a collaboration between these two odd minds. On Miller's piano solo, he feints a quote from Prokofiev's *Peter and the Wolf* before heading off on his own tangent once more, eventually running into a surprisingly beefy guitar-riff-laden middle eight, which gives the song great balance. The plum lyric line comes on the last verse when Warren sings, 'A bee got in my car and I ran into a wall': a line that always makes me grin and a plausible scenario at that.

It's a fine track, showing that the Warren muse is well and truly back on form, thanks to the catalyst of John Miller.

'Something About The Beatles' (Menage, Warren)

James Warren had an almost Messianic fervour about this track being a potential hit single – so much so that he later forced the issue when a version by The Korgis was released, to minimal sales. I suppose he had a point – with the right exposure, this studied homage to the fab four could possibly have done the business, but airplay was hard to come by for both the Stackridge and Korgis readings of this tune. A big ballad taken at a stately pace, Warren's voice and guitar gently weep to the sky in this evocation of the golden age of pop when four boys from Liverpool changed the world and all of our lives forever. His selection of co-writers during this time seem to have brought out the best in him, as Sarah Menage makes her first writing contribution to the album.

'Help Under Doors' (Miller, Warren)

A welcome example of the new Stackridge rocking out, Warren always touted 'Help Under Doors' as a nod to grunge, although in truth, this is closer to classic 4/4 rock than anything to come out of Seattle in the 1990s – Nirvana they are not. Nevertheless, it rocks like the clappers, and made a very effective live number for both the millennium lineup (who used it as a set closer) and the later reformation of the core four and their backing band. The rising middle-eight is well-judged and slides chromatically back into the final verse, which features a particularly nice lyric nod to Stackridge mythology in the line

'That's the way the rhubarb crumbles'. Driven home with some headbanging, insistent double-string lead guitar riffs from Warren, this track makes for a great change of pace.

'The Vegan's Hatred Of Fish' (Walter)

The first of two writing contributions from Crun Walter on this album, its triple-time intro throws the listener off the scent as the spirit of 'February In Shropshire' is momentarily recalled before we find ourselves swimming against the current in a slow underwater world. The subterranean tones of Mike Evans negotiate us through this dose of whimsy that doesn't quite make it as the humorous interlude it's possibly intended to be. Sounds fishy to me!

'Sliding Down The Razorblade Of Love' (Cook, West)

The preponderance of remakes on *Something For The Weekend* perhaps demonstrates a paucity of new, original material being produced at this juncture and the presence of this cover version written by long-established songwriters Roger Cook and Andy West cements that theory in my view. The arrangement of this lighthearted ode was perhaps an attempt to replicate the period charm of the flapper-era pastiche 'Anyone For Tennis', from the band's earlier *Friendliness* album. Charm it certainly exudes, but without quite matching the chutzpah of its illustrious predecessor, despite a flawless period flavour, enhanced by Richard Stubbings' impressive wind arrangement.

'The Youth Of Today' (Miller, Warren)

This song has a lyric that asks, 'Why are we afraid of the youth of today?' - a question the convoluted lyrics of this song attempt to answer.

The initial verses are based on a marimba-like sequencer section with a drifting feel, before a bathetic Reginald Dixon-style organ breaks the tempo, sounding as if it's rising from the pit, as such pieces of furniture were wont to do back in the 'good old days'. This leads into a swinging rhythm, driven by some playing on the bell of the cymbal, presumably by Tim Robinson. The middle eight ends with an authentic ambulance siren-style vocal by James, which modulates up a tone before a return to the languid opening arrangement.

Somewhat broken, despite its ambitious arrangement, this track doesn't quite cut the mustard to my ears.

'Have Faith In Love' (Warren)

Sounding like a straight transfer of the version on *Jim's Special Edition Easy Listening Christmas Album* – where it was titled 'The Crying Song' – this sounds more like a Korgis production than a Stackridge one. James Warren is at his most Lennon-like as his reverb-rich voice floats against an airy sea of synthesized sound, engendering a numbing sense of light relief after the sonic harassment of the previous track.

'Five-Poster Bedlam' (Evans)

Completing something of a soggy dip in the middle of the Stackridge comeback album, this violin and guitar extravaganza penned by Mike Evans impresses with its technical dexterity, whilst failing to engage on an emotional level, or is it just me? A rather breathless and inexplicable arrangement of variations with bursts of canned applause, this track quickly fosters a sense of overkill with its relentless semiquavers, and is one I could probably live without.

'Wildebeeste' (Miller, Warren)

At last, the Stackridge spirit of old asserts itself again with one of the album's strangest tracks. Closer to the trailblazing verve of that first eponymous album than anything else here, 'Wildebeeste' opens sounding like a direct descendant of the startling 'Essence Of Porphyry', with its leaping acoustic guitar figures leading into a welcome dose of Evans' violin-playing. He also takes the vocal on this in his unique style, as he relates a curiously surreal tale of Wildebeeste with attaché cases, heading east , set to a variety of unsettling rhythms. These include a verse perched atop some strangely dancing piano notes, a series of quick-fire, tongue-twisting choruses that cram a large proportion of the Oxford dictionary into each vocal salvo, and a bizarre mutated tango in the middle eight. This all eventually settles into an instrumental section that resembles a delightfully odd gambol across the veldt, as Mike Evans gives a demonstration of what a master violinist he is, wringing emotion from every phrase he plays. A song possibly devoid of any meaning in the conventional sense – unless it's intended as an oblique reference to mass extinction maybe – it remains a welcome addition to the tradition of surrealism displayed in many a previous Stackridge lyric. With a passing nod to an Arabic scale on the last verse, and one last syllable-crammed chorus, we're suddenly into the next track.

'Grooving Along On The Highway On A Monday Morning Once' (Menage, Miller, Warren)

Undoubtedly the longest ever title for a Stackridge song, this sees contributions from both of James Warren's recent collaborators and grooves along in presto waltz-time. Warren's wordy witticisms are well to the fore, and a clutch of well-known philosophers crop up unexpectedly in the middle eight – as Wittgenstein, Hegel and Kant receive a name-check – displaying Warren's propensity for sprinkling pseudo-profundities amongst the usual playful lyric flippancy. Mike Evans saws his violin in classic style, and the whole thing recalls English music-hall specialists Flanders and Swann, ending with a satisfying cod-classical climax.

'Someday They'll Find Out' (Warren)

This engaging and well-travelled slice of candy floss continues the lighthearted mood, and is again packed with linguistic mischief. Another transfer from *Jim's Special Edition Easy Listening Christmas Album,* there are a host of amusing couplets to enjoy, buoyed by a reggae rhythm driven by programmed drums. With a nod to The Beach Boys in the middle eight – including the mention of a naked Brian Wilson – Warren still manages to throw in the occasional profundity – the best of which is 'Are we men or merely apes with attitude?': a pertinent question indeed!

'Drinking And Driving' (Walter)

Crun Walter's second writing contribution appears as the penultimate track, in the shape of a harmless boogie shuffle with a slightly stiff rhythm. It's pumped along in bluesy fashion by the harmonica-toting Graham Smith: possibly he who wrote the lyrics to 'The Indifferent Hedgehog' for the band back in 1973. Lyrically, our bearded bass man returns to one of his passions – namely the automobile, which cropped up in his very first recorded lyric back in 1971 and would resurface again in the future. A warning about the perils of mixing alcohol and motoring, our driver is rightfully arrested before the song ends, hopefully without incurring any innocent casualties along the way.

'It Must Be Time For Bed' (Menage, Warren)

Another refugee from *that* easy-listening album, but this time with substantial input from an overdubbed Mike Evans, whose violin-playing lends the track a new dimensional depth. Entering in the most low-key fashion possible, James Warren's casual guitar picking on the slow verse and middle eight belies the sophistication of the chord sequence he's playing, littered as it is with minor-9ths, flattened-5ths and 11ths. It would be a test for anyone to work out the correct chord changes of this piece, given that the track – whether purposely or accidentally – seems to have been recorded *in the cracks*, making it sound slightly vari-sped.

The middle eight, in particular, evokes the spirit of Brian Wilson in full *Smile*-era mode, with a lovely set of changes. The late-night feel is matched by the resigned, world-weary lyrics, and the track is full of surprises for the first-time listener.

The piece evolves into an upbeat mode for an instrumental middle section, the material for this being cunningly derived from the movement to a flattened 5th that graced the opening verses. A distinct eastern feel permeates this energised passage, as a wordless chanting female voice floats disembodied in the aural ether (Sarah Menage maybe?), eventually joined by Mike Evans' violin before the whole thing dissolves into some manic *Tom and Jerry*-type piano doodling. This marks a brief return to the sleepy verse, on which Warren intones movingly, 'I know I'd rather choose, whatever I may lose, to live inside my dream' – a sentiment that's either scarily insular or a bold statement of standing by your beliefs and personal dreams in the face of adversity: it all depends on your viewpoint I suppose. The upbeat section is reprised as the neo-psychedelic feel that opened the album makes a comeback, complete with sample loops of the disembodied female chants that we encountered earlier. The sound appears to stretch and swim before the ears like the aural equivalent of a 1960s lava lamp before vanishing, leaving the briefest of codas with snatches of harmony from the verses, trailing away into the void. One of James Warren's most adventurous tracks, it confirmed that by the 1990s, he was at last back on track as a writer.

Additional Material

'Rope Of Pearls' (Davis)

The first of two Andy Davis demos recorded prior to him dropping out of the reformed Stackridge in 1998, this is a rather rough recording of a Byrds-like thrash with chiming 12-string guitars against an unrelenting drum machine. Maybe the band could've knocked it into shape had Davis not left the project, but it just feels like a half-formed idea in its released state on the 2007 Angel Air CD re-release.

'Sad Romantic' (Davis)

The second addition to the CD re-release was another Andy Davis demo that sounds formative at best, played along to a basic drum-box rhythm. Using two alternating guitar harmonics to drive the verse, this has something of a one-chord feel with a repetitive descending guitar riff insistently playing against the repeated harmonics. There are some strange keening lead guitar bends toward the end on single notes. This is another song idea in need of proper development, though.

'No Love In Her Heart' (Warren)

This initially-unused track makes a welcome addition to the 2007 CD re-release of *Something for the Weekend*, as James Warren – obviously still under the influence of The Beatles after all these years – strings together an ear-pleasing chord sequence full of nice surprises. It opens with an attention-grabbing *a cappella* half-verse before the backing kicks in – an effective device that was perhaps inspired by The Beatles' 'Nowhere Man' from the 1965 *Rubber Soul* album, which employed a similar method. With its lovely winding melody, this typically-Warren love song really should've graced the original album, as it's a fine piece of work.

Pick of the Crop (2000)

Personnel:
James Warren: guitar, vocals
Mike Evans: violin, vocals
Richard Stubbings: keyboards, flute, accordion, vocals
Ian Towers: keyboards, guitar, vocals
Crun Walter: bass
Tim Robinson: drums
Ruth Evans, Nina Smith: violin, percussion and vocals
Recorded live at Cropredy Festival, Oxfordshire, 12 August 2000
Producer: Stackridge
Engineer: Johnny Morris
Label: Dap
Release date: 2000

Pick of the Crop wasn't universally welcomed by Thrashers at the time, being a cut-down version of the millennium lineup's set circa 2000. Many preferred the two-volume unofficial *The Full Crop* to this official release of the band's Cropredy Festival performance on 12 August 2000, as the bootleg featured the unexpurgated set. It's true that *Pick of the Crop* does come over as a bit of a slapdash package, though the sound quality is generally good.

The front cover photo was shot by Crun Walter's son George, and shows the sort of multi-generational audience that the band were attracting at that time, with a young girl perched on her father's shoulders, holding up a stalk of rhubarb, in the centre of the shot. The band name is emblazoned across the top in blue lettering, with the album title printed in white at the bottom. Opening up the insert, there are sleeve notes provided by the band's then-manager Jennie Evans, printed in black on a wider audience photo and not too easy to read. The rear insert is a rather washed-out photo of Stackridge on stage at Cropredy with the track listing and credits printed in black: again, not easily legible. Interestingly, at the bottom of the picture, the legend *Official Bootleg No.1* is inscribed, despite this being a Dap Records release.

'Dora The Female Explorer' (Stackridge)

The opening track is an example of the loose approach to this live release, as instead of the whole performance, it fades in midway through. Why? What we do get on this version of 'Dora', is under two minutes of the last half of it. It's a more accordion-driven sound than previous variants, and though it jogs along in a jolly enough way, it's probably the least incisive of the different lineups' versions of this song, and has a light, airy feel.

'Lummy Days' (Davis)

It's interesting to hear a different flautist on the all-time Stackridge classic 'Lummy Days', after the original Mutter Slater version and the Keith Gemmell variation. But Richard Stubbings manages to put his own stamp on it. Although not as pure-toned as Slater or as technical as Gemmell, he does come up with a few interesting variations, including an extra bar playing at the end of the repeated sections leading into the central violin solo and the end piece. There is also some fluttering flute improvisation over the later half-speed section of the main melody where Slater used to do his *flute cartwheels*, which is interesting, although his improvising is slightly uncertain in places. The arrangement is as tight as ever, though, and the spirit shines through brightly on this evergreen composition.

'Grooving Along On The Highway On A Monday Morning Once' (Menage, Miller, Warren)
Lightly played on a marimba-like keyboard setting, James Warren regales the Cropredy crowd with his lighthearted ode to life on the road, Stackridge-style, as Evans fiddles away like the virtuoso he is, and the millennium lineup swing tightly in the background as the band plug the new album. It's an ideal, sunny ditty for a hot August day and goes down a treat with the Fairport Convention crowd, as you would expect.

'The Last Plimsoll' (Davis, Smegmakovitch)
Driven by a twin keyboard attack of piano and organ courtesy of Ian Towers and Richard Stubbings, respectively, James Warren provides the chunky guitar riffs and lead vocals on this 1973 classic. Always an action-packed live number, Stubbings swaps to flute towards the end for some solo improvisation, as the track moves seamlessly through its minor-to-major construction, to the delight of the crowd.

'32 West Mall' (Davis, Warren)
It's good to hear this acoustic gem back in the set after a long absence. It's the iconic tale of the early Stackridge Lemon's Bristol abode way back when, and there's some delightful three-part harmony singing to savour. There are even some atmospheric bird whistles thrown in, as of old! Note the authentic rising whistle that accompanies the line 'The old tin kettle's boiling' as the group harmonise over it: a wonderful touch to a charming rendition of this lovely little tune.

'The Road To Venezuela' (Davis, Smegmakovitch)
Ian Towers' takes the vocal for the classic *Man in the Bowler Hat* track, and he croons rather fetchingly, in my view. His recent cabaret background is strongly in evidence, but the quality of the song makes sure it's not too *chicken-in-a-basket*.

As usual, Mike Evans fiddles furiously and provides one of his inimitable variations on the violin-solo section. This is another winning performance from the band.

'Fish In A Glass' (Davis, Walter)

The second song in a row to feature new keyboard recruit Ian Towers on vocals, this *Mr. Mick* track made a welcome return to the Stackridge set in 1999 and stayed in the set through to this lineup's dissolution in early 2001. Always a Stackridge classic, this lineup give a good account of themselves on this multi-segmented tune dealing with the fate of old rock stars (much like 10cc's 'Old Wild Men' from the 1974 album *Sheet Music*), and the subject of this song is also an ageing rock star waiting for miracles, as were the 'Old Wild Men'.

Curiously, there have been three sets of lyrics for 'Fish In A Glass' throughout its life, although all with a similar thrust. The author of said lyrics was residing in the band at this point – namely Crun Walter – and this version features a previously unheard verse which evokes the writings of Oscar Wilde with reference to his famous eternally-youthful literary character Dorian Gray.

Ian Towers does a cracking job on the vocal, and the band turn in a tight performance with Mike Evans augmented by the violins of daughter Ruth Evans and her friend Nina Smith, covering the previously sax-driven Zappa-like themes in the instrumental first half of the piece. The girls definitely added a touch of glamour to the lineup, and future personnel variations would stick with this policy of vocal/violin-toting younger females.

'Something About The Beatles' (Menage, Warren)

The next two tracks are programmed continuously as one performance, displaying a bit of conceptual continuity, as the band's tribute to the fabs is linked with one of said band's lesser-talked-about numbers. James Warren sings his 'paean to the sixties', while the guitar solos of the album are replaced with Mike Evans' violin to good effect before we're suddenly into the next track.

'Old Brown Shoe' (Harrison)

This is a fine cover version of George Harrison's underrated shuffle that originally appeared on the B-side of The Beatles' 'The Ballad Of John And Yoko' single in 1969. Stackridge do it proud as Warren faithfully replicates the quiet Beatle's vocal and guitar lines, while the band get down and groove along splendidly. Warren's encyclopaedic knowledge of the Beatles canon proved to be useful for Stackridge throughout their career, as they included a plethora of fabs tunes over the years, often at the drop of a plectrum. Back in the early-1970s, when the band toured extensively with Wishbone Ash, the story goes that Warren and Wishbone guitarist Ted Turner would get together with their acoustics and could be found sitting in a peaceful spot playing and singing through whole Beatles albums. Anyway, we digress. All in all, 'Old Brown Shoe' is another fine Beatles cover from the band, and includes a startling *a cappella* harmony from the assembled cast (on the 'Doo doo, doo-doo-doo' bits towards the end of the song).

'February In Shropshire' (Davis)

Making a welcome return to the Stackridge set in 1999, Mike Evans' mercurial violin lines lead us into another romp through the inspired architecture of the brilliant 'February In Shropshire': surely the absolute peak of Andy Davis' composing career. Even more of a spotlight number for Evans than it was back in 1973/1974 when he shared the lead instrumental role with Keith Gemmell; here his expressive and fluent violin takes nearly all the plaudits as the band gallop through the ever-changing landscape of this pastoral beauty *par excellence*. The harpsichord section is extremely well played by Ian Towers, as it rises up in fluent waves to a late peak in the music just before Evans' gypsy violin break leads us into the final downhill charge through the main theme to the breathless conclusion of this elating tune. Wonderful stuff!

'Ruth Did You Read My Mind?' (Miller, Warren)

Next up is a romp through this quirky tale of a one-legged earless fellow and his series of unfortunate accidents at various locations around the globe – perhaps inspired by the Bonzo Dog Doo-Dah Band's western-slanted ode 'Bad Blood' from the 1971 album *Let's Make Up And Be Friendly*, where the subject loses even more body parts. All in the best possible taste of course! The music kicks up a tornado of sawdust with Mike Evans' frantic hoedown violin, juxtaposed against some meaty rock riffs to cook up a satisfying stew for a sunny outdoor festival.

'Help Under Doors' (Miller, Warren)

Closing the set with a more-straightforward boogie rock groove, this down-the-line rocker from *Something for the Weekend* seals the deal, getting the punters up and dancing. Another number with a false ending, this time it's employed by Warren to briefly introduce the band members (including 'Sex God, Crun!'), before another rocking blast of the chanted title, a tight ending and a shouted 'Good night!' from Warren.

Additional Material

After the reformed Stackridge hit the road in 1999/2000, their live set was mostly split between a selection of their 1970s classics and tracks from the new *Something for the Weekend* album. There were, however, a clutch of interesting covers that were occasionally slotted into the set. These included The Beach Boys' 'Help Me Rhonda', which was played quite a few times; The Beatles' 'Yesterday', which was generally performed by James Warren with acoustic guitar and brought into action in the event of an equipment malfunction, and the old Russ Conway number-1 piano instrumental from 1959 'Side Saddle', which was performed as a solo spot by new Stackridge pianist Ian Towers. Aside from these, a few random spontaneous covers were thrown into the set at various gigs, including the unlikely choice of Peter Green's 'The Green Manalishi (With the Two-Prong Crown)' – a 1970 hit for

Fleetwood Mac – and even a short blast of Deep Purple's 'Black Night' from the same year.

Towards the end of 2000, the band were obviously thinking about possible new material, as a brand new original called 'Happy Saffron' entered the set, but any hopes of more new material from this lineup were snuffed out by their dissolution in early 2001 due to band politics. 'Happy Saffron' was however happily captured for posterity on the unofficial *Live At Banbury Mill* CD, which made it easy for me to work it out for inclusion on my own *Prescription* CD in 2007.

'Happy Saffron' (Warren, Towers)

The only known writing collaboration between James Warren and Ian Towers, 'Happy Saffron' is an interesting song in that it's written using two languages. The verses are sung by Warren in French, while the choruses revert to English. To me, it's always evinced a calm Buddha-like feel, and the chorus chants of 'We could be half-awake and still be happy' have a definite Buddhist vibe to them, as does the song title – so much so that when I covered it, I re-wrote the French verses with English text and stayed with the karmic atmosphere induced by this gently rambling number. It's a pity no Stackridge studio version was ever attempted, but at least the song survived to have an afterlife of its own.

Lemon 2002 (2003)

Personnel:
Andy Davis: guitar, keyboards, vocals
James Warren: guitar, vocals
Mutter Slater: guitar, flute, keyboards, vocals
Crun Walter: bass
David Lord: keyboards
Recorded: Andy's Attic and Inner State, Bath, December 2002
Producer: Andy Davis
Engineer: David Lord
Label: Stackridge Lemon
Release date: 2003

Rumours abounded during 2002 that there may be hope of reconciliation between the previously-estranged Stackridge members, and the news that four of the classic lineup appeared to be gathering at Andy Davis' studio as Christmas approached was greeted with joy by Thrashers everywhere. The results of this tentative reunion were captured in the six-track CD *Lemon 2002,* which was made available by mail order in the new year. Even more cheering was the news that the band were hoping to get together to play some festivals in summer 2003, and they began reacquainting themselves with their back catalogue at rehearsals during the early part of that year. This plan hit the rocks when Mutter Slater pulled out, claiming he wasn't particularly interested in reliving his past again at the moment, and this left Thrashers feeling frustrated.

After the 1976 split, Slater had re-emerged briefly in the 1980s with a new gigging lineup called Rave to the Grave. In 1984 they'd released an EP of Slater originals under the title *There's Life in the Old Boy Yet*, and the music had a more blues/roots feel. In 1987 they followed this with an album of mostly covers called *Slease with Ease* on the Jolly Roger label. But not much was heard from Slater for the next decade or so, as he concentrated on earning a living outside of music. That he emerged to proffer a track for *Lemon 2002* was a cause for optimism among Thrashers. The new mini-album again proved to be more akin to a selection of solo tracks – occasionally enhanced by other members, but the writing was very strong, and the potential on display was tantalising, to say the least.

The front of the CD insert shows a lemon against an orange background, with the band name in white across a black background strip at the top. The album title is printed in black against the orange background, below the band name. The inside of the insert has the lyrics and photos of the core four Stackridge writers – including Slater and his bride Linda at their wedding – while the reverse of the insert displays the inside of a cut lemon against an orange backdrop, along with a short write-up on the CD contents. The back insert keeps the orange colour scheme, listing the tracks, writers and recording credits.

'Big Baby' (Genovese, Gidman)

This contentious cover of Rick Genovese and Gary Gidman's 'Big Baby' is a track that seems to have divided Thrasher opinion. Harder-edged than most Stackridge fare, it's an Andy Davis production with little evidence of input from other band members, though I may be wrong on that. Opening with some *Revolver*-style studio talkback, it retains a strong Beatlesque feel throughout but remains much more contemporary-sounding for all that. Great lyrics and a tough, slightly edgy production make this a winner for me, and it makes for a cracking first track on this new Stackridge offering.

'The First Name Of Love' (Warren)

James Warren's sole offering on *Lemon 2002* is this lovely acoustic ballad, in which he sharpens up his Rishikesh-style finger-picking, so reminiscent of The Beatles' *White Album*-era. Very McCartney in flavour, it's perhaps a distant relation of his 'Mother Nature's Son', and is definitely a song that could only have been written by a songwriter of a certain vintage.

As the gentle wisdom of the lyric unfolds, Warren is firmly wearing his reflective hat with not a whiff of whimsy in sight for a change. When he decides to write in this more-introspective style, he proves to be a master at it; the lyric finding its mark just under the ribcage of his target audience, of which the current writer is a prime example. As he sings of 'The furrowed face in the mirror' and 'The coarseness and the levity of once remembered youth', this boy knows exactly what he's saying: a bittersweet moment to savour. The ghost of Paul Simon is also invoked: another influence that has always loomed large in the Warren muse.

'A Wonderful Day' (Walter)

One of the highlights of *Lemon 2002*, this breezy pop tune continues Crun Walter's ongoing car fixation. Here he swaps the Triumph Spitfire of 'Drinking And Driving' for his reliable old Maestro van as he expounds the simple virtues of cruising along the B-roads: an antidote for the countless songs about speeding dragsters and highway stars.

With the band putting on something of a united front, Warren and Davis can be heard harmonising on this feel-good ditty, in a heartwarming display of togetherness. As the sun appears from behind the troubled clouds of the preceding track, and with the windows wound down, Walter invites us to share his car trek. There is some interesting vocal filtration going on during the spirit-lifting middle eight, and the song is full of bounce and vitality. There are many choice lyrical couplets to enjoy here too. My favourite one rhymes 'jumper' with 'Kuala Lumpur', and all in all, this is by far Walter's best solo composition up to this point. It also proved to be a real winner when it was integrated into the 2007 live set, and it's the kind of irresistibly unpretentious high-quality pop song that appears to be practically extinct in modern mainstream music.

'Charles Louis Dance' (Davis)

With a subtle and beautiful melody, this classical-sounding exercise from Andy Davis, conjures up mental images of decaying English dance halls from a century fast receding into the past. Poignant in the extreme and quite a tearjerker for this listener, it's the kind of instrumental interlude I always used to look forward to on a Stackridge album. The string and cello samples are excellent, and some of the chord changes in this stately piece recall the theme from the 1970s TV series *Randall & Hopkirk (Deceased)*. But the dark reverie of 'Charles Louis Dance' carries a deeper emotional resonance and an air of sad resignation that appears to permeate many of Davis' later compositions.

'The Final Bow' (Davis, Menage)

This triple-time folk-flavoured song that shares an obvious lineage with The Beatles' 'Norwegian Wood' (a track covered by Stackridge on a 1971 radio session) is a gorgeously sad song, beautifully engineered by David Lord, who does a sterling job on the entire *Lemon 2002*. The performance carries a subtle emotion as Davis' distinctive voice imparts a tangible sadness, especially on the rising chorus. The effect is entrancing and the melody gently affecting, as the folk-influence in Stackridge music proves to be alive and well.

'Beating A Path To Your Door' (Slater)

Mutter Slater provides the closing track to this mini-album with an offering that is unlike anything else presented here. By far the most-ponderous thing on this collection, it also aptly demonstrates the difference between Slater's writing and the styles of Davis and Warren, being much more openly ambient than the latter writers are wont to be. The music from the choruses sounds like a nod to the melody of 'Colours' from Phil Collins' 1989 album *...But Seriously,* but whether this is conscious or subconscious borrowing or just coincidence, is a moot question. Nevertheless, the track isn't without a fragile charm, as Slater sings in a cracked tone on a song dealing with entropy, growing old and the passing of time – a subject as fascinating as it is alarming to those of us pushing forwards into our second half-century.

The funereal pace is anticipated by the tolling of bells, before Slater croons over a slowly-drifting musical landscape of strummed guitars and a synthetic-sounding string wash, painting a portrait of slow decay and the inevitability of all things coming to an end – not a cheery thought and far too much realism for some people to take in their musical entertainment, I would guess. Oddly, it brings to mind nothing less than Pink Floyd – those past masters of musical doom-mongering, and this effect is enhanced by some Floydian slide guitar: presumably played by Slater himself.

In the absence of the usual verse/chorus structure, 'Beating A Path' relies on atmosphere to carry it through its considerable length. Whether this works or not will depend entirely on the mood and disposition of the listener, but in the context of the album, it certainly makes its mark as a contrast to the more-structured compositions of the other band members. Very much the product of a reflective, age-ripened mind, 'Beating A Path' certainly makes a distinct lyrical statement, enhanced by the drifting, ambient music that accompanies the vocal.

Additional Material

2005 was to be a great year for Thrashers, as Angel Air started to reissue the band's back catalogue and produced the excellent compilation album *Sex and Flags*, which brightened up the summer with its sparkling presence, and it was heartening to see a full Stackridge release hitting the shops once more.

Combining the best of the *Something for the Weekend* tracks with the whole of *Lemon 2002* and adding two unreleased Andy Davis recordings made for a superb album – lifted to even greater heights by the inspired programming where one track ran into another, very much like The Beatles' *Sgt. Pepper's....* Crun Walter's car song 'A Wonderful Day' even started to pick up airplay on Radio Two on the strength of this release, and the omens looked increasingly good for a Stackridge reunion. The additional two Andy Davis tracks that debuted on *Sex and Flags* were 'Bread And Water' and 'Dirty Nightingale', and were possibly recorded in 2002 at the sessions that included the *Lemon 2002* track 'The Final Bow', as the two additional tracks share the same folk-influenced feel and tonal palette.

'Bread And Water' (Davis)

Built on some delicious finger-picked acoustic guitar, this song of unabashed adoration finds Davis at his most lovelorn, as he equates existing without the love of his life as like 'living on bread and water'. Beautifully orchestrated by Davide Rossi, it also features his superb violin-playing. There is also some gorgeous harp decoration courtesy of Jenny Crook that lends the track a rich, harmonic feel. It's a song that amply demonstrates the difference Andy Davis could've made to the *Something for the Weekend* album had he stayed involved with the initial Stackridge comeback in the 1990s, giving a musical balance that's evident in spades on the inspired production of the *Sex and Flags* compilation.

'Dirty Nightingale' (Davis, Ferguson)

Another song from Davis/Ferguson, it taps into the folk-influenced side of Davis' muse with its triple-time and a winding, folksy melody. Instrumental interludes played on pennywhistle by guest musician Jamie Matthews, link up the verses.

Lyrically, Davis appears to be addressing either a woman who has fallen on hard times, or perhaps a lady of the night, the latter being the subject of a handful of songs in his portfolio through the years. Some subtle orchestration adds extra sonic texture, sounding particularly rich in the bass frequencies with a resonant cello to the fore. The melody sounds akin to a traditional Irish folk tune and has a timeless quality. Davis would revisit this track on his 2015 solo album *Desire Lines*.

The Korgis Kollection (2005)

Personnel:
Andy Davis, John Baker: keyboards, guitars, vocals
James Warren: guitars, bass, keyboards, vocals
Recorded: David Lord's Studio, 2001
Producer: David Lord
Engineers: Glenn Tommey, Guy Johnston
Label: Angel Air
Release date: 2005

During 2001, James Warren, Andy Davis and John Baker began to write and record again as The Korgis, with David Lord producing. Five new compositions were recorded but would sit in the can for another four years until Angel Air – in cahoots with the band – released the compilation album *The Korgis Kollection*. This CD featured remixed and partly-re-recorded versions of the band's previous output, in addition to the aforementioned five new songs.

The year before *The Korgis Kollection* was released, James Warren and John Baker jetted off to Belgium after an invitation The Korgis received to record a series of cover versions for Reader's Digest Music. These were mainly their interpretations of golden oldies from the 1960s to the 1990s. The first session went so well that they ended up making regular trips to the continent to record a plethora of covers over the next 16 years or so. Trying to collect all these tracks is fraught with frustration, as about 40 covers are spread over 19 compilation albums issued by *Reader's Digest* over 17 years. And to be honest, only the maddest Stackridge/Korgis fan would pursue the complete collection of these pleasant but essentially non-essential recordings. In amongst the covers, the band did throw in the inevitable version of 'Everybody's Got To Learn Sometime', which featured on the Dutch five-CD compilation box set Liedjes *Die Troost Brengen (The Sound of Silence)* released in 2006. This wasn't a new version of the hit song, but the 1992 remake that was previously available on *This World's for Everyone*.

Also released in 2005 by Angel Air, was a Korgis' *Unplugged* DVD, which consists of the trio version of the band that had formed the core of the 1990s lineup that recorded the 1992 album *This World's for Everyone*. The DVD was recorded live somewhere in Bristol, and is one of those pleasant-enough additions to the collection without being essential listening, as all the songs featured have studio versions on various Korgis-related albums. Having said that, it's instructive to hear these varied compositions in a stripped-down format, as it illuminates the quality of writing, and that's a good test for any song.

The more humour-slanted songs like 'Cold Tea', 'Dumb Waiters' and 'Young 'N' Russian', fare less well than some of the ballads, and the top-quality songs like 'All The Love In The World', 'Everybody's Got To Learn Sometime' and 'It All Comes Down To You' still sound sublime in this format. The trio's harmony singing and playing are excellent, as you'd expect, and as a one-off concert with an audience present, this would have been a winner. It's a shame the band didn't go for that option, rather than recording live in a rather sterile room. The self-conscious spoken introductions to the songs also come over sounding a bit odd due to lack of an audience to respond to, and this album is one for the hard-core fan rather than the more-casual listener. However, the five studio tracks that were released on *The Korgis Kollection* are excellent and well-worth adding to the collection for any dedicated fan of the band, and these are discussed below.

'It All Comes Down To You' (Davis, Baker, Warren)

This is the perfect example of how to write a great song using just a handful of chords. With a sweeping European feel to its expressive melody, and an arrangement built on a complex mesh of different keyboard sounds, including piano, string samples and harpsichord, this is a track with a singular and mesmerising feel. Although virtually the same chord sequence runs through both verse and chorus, the skill employed in the melodic construction makes the two sections feel quite different from each other, giving the song a naturally perfect form. Some fine Warren wordplay completes this co-write by the three Korgis and indicates the band is firing on all cylinders in the songwriting department as the new century dawns. It's all wrapped up in a beautiful production by David Lord, and makes for another impressive addition to The Korgis' canon.

'Find Yourself Another Fool' (Davis)

Andy Davis offers up this quality pop song underpinned by medium-tempo piano with a strong lead vocal by John Baker. It's a well-constructed melody with a chorus vocal that moves to a higher register than the verses, to good effect. Bereft of a middle eight, it relies on its considerable atmosphere to carry it through, which it just about does. Although not by any stretch a major composition in The Korgis' songbook, it manages to hold its own in the company of the other new high-calibre pop songs presented here.

'That's What Friends Are For' (Davis, Ferguson)

Always one of my favourites of the Davis/Ferguson songs, this laid-back country ballad is beautifully sung by John Baker, with backing harmonies from Davis and Warren. What sounds like reversed guitar samples, can be heard forming an atmospheric matrix in the right-hand channel, and the understated arrangement based on Davis' acoustic guitar feels just right.

Although it's a remake of a song that first appeared on the *Andy Davis Band* album in 1994, it has travelled well, with this being the definitive version. With its timeless sentiment of altruistic amity and a simple but perfect musical form, this song deserves to become a much-covered standard.

'I Wonder What's Become Of You' (Baker, Warren)
Another disarmingly simple pop tune that's likely to lodge in your head after a few listens, this song displays an elegant construction, with a verse opening section that moves up and down over a few chords, and a perfectly-formed repeated middle eight that sounds like James Warren in classic pop mode. Hugely listenable, this track maintains the high standard of pop songwriting in evidence on these Korgis 2001 sessions, and is another welcome addition to their songbook.

'Come To Me' (Warren, Lord)
James Warren collaborates with David Lord on another of those sweeping arrangements, with a strong European vibe dominating and a chorus built along chromatic lines via a descending sequence that's a bit too close to ELO's 1971 single '10538 Overture' – it even quotes a motif from Roy Wood's French horn part on that song.

The middle section displays a complex chord arrangement moving through several modulations that strongly recall Brian Wilson's *Smile*-era work: a recurring influence. It's another interesting track, with the only negative being the repeated chorus chant of the title, that's a bit overdone on the long fade.

Love And Hate – Mutter Slater (2006)

Personnel:
Mutter Slater: guitar, vocals
Richard Edwards: slide guitar
Clive Ashley: tenor and soprano saxophones
Chris Lonergan: bass
Ady Milward: drums, backing vocals
Robbie McIntosh: guitar
Ben Waters: piano
Tom Hughes: organ
Ray Ashley: slide trombone
Recorded: Mojo Studios, Torquay; Loudbox Studios, Yeovil, 2006
Producers: Mutter Slater, Steve Kitch
Engineers: Leo Brown, Steve Kitch
Label: Thoroughbred
Release date: 2006

Before he finally rejoined Stackridge in 2007, Mutter Slater first had some unfinished business to attend to in the form of his latest batch of solo compositions. He'd been playing the West Country bars with a local raunchy blues/rock outfit that he put together under the name Little Dixie and the Kickass Rhythm Section, and his latest batch of songs were very much an exercise in American influences. This moniker had come from a family connection, as his father was referred to as Dixie, therefore, his son adopted the *nom de plume* Little Dixie. By the time he had an album ready for release, the band title was shortened to just Little Dixie.

'Golden State' (Slater)

Displaying a great overdriven guitar sound, 'Golden State' opens the first of Mutter Slater's series of band albums serving to display his solo songwriting. The mid-tempo is enhanced by some fat descending electric guitar arpeggios, giving the track a characteristic feel. Slater intones his unease at existing without the object of his desire, as he 'Can't move a muscle' since parting from his loved one. The 'Golden State' he's referring to is not California but the ideal state of mind that he yearns to return to via reconciliation with his estranged partner. The band are tight and impressive on this solid opening track, with the first appearance of his go-to saxophone player Clive Ashley, who would remain a collaborator for many years, even playing occasional duo gigs with Slater.

'O.K.' (Slater)

Kicking off with overdriven wah-wah guitar, this track blusters along in a blues rock style, as Slater's lyric deals with the subject of domestic quarrels: hopefully not written from an autobiographical perspective. Fights rage over Sonny's tonsillectomy, food preparation, and even arguments about the rules of fighting, detailing a far from happy domestic situation. As the enmity escalates, the police make an appearance and rough up the protagonist further, arresting him for disturbing the peace. This is a decent rocker that moves along smartly enough to be enjoyable.

'Til The Sun Goes Down' (Slater)
This excellent rocking track motors along, building up a fair head of steam and coming on like a cross between the Chuck Berry song (and Buddy Holly hit) 'Brown-Eyed Handsome Man' and an up-tempo Jackson Browne number. This is one of the most neatly-constructed songs on the album and a thoroughly engaging one with a perfect turnaround chorus and a repeated middle eight. Again, Clive Ashley excels on sax, providing melodic reiterations after the choruses, and also contributes a freewheeling solo which is followed by a cool, rocking piano solo from Ben Waters, who is impressive throughout the album.

'Sea Of Tears' (Slater)
Another well-constructed song, 'Sea Of Tears' has an effective four-chord verse and a chorus that's liable to stick around in the cranium after a few passes. Blowsy sax carries the track, including a brief solo, and Slater regales us about another lost love, his crying exceeding the perennial river to become a whole sea.

'Broken Wheel' (Slater)
This track is an attempt at an acoustic slow blues that, to my ears, doesn't work so well. Slater's vocal goes a tad over the top in places, especially on the coda. The main point of interest is some excellent bluesy barrelhouse piano from Ben Waters, but it's not quite enough to rescue the track.

'Sweet Larraine' (Slater)
This boogie sounds almost akin to Status Quo in places, as Slater goes to town over his feelings for 'Sweet Larraine' (strange spelling!). Rocking along like the clappers, this is another highly listenable track. The up-tempo numbers definitely suit his voice better than the slower tracks.

'For Right Or Wrong' (Slater)
This is a triple-time song with a bluesy feel, and mooches along slowly in the mould of a torch ballad such as the Ragavoy/Weiss soul classic 'Stay With Me Baby', which Lorraine Ellison made famous in the 1960s. Slater testifies 'Love me for right or wrong' mightily on the choruses, with his usual 100% vocal commitment.

'Hey! Bartender' (Slater)
Back with up-tempo rock, after yet more woman trouble, Slater heads to his local boozer in an attempt to drown his sorrows. Our sozzled troubadour

has one too many as he perches on a barstool and serenades the bartender with this ode to his former woman. The music has an engaging mid-tempo lope, accentuated with some tasty slide guitar licks, occasional stabbing sax embellishments, and more excellent barroom piano.

'Life Ain't Fair' (Slater)

This track makes for a refreshing change of pace, coming on like a cross between Tex-Mex and ska. Opening with Clive Ashley's sax and Ray Ashley's almost comical trombone sliding around and sounding like Mariachi music, the tempo eventually settles into a fast bluebeat rhythm as Slater delineates just why life ain't fair.

'Love And Hate' (Slater)

Closing with a ballad, Slater weighs up the two sides of this fractious-sounding relationship with a soliloquy to love and hate. It doesn't add up to a great deal, but the overly-long running time of nearly eight minutes *does* allow for some saxophone doodling and a slide guitar solo *en route*.

Jim's Easy Listening Album (2006)

Personnel:
James Warren: vocals, guitar, bass
Glenn Tommey: drum programming, percussion, keyboards
Rod Bowkett: drum programming, percussion, keyboards, bass
David Lord: keyboards, string arrangements
Louise Anderson, Tony Barbie, Sarah Mitchell, John Baker, Helena: backing vocals
Charlie Aggett: vocals
Will Gregory: tenor saxophone
Paul Burchill, Al Thomas: guitar
Kit Morgan: nylon guitar
John Miller, Andy Davis, Richard Stubbings: keyboards
Recorded by Jim at home; Glenn Tommey in his garage, and at David Lord's flat, 1995, 2006 (New tracks)
Producers: James Warren, David Lord, Glenn Tommey
Engineers: David Lord, Glenn Tommey
Label: Angel Air
Release date: 2006

Stackridge reunion rumours refused to go away, and the core four members would all eventually warm to the idea of giving it one more go. The obvious missing element was Mike Evans – a casualty of the management politics that initially prevented the Stackridge name being used by any of the other members for their nascent plans. Happily, this was eventually resolved, and Stackridge were able to be reborn and reinvented yet again, but without the luxury of Evans' violin-playing.

The first steps towards an anticipated reunion occurred when James Warren and Crun Walter got fed up with waiting for the others to make up their minds, and combined forces with musicians from a Beach Boys tribute band called Surf's Up, and scheduled a gig in Bath during summer 2005. This was advertised as an evening with 'The Next Best Thing' – presumably to avoid using the 'S' word – but thereafter became known as James Warren and Friends. This lineup brought former Korgis keyboard player Glenn Tommey back into the fold, along with drummer Andy 'Codge' Marsden, who concurrently played alongside Warren in his covers band The Blue Meanies. The vocal trio of Sarah Mitchell, Louise Barbie and Tony Barbie gave the vocal department harmonic depth, and local Bristol guitar hero Paul Burchill initially played lead guitar, later to be succeeded by Nigel Newton.

The live set featured a generous sprinkling of Stackridge classics, alongside Korgis and Beach Boys covers, with a truly marvellous arrangement of Crosby, Stills, Nash & Young's 'Carry On' that rivalled the original. The remainder of the set was made up of a handful of excellent new James Warren songs that would see the light the following year when they were added to the best of his 1995 recordings from *Jim's Special Edition Easy Listening Christmas Album*.

I caught up with Warren and the gang at the Prom Wine Bar gig in Bristol on 15 October 2005, and chatted with him and Crun Walter about future plans. The latter was still holding out hope for a full reunion, and yearned to make 'one more perfect album' with Stackridge. When I asked him if any of the as-yet-unrecorded *lost* compositions of old would be considered for a potential album, he confided, 'I'd really love to record 'February In Shropshire': one of the best things we ever did', and I had to agree with him on that one.

During the set, I chanced upon none other than Andy Davis in the audience and asked him whether he'd be stepping up for a guest appearance that evening. 'Not tonight', he replied: always a man of few words!

In 2006, Angel Air released the brilliantly programmed second imprint of *Jim's Easy Listening Album,* which trumps the original 1995 version, with the inclusion of eight new songs of exceptional quality added to the best seven tracks from the 1995 version. Superbly arranged, performed and recorded, the new additions lift this album up to the level of greatness, making *Jim's Easy Listening Album* the finest James Warren solo release so far. The tracks selected from the 1995 edition were 'The Leaving Time', 'Can't Get Her Out Of My Head', 'Money Talks', 'The Frozen North', 'Someday They'll Find Out', 'Love, Death And Photographs' and 'We Didn't Get Along'. But it was the new songs that were the most impressive and are looked at below.

'Hope In My Heart' (Warren, Davis)

The eight new numbers here show the Warren muse operating at peak proficiency, as this – the one new collaboration with Andy Davis – amply demonstrates. With a verse built on clusters of three to five notes crossing alternate bar lines, there is space for the melody to breathe, giving this love song an expressive, uncluttered feel. The chorus is memorable and will soon have many a listener singing along with it. This is superior pop songwriting at its best.

'Can't You Hear My Heart Calling' (Warren, Tommey)

With a sophisticated melody, this track shows that Warren had been mugging up on his Burt Bacharach songwriting techniques in the run-up to this project. On an album full of rhythmic variety, this quality 3/4 ballad also revisits Brian Wilson territory, with its effortlessly-winding melody soaked in rich vocal harmonies. Featuring a lineup employing many of the musicians from the concurrent James Warren and Friends, a real consistency of feel is maintained throughout these new recordings. Also, most of the new songs here were in the live setlist at the time.

'I Guess It Means We're Falling in Love' (Warren, Tommey)

A cool electric piano opens on this undulating melody that yet again shows a distinct Brian Wilson influence. It's a lovely arrangement, with finely-crafted key modulations worthy of a master songwriter (which Warren at his best can be) and is another quality collaboration with future Stackridge keyboard player Glenn Tommey. After one of the key shifts, an intricate, wordless vocal arrangement cascades past our ears, with harmonies abounding from both male and female vocalists. Warren's lyric – as ever on this album – is on the subject of love, with the hopes and doubts of a new love mingling together rather uncertainly.

'You've Got The Love That Matters' (Warren, Baker, Tommey)

This song is another mid-tempo piano-driven love song, which – with its authentic orchestra samples – brings to mind nothing less than those purveyors of perfect musical smoothness, The Carpenters. Not that it's all velvet-toned – a nifty George Harrison-style electric guitar arpeggio, cuts loose for a welcome middle eight before we resume with the catchy chorus. It all ends with more of the slightly-overdriven guitar to bring another fine piece of pop songwriting to a satisfying conclusion.

'The First Kiss' (Warren, Tommey)

This sunny, upbeat love song is absolutely joyous in its summery feel. Unremittingly up and optimistic, it really nails that just-fallen-in-love feeling. With a brisk walking bass and bracing jangly 12-string guitar support, 'The First Kiss' is the ultimate feel-good pop song with breezy harmonies and a Byrds-like 12-string guitar solo that closely follows the melody line. There is a false ending that precedes a glorious perpetually-descending coda, before finally closing with a nifty guitar turnaround. Glenn Tommey certainly proves his worth as a Warren collaborator of substance, judging by the quality level of his five co-writes for this album.

'Never Gonna Make It Better' (Warren, Bowkett)

Renewing old bonds from their writing experiences back in the transitional 1973/1974 Stackridge lineup, Rod Bowkett makes a welcome appearance after his successful first album as producer/writer for singer Corrine Bailey Rae. With a delicious minor-key melody wound around a sophisticated chord sequence, this is an example of classic ballad writing at its best. The bridge melody that links the first verse to the chorus is strung over a descending chord sequence that displays an almost classical grace. It finally falls into a chorus that sears into the brain cells. In other words, it has a memorably catchy chorus.

'This Love Isn't Good For Us' (Warren, Baker, Tommey)

With delicate nylon guitar – presumably played by session man Kit Morgan – this touching melody also boasts support from a delicious orchestral arrangement by David Lord, with cello and oboe most prominent. There are also some subtle percussion additions, treated with reverb and repeat echoes that drift across the soundscape (I'm a real sucker for this sort of thing, check out The Beach Boys' 1971 masterwork *Surf's Up* for some great examples of this technique). The quality remains high on a song that carries a lot of feeling as Warren shares the lead vocals with one of the female session singers, to wonderful effect.

'So Much Love' (Warren, Bowkett)

Another fine collaboration with Rod Bowkett, this syncopated track has a terrific Latin-percussion backing over a brisk samba-like rhythm that seems to float against the other instruments. It's an infectious groove, and the song is joyous in both its verve and lyrics, and as Warren emotively sings 'I lost my way, I'm coming home', you feel he really is back in peak form after his artistic dip back in the mid-1980s. The coda shows a Crosby, Stills & Nash influence, as close-harmony vocals revolve around, and the backing dips, leaving just the vocalis to close this superb track.

'Everybody's Got To Learn Sometime' (Original 1978 demo) (Warren)

An almost obligatory inclusion on a James Warren album, yet another version of the song appears here to close this excellent album. This time though, it's another appearance of the ultimate original, being Warren's first demo of his new song, recorded in November 1978 and previously available as a bonus track on the first edition of this album. Technically, it could've been included on the *The Korgis* debut album that appeared a year later, but it was held over until the second album *Dumb Waiters,* in 1980. The demo shows that the magic was there from the start in this stripped-down version sans violin solo and with Warren's bass much more to the fore. It's nice to hear as a piece of history, the song that has become a virtual standard.

The Forbidden City (2008)

Personnel:
Andy Davis: guitar, keyboards, vocals
Mutter Slater: flute, vocals
James Warren: guitar, vocals
Crun Walter: bass
Glenn Tommey: keyboards
Nigel Newton: guitar
Rachel Hall: violin
Sarah Mitchell: violin, percussion and vocals
Andy 'Codge' Marsden: drums
Recorded live at The Rondo Theatre, Bath, 1 April 2007
Producers: Glenn Tommey, James Warren, Andy Davis
Engineers: David Lord, Dave Tommey
Label: Angel Air
Release date: 2008

In 2006, Glenn Tommey oversaw the remastering of a compilation of classic Stackridge tracks, and Angel Air released this under the title *Purple Spaceships Over Yatton – Best of Stackridge*. A newly recorded version of the title track was included, and the compilation is very well put together, with Tommey's remastering job giving the tracks a glossy sheen. All the tracks featured were drawn from the 1970s variants of the band: mostly from the first three MCA albums, plus two from the Rocket catalogue. Apart from the new recording, one additional unique facet of the album was that the two halves of the *Friendliness* title track had been edited together into a single track for the first time, which worked really well.

However, the new version of 'Purple Spaceships Over Yatton' is the reason for Thrashers to obtain the compilation, as Davis, Warren and Walter – along with Glenn Tommey and Codge Marsden – cooked up a new arrangement of the classic Walter/Davis instrumental. The notable absentee was again Mutter Slater, and though the new recording is a stunningly strong track, the absence of Slater's flute is a definite missing element, and it's a pity this was recorded before he again hopped aboard the good ship Stackridge. Having said that, the new version is a mighty and muscular reading of 'Purple Spaceships', that highlights a brand new arrangement that would form the matrix for the ongoing live versions to ensue once Slater rejoined the band at the start of 2007.

The 2006 recording of this epic is much more spacey than the 1972 studio version and is more of a band performance than an orchestrated piece. The first half has a fascinating sampled cello arrangement that enhances its pensive feel, and there occurs one of those frankly odd Stackridge moments as Crun Walter and one of the other band members engage in an incomprehensible discussion about haddock (of all things). This is perhaps a reference to a feature from their live performances during the earliest 1970s gigs when Slater and Walter would perform an occasional skit of two neighbours nattering over a garden fence about bizarre subjects. The second half really misses Slater's flute, though, as it's replaced by a keyboard solo, and this passage feels a touch anticlimactic after the tension of the first section.

Happily, it wasn't long after this release that Mutter Slater once again threw in his lot with his old buddies, and the reunited Stackridge debuted at the Rondo Theatre, Bath, on 24 February 2007, following this with a gig at London's 100 Club on 16 March. For these first two gigs, they employed violinist Katy Salvidge, but by the third gig, she was replaced by young violin virtuoso Rachel Hall. This gig was to be a special one, as they returned to the Rondo on 1 April to record a live album/DVD. These were subsequently released by Angel Air Records in early 2008 under the curious title *The Forbidden City*. Various Thrashers – including myself – were interviewed in the street outside the Rondo, and these interviews were included on the DVD. It proved to be an enthralling evening for Thrashers, and I was delighted to be in the front row, right in front of the recently returned Mutter Slater. Watching and hearing him play flute on 'Teatime' once more, was a sublime experience, and I was thrilled to witness him back with Stackridge again.

'Fundamentally Yours' (Davis, Smegmakovitch)

Disc one of the two-CD set opens with an arrangement faithful to the studio version of the lead track from *The Man in the Bowler Hat,* to the delight of the partisan audience. The band fall back into their customary roles with a professional ease that comes with their combined experience, and are ably supported by the new recruits, as the largest live lineup the band ever had, opens a new era.

The album production is good and the stereo placement reflects the stage lineup from an audience perspective. Over the next few years, the band would slim down as various musicians flew the coop but for their impressive renaissance, the essential core-four would remain the heart of the band until 2010.

'Dangerous Bacon' (Warren, Smegmakovitch)

Sticking with their most high-profile album, James Warren's second vocal in a row revisits this timeless pop melody. Nigel Newton's guitar solos sound carefully worked out and somewhat perfunctory: as if he's learnt them from the album. At the time, it seemed an odd move in having an extra guitarist just for lead solos, especially with a virtuoso like Andy Davis in the band. But throughout the gig, I had the feeling that Davis was regaining his stage confidence after such a long layoff. But it wouldn't be long before he hit his stride again.

'Grooving Along On The Highway On A Monday Morning Once' (Miller, Warren, Menage) Yet another James Warren vocal leads us through this whimsical track from *Something for the Weekend* as the studio version is pretty much faithfully replicated. Rachel Hall, in particular, is playing the old Mike Evans violin solos.

'The Volunteer' (Davis, Smegmakovitch)

After Andy Davis' amusing introduction to this anti-war song – 'Just to show we're up to the minute, it's about the Crimean war' – Mutter Slater steps up for his first vocal of the evening, as he regales us with the salty tale of life in the British army in the late-19th century. His vocal is ably supported by some fine violin counterpoint from Rachel Hall, and the arrangement closely follows the *Extravaganza* version. It closes with a replication of Evans' violin solo by Rachel Hall, followed by Davis' usual country guitar solo.

'Syracuse The Elephant' (Walter, Davis)

As Crun Walter announces 'A song about an iguana', the band crash into a reading of their ode to a misplaced elephant, as Mutter Slater's flute once more plays the overture as of old, and Andy Davis regales the sad tale. He subtly alters the verse melody, giving it a more sinuous line than the studio version, and it sounds rather good. James Warren harmonises on the choruses, and Rachel Hall again sticks with the original violin arrangement in the central section. The studio waltz section is ejected from this arrangement, and it piles into the flute-led *jungle* passage before the final verse and chorus take it to the coda, completing a rather neat reading of this elephantine arrangement.

'Anyone For Tennis?' (Warren)

Prior to the band's rendition of James Warren's Charleston classic from *Friendliness,* he warns us that it contains 'some unreasonably high notes'. But he needn't have feared, as his pipes sound in good nick this evening, and he gives a sterling performance. The main differences between this and the 1970s live version are the omission of Mutter Slater's woodblock, whistle and his 'Wakey wakey' clarion call. But it's still a charming execution of a quaint ditty.

'Wonderful Day' (Walter)

As an introduction to his solo composition from the *Lemon 2002* mini-album, Crun Walter encourages the audience to recite three Polish phrases back to him, and then tells the assembled throng that they've 'just made a date with a gay Polish welder!', to which James Warren adds, 'I'm sure you'll have a wonderful day!', cueing Walter's song of the same name. It's a wondrous song and beautifully harmonised, bringing a welcome dose of sunny pop to the set. Everyone plays their socks off again, and this lineup proves to be impressively tight.

'Ruth, Did You Read My Mind?' (Warren, Miller)

Warren's hoedown-influenced stomper is performed close to the original studio arrangement: as many numbers *are* in the reformed band's debut set.

On this performance, the twin violin riffs of Rachel Hall and the ever-smiling Sarah Mitchell work extremely well together. Hall is the virtuoso of the pair, but Mitchell's versatility proved useful to Stackridge during this incarnation. In the future, in addition to violin, she would occasionally play keyboards and percussion as their renaissance flourished going forward from this point to their new artistic peak in 2009.

'Friendliness' (Warren)

Slater then introduces a number that had never before been played on stage (and one on which he didn't feature), as we're treated to a unique live rendition of both parts of the *Friendliness* title track, expertly combined into one seamless performance. As Warren plays the passing chords, Davis underpins with a single chord on the verses, as their vocal harmonies meld beautifully on this adventurous little piece. Some lovely ethereal vocals by Warren and the two girls, light up the glorious *musical box* section with an authentic celeste sample provided by Glenn Tommey, which weaves a beguiling spell. On the coda, he drifts off into some tinkling piano as Rachel Hall improvises on her violin.

'Dancing On Air' (Slater, Bowkett)

'What key is this song in?', enquires James Warren, as Crun Walter replies 'D'. The band then relax into a number first introduced by the *Extravaganza* lineup back in 1975: Mutter Slater's tribute to the era of Fred Astaire and Ginger Rogers. Slightly shorter than the original (but much longer than Slater's 1976 single version), there's still a substantial instrumental introduction, featuring Davis' laid-back guitar and Rachel Hall's perfect period violin chops. Slater alternately whistles and croons on this tale of high society and a night on the town with his gal. A real charmer of a performance, it was great to hear this back in a Stackridge set after 32 years. As the song comes to a close to waves of warm applause, Slater utters, 'It was really nothing'.

'Fish In A Glass' (Davis, Walter)

This *Mr. Mick* epic sees the band getting down to some serious playing, as the Zappa-like opening is again driven by Crun Walter's thunderous bass line, and the violin section combine beautifully with some big string washes by Glenn Tommey. The ever-reliable 'Codge' Marsden thumps along enthusiastically, as lead guitarist Nigel Newton replicates Andy Davis' usual electric guitar part; Davis concentrating more on his vocal. The choruses sound very strong vocally, with massed harmonies really filling out the sound, bringing the first half of the show to a satisfying close.

'Lummy Days' (Davis)

The much-anticipated 'Lummy Days' starts the second set, with Mutter Slater first explaining that the title – based on 'one of Andrew's father's sayings' –

could've easily been 'In Nan's Room Behind The Clock' instead: a less snappy moniker for sure! It was certainly a high point of the gig and sounded every bit as magnificent as of old, with Crun Walter's bubbling bass line dovetailing with Tommey's piano and Davis' guitar. Rachel Hall effortlessly powers through the intricate arrangement on her violin, and Slater's flute alternately pipes, trills and performs huge cartwheels of note flurries to a rapturous reception from the crowd.

'If I Had You' (Rachmaninoff, Davis)

The first of the evening's Korgis' tunes, Warren introduces it as 'Andrew's greatest hit!', before the mandolin-toned guitars ring out and Warren employs his best choirboy voice: which works well on the chorus harmonies with Davis' lower tones. Nigel Newton plays Davis' original solo note-for-note but picks it rather than using the slide that gave the studio version that something special. Also, Rachmaninoff now gets the credit he's due, despite his borrowing of the tune from Paganini!

'Teatime' (Walter, Davis)

One of the real treats of the evening, Mutter Slater once more sets sail on his beautiful flute arrangement, combining perfectly with Hall's violin to give that distinctive medieval feel to the first half. He throws in some liquid flute improvisation on the laid-back middle section before heading for the heavens, as Crun Walter's bass and Codge Marsden's drums pile in for the energetic two-chord vamp at the end. This also gives Hall a chance to stretch out with some frantic violin on the coda, bringing this timeless song to a towering climax.

'Happy In The Lord' (Welton)

With Mutter Slater mumbling 'If I get this right, it'll be a miracle', Glenn Tommey's church organ-like chords open a reading of Phil Welton's tongue-in-cheek song: one of the rare Stackridge cover versions. Slater gives a sterling performance at the top of his range on this *Extravaganza* song, as the band rock away, and on the coda he performs a variation of Tony Ashton's eccentric rap that closed the original, adding the afterthought 'I think I'll lie down in a darkened room now!'.

'Help Under Doors' (Warren, Miller)

Stackridge rock out a little on this eccentric song from *Something for the Weekend,* as James Warren takes the vocal and provides some lead guitar soloing. The violin/synthesiser duet in the middle section is as odd as on the original studio version, and at one point towards the end, all three of the front line are playing guitar, panned across the stereo spectrum with Nigel Newton stage left, Warren in the centre and Davis out to the right, making for a satisfyingly raunchy ending.

'Everybody's Got To Learn Sometime' (Warren)
The second Korgis offering is a subtly built-up arrangement from just keyboard and vocal to full band. Nigel Newton's guitar arpeggios enter the fray from the second verse onwards, while Andy Davis picks sympathetic guitar notes on the higher octave, and the drums enter with perfect timing by the second chorus. Hall's violin copies Stuart Gordon's original solo from the hit single: sounding as emotional as ever. This song would develop going forward, as Davis would later add much more guitar, including a solo on the coda. But this evening the more-stripped-down version still sounded sublime.

'The Road To Venezuela' (Davis, Smegmakovitch)
Back to *The Man in the Bowler Hat* next for another South American excursion via this ever-popular song. With Andy Davis swapping back to acoustic guitar, he proves to be in fine voice, joined by James Warren on the choruses. Through the years, the central tract of this song has been host to many different violin solos, and tonight is no exception as Rachel Hall improvises her way through her own set of variations, sounding wonderful. She's a superb musician who – after her two-year tenure with Stackridge was over in 2009 – went on to grace the excellent progressive rock band Big Big Train for nine productive years.

'Can Inspiration Save The Nation?' (Davis, Walter)
This little gem proves to be a welcome addition to the set and is performed via a stripped-down arrangement of Davis' guitar chords, Slater's flute riffs between verses, and some tasteful organ from Glenn Tommey on the middle eight. It's a rather short but very lovely song, with Davis rendering Crun Walter's rather poignant ecologically-slanted lyric, written back in 1975. The flute riffs, though, are of an even older vintage, having been rescued from the ever-influential but still-unrecorded 'After The Tetracycline' from 1974.

'The Galloping Gaucho' (Slater, Smegmakovitch)
Mutter Slater takes centre stage next as he relates the cheery tale of the 'boss-eyed blade on his last crusade' – the galloping gaucho himself – and it proves to be a heap of fun as always. Lots of audience participation is in evidence on the pauses between the verses, with long Thrashers chants of 'Whoa-oa-oa-oa!', before Slater resumes his next verse. With Glenn Tommey's fat trombone riffs in the driving seat, it sounds fabulous, and Slater gives his all in the vocal department. The violin/flute jig instrumental passages tumble along irresistibly, and Rachel Hall's violin negotiates the counterpoint melody on the climactic verse, bringing the track to a storming conclusion.

'The Last Plimsoll' (Davis, Smegmakovitch)
We stay with *The Man in the Bowler Hat* for a full arrangement of 'The Last Plimsoll'. It moves along smartly, and sees a welcome return for Mutter Slater's explosive flute soloing on the second half, which he delivers with gusto. This

arrangement would eventually be truncated on future gigs, but tonight we're treated to the complete *Bowler Hat* studio arrangement.

'Something About The Beatles' (Warren, Menage)
Always one of Warren's favourites, this *Something for the Weekend* song slots in nicely towards the end of the set, and brings forth from Nigel Newton, his most expressive guitar solo of the evening. Where he'd been playing tight arrangements on the other tracks, here he cuts loose with some hot improvisation that lifts the track up a fair notch.

'Slark' (Walter, Davis)
As Slater opens 'Slark' with that timeless flute riff, we are once more transported to the mythical Somerset landscape that sprang from Crun Walter's fertile imagination way back when. On the first verse, the original 'creosote car' has become a 'big black car', and Andy Davis also replaces the next original line with 'When a noise like thunder made me drop my cigar', which scans beautifully, it must be said. The big difference from the last time Slater performed it over 30 years before, was that this version followed the 1972 single arrangement rather than the ever-expanding album arrangement of old.

'Do The Stanley' (Wabadaw Sleeve)
Inevitably, the dance craze of 1973 returns once more to the Stackridge set, as Slater invites the assembled Thrashers to 'cut a rug' to the stomping rhythm. With Glenn Tommey's trombone driving it along, it more closely resembles the brass-inclined single version. With less energy than of old, Slater is a bit more static on stage these days, although he gives his all in the vocal department, as ever. In place of his usual join-in exhortation, 'Cor blimey!' towards the end, he sings the amusing 'Gawd 'elp us' as the number hits its climax to much applause from the assembled throng, who bring the band back for an encore.

'Dora The Female Explorer' (Stackridge)
What better climax to a Stackridge gig could there be than to close with a spirited rendition of the debut single? Slater chugs once more on his trusty harmonica, as those irresistible violin riffs from Hall and Mitchell power along this tribute to the world's greatest female adventurer, as James Warren gives his usual fine performance on lead vocal.

This gig marked the start of a glorious spread of live dates over the early years of the 21st century, signalling that Stackridge were back and sounding as great as ever. Emotions had run high this evening, as Thrashers all looked forward to following the band into a promising musical future, and so it would prove to be.

Riding a Hurricane – Mutter Slater Band (2008)

Personnel:
Mutter Slater: vocals, acoustic guitar, flute
Chris Lonergan: bass, slide guitar
Ady Milward: drums, backing vocals
Recorded at Mojo Studios, Torquay, Devon, 2008
Producers: Billy Bragg, Leo Brown
Engineer: Leo Brown
Label: Thoroughbred
Release date: 2008

In between his mounting Stackridge engagements, Mutter Slater found time to form the first lineup of the Mutter Slater Band. To produce his latest batch of solo compositions with a stripped-down three-piece set up, he'd engaged none other than the 'Bard of Barking' and big fan of the Slater voice: Billy Bragg. Very different from his Stackridge writing style, Slater pursued his love of more blues-based material on this excellently-produced album.

The two musicians employed for this project had both featured in Slater's previous aggregation Little Dixie, and proved to be perfect for these bluesy tunes.

'Excuse Me Ma'am' (Slater)

Opening an album that focuses on a mainly acoustic trio format, this song is driven along at a medium pace by Ady Milward's brush work, Slater's acoustic strumming and Chris Lonergan's bass. The lyric's thrust is along the lines of waking up in a strange bed with an even stranger woman lying beside you, after an overdone night on the town, as Slater sings 'Excuse me ma'am, I appear to be in your bed'.

Some tidy wordplay paints the scene, and with its amiable shuffle, it makes the perfect opening track.

'Sunday Running Wild' (Slater)

Sounding very much influenced by John Lee Hooker, this stalking acoustic blues – again powered by brushed drums – is a further tale of being let off the leash: in this case, once a week on a Sunday. Chris Lonergan's overdubbed slide guitar, stokes that John Lee blues feel, and this has an attractive groove. On the fade, Slater even gives a patent Hooker 'How-how-how-how' grunt: very authentic it is too!

'Strangers In One Room' (Slater)

A ballad with a swaying two-chord verse, the lyric is a reflection on that feeling after love has gone wrong – quite poignantly expressed in the chorus line 'How can a love just die, and yet the world still turns': an emotion often felt after deep loss. This is an effective and likeable ballad.

'Pig In The Middle' (Slater)
A pulsating acoustic rocker, this is breathlessly fast, and like much of this album, it has a great live-sounding feel. The lyrics tell the tale of a struggle to free a woman from a man who is mistreating her and using her like 'some goddamn house appliance', as well as attempting to sell her to 'his creepy little clients'. This elicits the passionate bellow from Slater, that he 'Wouldn't treat no woman like that'. In common with the rest of this album, it has a lovely crisp production.

'The Price' (Slater)
A dead slow blues, 'The Price' details the gory aftermath of a relationship, and the battles over possessions that ensue. Musically it's a straight blues with not a lot of action going down, and relying on Slater's admittedly heartfelt vocal to carry it. Somewhat inexplicably, this song was revamped on his next studio album six years later, but with a marginally-different arrangement.

'Last Train From Heartache' (Slater)
Opening with a hooky riff that later serves as a chorus, this track rocks along agreeably. Lyrically we're back in mistreated-woman territory, as the song's subject attempts to board the train and head for the hills, and who can blame her? In his usual blues-flecked vein, it features multitracked vocal replies at the end of each verse, and has a satisfying gritty feel to it.

'God's Gift' (Slater)
The intro chords and rhythm bring to mind Mason Williams' influential 1968 single 'Classical Gas'. With its thumping downbeat, this rocks along smartly, with the gift in question being an arrogant know-it-all rock star who reckons he's a 'walking marvel', and only walks and talks when he gets paid. Slater revisited this subject on his next album with 'We're In The Money'. Despite the acoustic rhythm section, this track kicks up a fair bit of dust with its driving forward momentum.

'Only The Dues to Pay' (Slater)
We are back to the slow blues on this ballad, as Slater gives his all vocally. His singing style is always heartfelt. It's mainly carried by its bluesy feeling more than any big musical surprises. But if you're in the mood for a slow blues, this one will fill the prescription.

'Moth To A Flame' (Slater)
A slow guitar prelude opens this track before it ups the tempo and Slater regales the tale of the eternal woman who seems to attract most of the male population.

Several tempo shifts carry the track along agreeably enough, and it's an okay track without being anything exceptional.

'Riding A Hurricane' (Slater)

The title track saunters along with further brushwork from drummer Ady Milward, and Slater strums diffidently at a guitar chord as he expounds on his philosophy of life. A call-and-response vocal chorus muses on the fact that – far from being a breeze – life can feel akin to riding a hurricane at times. A brief coda sees the first appearance of Slater's flute on this album, but it just plays a repetitive riff a number of times until it moves into some tantalising soloing that is sadly faded after five seconds, just when things were suddenly getting interesting. Never mind. It's reflective and laid-back in the extreme.

'Triumph Bonneville' (Slater)

Back in John Lee Hooker territory, this grooves along with some great blues slide guitar driving it. The music picks up a fair lick and generates surprising power from its mainly acoustic propulsion. It's the story of a leather-clad beauty breezing into town on said motorcycle, stirring up lustful emotions in the troubled boys frequenting the local bar. The lyric goes from the male protagonists amiably 'Putting the world to rights and mourning the 8-track tape' to a full-fledged fist fight, after the arrival and subsequent departure of the slinky female and her motorcycle, leaving mayhem in her wake.

'I'm Holding Your Picture' (Slater)

A song destined for bigger things, this is Slater's formative version of a song that would soon be revamped with Davis for a new Stackridge album. This recording proves that Slater brought the bulk of the song to the Stackridge sessions. Both the verse music and the instrumental middle eight were already present, and it just needed the choruses that Davis later added. It still carries itself well in this arrangement, though, and is one of Slater's best latter-day compositions, sympathetically painting a portrait of a soldier in a trench somewhere, poring over a picture of his loved one taken back in better days. The coda sees a further Slater flute contribution to this album, but it's only a tentative melodic restatement of the tune.

A Victory for Common Sense (2009)

Personnel:
Andy Davis: guitars, keyboards, vocals
James Warren: guitars, bass, vocals
Mutter Slater: flute, acoustic guitar, vocals
Jim 'Crun' Walter: bass, acoustic guitar
Glenn Tommey: keyboards, trombone, backing vocals
Rachel Hall: violin
Sarah Mitchell: violin, backing vocals
Eddie John: drums
Andy 'Codge' Marsden: drums ('Boots And Shoes')
Mark Frith: programming
Chris Hughes: percussion
Davide Rossi: string arrangements
Recorded: Ashley Manor, Wiltshire, Spring 2009
Producer: Chris Hughes
Engineers: Mark Frith, Chris Hughes
Label: Helium
Release date: July 2009

After the core four Stackridge writers reformed with the flexible nine-piece lineup in 2007, the band forged forward with an ever-expanding gig calendar – though nowhere near as extensive as the old days, they still managed 16 gigs in 2007 and 31 in 2008 as they welcomed additional Stackridge classics back to the set.

To celebrate the band's return to the Glastonbury stage on 29 June 2008 (38 years after they famously opened (and closed) the very first festival at Worthy Farm, Pilton in 1970), an interview and acoustic session was recorded for *The Guardian,* and appeared in a podcast on 31 May 2008. During the interview,, Andy Davis and James Warren both spoke about that very first festival, and the band played several numbers *unplugged*. The first was an excellent relaxed acoustic version of the Bowkett/Slater 1930s-style charmer 'Dancing On Air', followed by a lovely version of the first part of the song that opened that very first Glastonbury festival: 'Teatime'. Mutter Slater's flute tone is surpassingly beautiful, and violinist Rachel Hall faithfully replicates Mike Evans' lines of old, as James Warren gives a fine vocal rendition supported here and there by harmonies from Andy Davis. It's just a pity it comes to a close after the song section, omitting Slater's gorgeous flute passage. It's still a wonderful performance, though, and it's so good to hear the band sounding stripped down to acoustic for a change. There were rumours at the time that they were considering a complete live acoustic album, but sadly this never came to pass.

However, 2009 brought delightful news for Thrashers, with the announcement that Stackridge had signed a three-year/three-album deal with Helium Records. The thought of a further trio of Stackridge albums in quick succession was surely a cause to celebrate wildly, and the future for the band at this point looked distinctly rosy. News soon broke about the sessions for the first of these releases, and a tentative tracklist was mentioned. This would end up differing from the final selection in several ways, and the obvious absentee when the album emerged was a mooted instrumental known as 'Fluffy Bunny', which was originally slated as the opening track. By the time the album appeared, this track had evidently hopped off somewhere and wasn't included. It was also rumoured that a remake of the Davis/Ferguson song 'The Chrysler Girl' may be in the running for the first Stackridge studio project since *Lemon* 2002.

On 11 June 2009, I had the privilege of attending a playback session for the newly-recorded album *A Victory For Common Sense* at producer Chris Hughes' Ashley Manor Studio, set in the rolling hills of Wiltshire. An invited selection of Thrashers attended, as well as band members, including Warren, Davis, Walter, Tommey, and none other than Bill Blake (aka Billy Sparkle), who I'd last seen with the band in 1973! Veteran manager Mike Tobin was also in attendance: he really worked his socks off for the band during this second spell as their manager. When we were all settled in, Chris Hughes ran the master mix, and we were treated to a preview of the new album. It was obvious from the first note – a howl of guitar feedback leading into a rocking rendition of the stage favourite 'Boots And Shoes' – that this new Stackridge album was going to be different from any of the releases that preceded it. The general tone of the album was darker and at times heavier, dominated by Davis' underrated guitar skills, more of which later.

The writing setup also differed from past projects in that it was heavily collaborative, with all four main Stackridge writers pitching in, aided and abetted by the considerable arranging skills of keyboard player Glenn Tommey. This new method of composition becomes particularly apparent in the second half, in the form of more expansive and exploratory arrangements, contrasting with the more compact compositions of the first half. The track programming bears some comparison with the band's 1974 album *Extravaganza* in this respect, as it appears to have been created with a vinyl mentality – the music clearly delineated into a side one/side two format of contrasting styles – although the music is on the whole very different from that album.

After the release of *A Victory For Common Sense*, the band performed an album launch gig at Bush Hall, London, on 16 July, followed by a promotional tour during which they took a few days off in August to film live studio performances at Chapel Arts Centre in Bath that were subsequently released as the *4x4* DVD at the end of 2009. The run of gigs continued into the spring of 2010, by which time Mutter Slater was getting itchy feet and announced he would again be leaving the band to concentrate fully on the Mutter Slater Band: forcing the remaining members to regroup without him.

On the back of a brief tour of Japan, Stackridge were offered a slot on the American CBS TV special *Craig Ferguson's Late, Late Show*. Amazingly, Slater agreed to return for a cameo appearance with the band, and after flying out to Los Angeles, they recorded a somewhat truncated version of 'The Last Plimsoll' for broadcast later that month. It was a one-take performance that delighted the recording technicians and band alike, and there was a brief hope that this blaze of publicity might encourage a late flurry in sales for the current album. On the face of it, it seemed surprising that they chose a track from one of their 1970s albums rather than a newer song, but this choice was heavily influenced by the fact that the host had used said tune as his unofficial theme music during high profile stand-up comedy gigs at Madison Square Garden and the like. It was quite a blast for Thrashers to view their beloved band performing on American TV 41 years after they first formed in 1969! The eagle-eyed would spot that drummer Eddie John had gone AWOL, though, replaced on this occasion by ace session man Jerry Marotta, who had history with the band, having played drums on many Korgis tracks back in the 1980s. Eddie John would, in fact, continue as the Stackridge percussionist right through to their final gig. It seems he may have missed the CBS broadcast due to a dislike of flying.

Back in the summer of 2009, though, Thrashers were wildly celebrating the release of a full Stackridge studio album, with the promise of more to come. The CD appeared in a gatefold card sleeve with the core four lining up on the front in a monochrome photo set against a white background – from left to right, Walter, Warren, Slater and Davis, all staring uncertainly out from the cover. Further black-and-white head shots line up on the rear of the gatefold sleeve, the track credits above them. Opening up the gatefold reveals a colour shot of the core four posing around two tree trunks, with the album credits printed alongside them. The opposite side of the inner gatefold consists of a photo collage of the musicians on the album.

'Boots And Shoes' (Davis, Warren)

As previously mentioned, the band's guitar-dominated version of 'Boots And Shoes' starts with a howl of feedback from Andy Davis' guitar and quickly blows the old Korgis studio version into a cocked bowler hat. With a relentlessly kicking rhythm section featuring some tasty bass runs pushing into the choruses and Davis' searing guitar fills, the track powers along with tight vocal harmonies from Davis and Warren.

Drummer Andy 'Codge' Marsden had originally played on the majority of the album's tracks, but producer Chris Hughes' modern approach meant that a lot of the album's percussion ended up being replaced by drum programming. Although this meant everything sounded as tight as a drum (as you would expect), a degree of Stackridge's warm, organic feel became inevitably lost to strict timekeeping on many tracks. According to 'Codge' though, the drumming on 'Boots And Shoes' is indeed by him before he quit the live band to be replaced by Eddie John (sometime drummer with Bristol area band The Harrisons, and prior to that with Thin Air). The perfect album opener, the song sets up the new 21st-century Stackridge sound, with more stress on the rock element than previous incarnations.

'The Old Country' (Davis, Warren, Slater, Walter)

Although there is less emphasis on the band's lighter, more whimsical traits on this album, some of the inevitable playfulness inherent in the Stackridge DNA surfaces on this lyric – a Mutter Slater-led romp through one of the most perfect slices of pop/rock you could wish for. 'The Old Country' is the first of three loosely-linked consecutive tracks known unofficially as 'The England Suite'. This track is classic Stackridge all the way, as Slater tells the tale of an ex-pat whose loyalties are split between the Antipodes and good old Blighty, set to a martial rhythm with chiming guitar work. His vocal sounds somewhat treated and possibly slightly vari-sped, probably via that scourge of 21st-century recording, autotune. Thankfully the results here sound clear, high and handsome, avoiding that horrendous default setting that has plagued the majority of contemporary pop vocals since its invention.

The middle eight is a shining example of quality songwriting at its best and moves into one of those vintage Stackridge moments for the first flurry of Slater's beautifully-recorded flute in a bridge section of pristine perfection. This leads into the raucous final verse and a classic turnaround ending, recalling the pop genius of Ray Davies at his peak. Some witty bass riffs decorate the bridge and fade out (including several amusing quotes from the nursery rhyme 'Polly Put The Kettle On'), completing a faultless band performance.

As both James Warren and Crun Walter are credited with bass on the album, it becomes a guessing game to spot which of them it is. Judging by the style, I would bet on it being Walter on most of the tracks, including this one.

'Waiting For You And) England To Return' (Warren, Davis, Tommey, Slater)

The awkwardly-titled third track opens with a gentle acoustic guitar accompanied by the plaintive voice of James Warren, recalling a fast-fading age of friendly bobbies on the beat, old country buses, village greens and rustic English life, all set to a folk tune of such poignancy that many a Stackridge fan may well find themselves moist-eyed when listening to it. The lyric cleverly combines the universal and the personal, as if the protagonist has suffered a deep loss and that a return to the rapidly-vanishing values of the past could somehow ameliorate this bereavement.

The song, however, carries a far deeper resonance of loss and the passing of a golden age in this fast-shrinking modern world, and a bittersweet pall of almost unbearable sadness and longing hangs over the choruses. The middle section is quite wonderful, as Warren's piping vocals are replaced by the baritone richness of Andy Davis' voice, making for a marvellous contrast. A clever variation finds them singing harmony together – always a wonderful sound – before falling back to Davis' voice alone. There then follows a roll of tympani and a truly tearjerking return to the Gaelic sweep of the touching verse melody as it's taken up in all its glory by Sarah Mitchell's expressive violin, creating one of the most beautiful moments in the entire Stackridge canon. A final brief return to the verse follows, this time with Davis' vocal superimposing the melody from the middle eight as a counterpoint to Warren's rendition of the verse melody – providing the final artistic brushstroke to complete a shining example of late-period Stackridge songwriting genius.

'Red Squirrel' (Davis)

The sound of birdsong leads into the third part of 'The England Suite'. Here we move from the sad resignation of the previous track, to a lyric that teeters precariously between patriotism and xenophobia, as Andy Davis relates the tale of the red squirrel's battle for survival against the interloping grey variety. It's a riff-driven mid-tempo song based around a cyclical guitar figure and the chord sequence is a touch obvious, so extreme dynamics are employed to add interest, moving from gentle picking to a towering wall of noise bolstered by guitar fireworks. To my ears, it's not enough to rescue it, as this progression soon palls on repeated listens and starts to outstay its welcome.

Lyrically, it does manage to add yet another geographical West Country reference to the Stackridge songbook in the shape of the quaintly named Somerset village Nempnett Thrubwell. The coda brings an unexpected flurry of leaping piano figures as the rhythm fades out underneath: possibly the most interesting musical point; I'm a sucker for random tinkling pianos!

'North St. Grande' (Slater, Davis)

To close the first half of the album, Mutter Slater offers a kind of Mississippi Delta waltz. It was initially recorded as 'I'm Holding Your Picture', and closed the Mutter Slater Band's 2008 album *Riding A Hurricane*. Slater brought it to the table at the band writing sessions for *Victory,* and Andy Davis appended the catchy Yuletide chorus, effectively completing what previously felt like an incomplete song.

With great attention to light and shade, Slater relates the story of a soldier in the trenches of a far-flung war-torn outpost approaching Christmas time, holding a picture of his loved one dancing at the mythical North Street Grande ballroom in Yeovil. Sounding amazingly like an English version of The Band – those Americana pioneers from the late-1960s – Stackridge negotiate this tricky arrangement with the grace it deserves, building up to those oh-so-sing-along choruses that mark this song out as a potential Christmas perennial. It did see release as a Christmas single in 2009 when a re-recorded version hit the seasonal market but sunk without a trace like every Stackridge single before it.

Following the first chorus, the violin-led instrumental interlude is delightful and sounds like a tipsy New Orleans funeral parade, and it's one of those passages that could only be Stackridge, with a repeated chorus to take the song to its denouement.

'Long Dark River' (Walter)

The second half of the album kicks off with the atmospherically-meandering 'Long Dark River', a solo offering from Crun Walter but very different from his other recent solo compositions for the band, which dealt with cars and vegetarianism.

The subject appears to be a musing on mortality, with Stygian references to impending doom and finality ('Just avoiding the long dark river for another year or two'). It's a sombre subject, and the album's remaining tracks also chart darker waters than the band have previously sailed.

Setting up a drone atmosphere once heavily used by George Harrison, the meshing guitars and subterranean bass move this mid-tempo concoction along with a trance-like atmosphere that indeed takes the listener on a kind of mood voyage, with rich vocal harmonies in the chorus, buoyed by the voices of Sarah Mitchell and James Warren behind Andy Davis' lugubrious lead voice. The song part leads seamlessly into a repeated rising rock riff that strongly recalls late-1960s bands like Cream, and is perhaps a nod back to Davis and Walter's blues roots in Griptight Thynn. It builds until it punches out more dramatically, accompanied by splinters of blazing guitar from Davis that bring it to a climax after just over seven minutes.

'Lost And Found' (Davis, Warren, Tommey)

Arpeggios abound on this album and also open this track, which features a gorgeously stratospheric and sinuous vocal line from James Warren. The lineage of this track can be traced as a progression from the experimental Warren closing track from the *Something for the Weekend* album – 'It Must Be Time For Bed' – as it also employs a convoluted chord structure to guide its winding melody. The rhythm section is really punchy and tight, hitting a groove reminiscent of Swindon band XTC in their 1980s era, and it gets quite funky in places too. The track also has a cooking harmonica-tinged synthesizer solo that leads into some bluesy lead guitar from Andy Davis, recalling Eric Clapton at his 1960s best when he was deified by fans as 'God'. With an almost psychedelic coda over that punchy groove, Mutter Slater adds some Eastern-sounding flute as Davis' guitar screams to the heavens, sliding up the scale into infinity before a staccato ensemble figure recalling The Kinks' 'You Really Got Me' brings the track to a juddering halt. 'Lost And Found' displays an intangible quality that's difficult to put your finger on, but it's opaque and nebulous, and remains intriguing.

'Cheese And Ham' (Davis, Warren, Tommey, Slater)

This started out as a Davis/Warren song that the band chipped in on and is again exploratory in nature, with a dark lyrical overtone that paints a picture of child abuse. A ticking clock and fairground Wurlitzer open proceedings before the softer verses representing the frightened child hiding in a cupboard under the stairs are intoned by James Warren, and the harder-edged choruses representing the father figure admonishing the child are sung by Andy Davis. It's the second song in a row to mention 'father issues'.

It has several interesting rhythmic shifts juxtaposing 5/4 and 4/4 tempo on different sections, and these are skilfully interlinked. The verse/chorus structure soon wanders off into more progressive-rock-influenced territory, including a brief Stravinsky-like orchestral passage reflecting perhaps the continuing and far-reaching influence of Frank Zappa on the Stackridge muse. The track ends back with the ticking clock – perhaps the child is again sheltering in the cupboard under the stairs: another disturbing image for us to ponder. In the last analysis, 'Cheese And Ham' feels like an interesting experiment rather than a classic song.

'The Day The World Stopped Turning' (Davis, Warren, Tommey)

The final track on *A Victory for Common Sense* originally went under the working title 'Eric The Epic', and runs for over 11 minutes, making it the second-longest Stackridge studio track after the 14-minute 'Slark' on their debut album. 'The Day the World Stopped Turning' is a kind of apocalyptic puzzle, with different sections bolted together using some fluttering Mutter Slater flute to smooth the transitions.

The first section is a long slow build, opening with cool electric piano joined by a cooking organ passage before Andy Davis lets rip with a slide guitar solo that could be mistaken for Pink Floyd guitarist Dave Gilmour. This passage exudes a similar vibe to the ideas explored on Slater's track 'Beating A Path To Your Door' from the *Lemon 2002* mini-album: oddly so, as Slater isn't included in the composing credits on this one. Davis sings this section with lyrics suggesting some disaster has occurred in the middle of the night, but this idea is never really expanded on as the piece moves forward.

The second segment sees a slight rise in tempo as James Warren's vocal relates a search for identity invoking 'Round pegs in square holes'; the tone of the message seeming to be *adapt and survive*: perhaps in answer to some of the quandaries pondered earlier in the album. The standout section is the middle movement, in which the tempo shifts up another gear, ostensibly for an extended Mutter Slater flute solo as only he can provide, beautifully recorded by Chris Hughes and Mark Frith, capturing the elusive spirit of Slater's flute in all its glory with just the right amount of sonic spice and herbs in the reverb department.

This is the best album for Slater flute cameos since *The Man In The Bowler Hat* in 1973. After a reprise of Warren's vocal section, Davis returns once more with some decent Dave Gilmour-style slide guitar, and that unsettling middle-of-the-night feeling that something is terribly wrong is resumed. Unfortunately, the track's inordinate length starts to pall a bit by this stage until Slater again comes to the rescue to lift the spirits with some more fluttering flute improvisations, which are the best thing about the entire track for me.

Additional Material

'Seek And You Shall Find' (Davis, Warren, Tommey)

This was the one track from the *Victory* sessions that wasn't included on the album, although it was made available at the time as a download. It evinces a very James Warren vibe, and though credited as a co-write with Davis and Tommey, it feels more like Warren territory. Sporting triple-time, the tune echoes George Harrison in the almost mantra-like feel: very hypnotic with hand-played percussion. In a live setting, Eddie John would sit on a large wooden box, playing it percussively with his hands, while Crun Walter would shake a tambourine. With the Warren-intoned verses split with jig-like violin interludes, it lifts into a strong harmony-cushioned chorus on which we are advised to 'Forgive and then forget'. With a mostly acoustic feel, the only electric interludes are some cutting guitar lines by Andy Davis on the choruses. With its trance-like feel, this is a lovely track, and personally, I would've included it on *Victory*: probably in place of the less musically interesting 'Red Squirrel'.

4X4 (DVD) (2009)

Personnel:
Andy Davis: guitar, keyboards, vocals
James Warren: guitar, vocals
Mutter Slater: flute, vocals
Glenn Tommey: keyboards, trombone, vocals
Claire Lindley: violin
Sarah Mitchell: keyboards, violin, vocals
Recorded: Chapel Arts Centre, Bath, August 2009
Producer: Chris Hughes,
Engineer: Mark Frith
Cameras: Bill Blake, Stephen W. Tayler, Ian Clutterbuck
Label: Helium
Release date: November 2009

'Red Squirrel' (Davis)

These filming sessions were put together over a few days in August 2009, the title *4X4* being a reference to the number of tracks recorded and the original core-four Stackridge writers. Starting with Andy Davis' 'Red Squirrel', makes for a bit of an anticlimactic start, really, but this version does differ slightly from the studio take on *A Victory For Common Sense* in that Mutter Slater blows a few nice flute flurries, especially in the quieter verse after the middle eight.

'North St. Grande' (Slater, Davis)

Things improve considerably with the second track, as Slater leads the band through the rearranged version of 'North St. Grande'. Starting with the Yuletide chorus, this is essentially the single version that was released for the 2009 festive season. The band turn in a fine performance, as Slater gives a convincing vocal rendition, and new-recruit Clare Lindley on violin gets a chance to shine, underpinned by Glenn Tommey's ever-entertaining trombone on the woozy instrumental section, which is led by Slater's flute melody.

'Lost And Found' (Davis, Warren, Tommey)

Sounding almost neo-psychedelic, the band turn in an electrically-charged live version of 'Lost And Found' that far outshines the studio take. It's beautifully recorded, and James Warren turns in a dynamic vocal performance on this atmospheric song. The real meat-and-spuds though are the instrumental sections, extended for some really hot soloing and starting with Clare Lindley's attacking electric violin solo through a Marshall stack that raises hairs on the back of the neck with its sheer verve. Andy Davis then takes over in top form with some expressive guitar that cooks up a great feel over a funky, tight groove from the rhythm section. Mutter Slater gets his turn to shine though, with some of the most visceral flute-playing of his entire Stackridge output, and the way his playing morphs into a flute/violin duet is something to behold. As Slater's stunningly fast and fluent flute lines appear to head skyward, the whole thing judders to a halt on its hammering riff, completing one of the most impressive live performances captured by this lineup – underlining how stunning the 2009 variant of the band could be on a good night. Brilliant stuff indeed.

'Slow Train' (Flanders, Swann)

The band's cover of one of Flanders and Swann's best songs was a welcome addition to the set, and for me, the film of this track remains one of the most moving visual moments of Stackridge music ever captured.

Written back in the early-1960s as a commentary on the swathing Beeching cuts to Britain's railways, it was an unusual one for the normally tongue-in-cheek satirical duo, as it was a more serious number. The Stackridge performance really draws on the song's pathos, as gathered around one microphone, the core four of Stackridge take turns to approach the mic for a verse, backed by keyboard chords from Glenn Tommey. Andy Davis starts off with the first verse of the song's parade of long-lost station names that, back in the day, led to some remote communities being virtually stranded and left with no rail links at all. Mutter Slater takes the first two lines of the second verse before James Warren chips in to complete it. Up steps Davis to render the middle eight, joined after two lines by Slater, Warren and Walter in harmony. The final verse is left to the rarely heard Crun Walter singing voice, touchingly joined by his harmonising bandmates on the refrain 'from St. Erth to St. Ives', followed by a momentary pause.

The finale, however, takes the song emotionally beyond its comment on the loss of the 1960s railway network to a more universal interpretation, as the core four movingly sing 'They've all passed out of our lives on the slow train', bringing to mind the metaphorical slow train of the passing years and the inevitable sense of loss we humans feel as the arrow of time flies on into the future. As the band chant out with a few repeats of the 'Slow Train' refrain, a subtle sound effect of the clickety-clack of a locomotive's wheels on the rails plays out an exceptionally moving performance, rich in poignancy.

For whatever reason, the original three-year/three-album deal became nullified going forward, *4x4* being the last Stackridge release on Helium Records, and essentially this marked the end of Mutter Slater's recording career with the band. Although, he did return for a pair of live guest appearances – one for CBS TV the following year, and another on the final Stackridge gig six years later, when he stepped up for a couple of numbers.

Limited Edition Spring Tour Single (Stackridge 2011)

Recorded over a bicycle shop in Somerset
Date: May 2011
Engineer: Andy Davis
Producer: Stackridge
(No detailed writing credits included)

'Beside The Sea' (Stackridge)

The lead track on the 2011 *Spring Tour Single* was the maddeningly catchy 'Beside The Sea', which had entered the live set back in September 2010. As there are no writing credits on this release, it remains uncertain who the main instigators are. But judging by the various styles on show, it's possible to spot various composing traits. When I saw the band perform this song at the Polish Club in Bristol in 2010, it was rumoured that the recently-departed Mutter Slater could've had a hand in writing it, along with Crun Walter. There may also be a touch of James Warren about it too, but the mystery remains.

Opening with a jolly violin riff which has a definite end-of-the-pier feel to it, Clare Lindley follows with a pre-quote of the later chorus melody before the song modulates down for the first verse. The lyrics go for a kind of saucy picture-postcard humour, including the line 'Just don't share his 99', toned down from the spicier live rendition of 'Just don't lick his 99'. With a tilt at rewriting the old music hall song 'I Do Like To Be Beside The Seaside', the admittedly-catchy chorus appears to fold around on itself one too many times, sounding a bit too wordy and claustrophobic. Andy Davis plays an arranged guitar solo to break it up, and the slowly-picked melody of the last part is reminiscent of a passage from The Divine Comedy's brilliant 'The Plough', from their 2006 album *Victory For The Comic Muse* (possibly coincidence). We return to the jollity of the opening jig for the coda, with a laughing-sailor effect over an upward modulation of the violin riff toward the close. The relentless merriment of it all, made it a good one to leap about to at gigs!

'Dummies' (Stackridge)

The second track is a much more reflective piece of work. Again, with no credits, it requires some detective work to make a best guess at the composers, but this definitely sounds more like Andy Davis' work, possibly with some contributions from Clare Lindley on the violin arrangements.

Opening with a drifting violin melody before settling on a throbbing bass pulse, 'Dummies' generates quite an atmosphere, and has an intriguing mysterious feel as it alternates between pulsing and drifting sections. On the verses, Davis sings, 'Are we for real or are we pixels on a screen', in a song that's perhaps influenced by the digital lifestyle we find ourselves slipping ever deeper into. The verses are separated by slowly descending, floating violin triplets from Lindley that maintain the pensive ambience. Towards the end, there's a repeating three-chord build-up which stokes the portentous feel until the tension is finally released back into the drifting violin melody that started it all. So ends a thoughtful, contemplative track that seemed to augur well for a possible future Stackridge album. Unfortunately, that album never came to pass, and the two tracks on the May 2011 *Spring Tour Single* were the last studio recordings released by the band, despite the fact they carried on playing live for another four and a half years. It was definitely a missed opportunity.

AbsoBloodyLutely – Mutter Slater Band (2014)

Personnel:
Mutter Slater: vocals, guitar, flute
Chris Cleaver: guitar, slide guitar
Clive Ashley: saxophone, backing vocals
Chris Rickard: organ, backing vocals
Ian Oliver: bass
Dan Wheeler: drums, backing vocals
Recorded: Olive Tree Studios, Dorset, 2014
Producer: Mutter Slater, Chris Cleaver
Engineer: Tom Hughes
Label: MSB
Release date: 2014

Meanwhile, Mutter Slater had been busy in Bridport gigging with his own re-jigged band, who headed for a local recording studio in 2014 to cut their next album. Managing the production and engineering duties from within the band ensured a purity of vision, and the recent gigging had helped cement the band into a formidable musical unit, making this album their most potent statement of intent yet.

'We're In The Money' (Slater)

Immediately catching the ear with a brilliant guitar intro, this starts the best Mutter Slater Band offering yet. Chris Cleaver's guitar-picking is a revelation throughout this album, and the introductory riff underlines why. With a superb touch to his playing and a liquid fluency, Cleaver is a real find who seems to choose what is just right for each track he plays on. Beautifully recorded, and with just the right amount of reverb, the opening lick nails the atmosphere on this pummelling up-tempo track.

Mutter Slater paints a portrait of a coked-out superstar and his strung-out companion with more money than sense, practically exiled within a sprawling mansion so big that they 'think there's a gym somewhere within'. The jeering chorus repeating the song title is underpinned by that classic intro riff, and really hammers the track along. Painting a picture of debauchery with the lines 'There's a car in the pool/Don't it look cool' and an inability to hold onto any cleaning staff due to the fact 'They couldn't stand the stink or the screaming', you don't know whether to feel repulsed by or sorry for the protagonists. Obviously not written from personal experience, but one of Slater's story songs, this salutary tale tells the all-too-familiar yarn of oft-undeserved privilege taken to extremes.

'The Price' (Slater)

The only misstep on the album is this re-recording of the deadly slow blues first heard on Slater's 2008 album *Riding a Hurricane*. As such, I have essentially dealt with it there, as this version is minimally different from the original take. Slater must obviously have rated it to record it again. Either that or he was a song short for this collection.

'Bridport' (Slater)

Very much an autobiographical song, 'Bridport' is Slater's homage to his second-adopted home town (Yeovil being the previous one). As a recently settled native of Bridport, the lyric displays his love for the Dorset town he longs to return to after his travels on the road. With some fine lyric couplets – my favourite being 'The shitty seagulls in the sky/Will be the apple of my eye' – there are mentions of his wife Linda and arriving back with 'luggage full of songs'.

The music displays a Van Morrison influence, with a mid-tempo drive that motors happily along, with the repeated middle eight sounding melodically similar to his fine 2006 song ''Til The Sun Goes Down'. All in all, it proves to be an enjoyable romp.

'The Old Dog' (Slater)

This is one of those Slater tracks invoking an atmosphere of creeping menace – something he's so good at – enhanced by some incredible slide-playing by Chris Cleaver and raising the ghosts of blues players past. With another really tasty riff, the doom-laden feel of impending danger is palpable as the track progresses with an authentic 'Hellhound On My Trail' vibe, as Slater laments 'When my breath is getting shallow' and 'my will has taken flight', this mysterious menace will eventually hunt him down 'in a corner of the night'. Whether this is the spectre of the Grim Reaper, an overactive imagination or a more-human threat, we never find out. This is a great track and worth the price of entry for the guitar-playing alone.

'AbsoBloodyLutely' (Slater)

A more extended slow burn, jazz-funk workout, the title track is an ironic comment on the pernicious effect of television on public perception, and the 15-minutes-of-fame syndrome, with hard-sell merchandising channels and the exploitation of less fortunate 'ne'er do wells' in the name of entertainment, coming into the firing line. Sung in Slater's alto voice, he pushes the top of his vocal limit, but it suits this laconic song very well. There's some really funky bass-playing from Ian Oliver, and both Slater's flute and Clive Ashley's sax give the track a real jazzy vibe. There are also some great lyric phrases to enjoy throughout, with 'He's the golden one with screaming teeth' in reference to the host of some TV programme, being a particularly memorable image. Also, the pointed comments on reality TV – 'ASBO on the mantelpiece' and a 'Duffle full of fags' – are equally-striking phrases to describe the typical goggle-box viewer's reaction to the unfortunates featured on this form of entertainment.

'Think Of Me Once' (Slater)

A medium-tempo pop/rock number, 'Think Of Me Once' starts with its hooky chorus and is a song relating relationships to musical metaphors, like 'Romance leads a merry dance' and the 'tear-stained barroom piano'. It's not a major track musically, but it moves along smartly and features a Clive Ashley sax solo that brings to mind Phil Collins' 'All Of My Life' from his 1989 album *...But Seriously*. After said solo, there's a key drop for a brief flute interlude before the final verse. The chorus is memorable enough to quickly sink in, and you may well find yourself whistling it after a few listens.

'The Boy' (Slater)

Displaying a more acoustic feel, this up-tempo country-tinged song has a bouncy rhythm with a lighter sound than most of this album. One of Slater's story songs and set in the back of beyond somewhere out in the American Midwest, it tells the tale of a strange boy who turns up in a hick town, sitting in the gutters and acting weirdly, with the inevitable consequence of freaking out the locals, who end up shunning him. With the persecution of the outsider as its subject, the story unfolds and sees the townsfolk grow so paranoid about the boy that they end up neglecting their crops and animals: so intent are they on keeping him under surveillance. By the end of the song, their lives are ruined, but 'That boy is doing fine'.

Amongst the musical delights are a Chet Atkins'-style country guitar solo from Chris Cleaver, and some hot sax from Clive Ashley, both underpinned by a Slater solo on that most rarely-heard instrument, the Jew's harp.

'Cindy Lou' (Slater)

With a raunchy roots-rock drive, 'Cindy Lou' is the tale of a regular guy falling for a famous girl who is gallivanting around the globe, while the poor guy laments, 'Won't you please come on home Cindy Lou' in the choruses. Slater always sounds effective on upbeat numbers like this, and he gives this one some real vocal grit. Great slide guitar from Chris Cleaver propels this rocker, making for an enjoyable ride.

'The Unforgiving Man' (Slater)

Opening with drifting flute and heavenly organ chords, this morality tale employs biblical metaphor to make a point. The tale begins with the Devil and his buddies raising a toast to the unforgiving man, celebrating the notion that 'Nothing helps us more than the settling of the score that satisfies the unforgiving man'. Slater's language is telling, and there are some great lines – I really like the phrase referring to Old Nick: 'He raised a carbine claw and pointed to the pit'. The couplet at the heart of the song is based around the biblical quote ''Vengeance is mine' said the Lord', as Slater rejoins 'Ha, he really ought to hear himself someday', pointing out that the head honcho of this particular belief system comes across as a pretty unforgiving deity himself on occasion.

The music displays a compressed power with a strong sense of unresolved tension as it slowly moves through its six-and-a-half-minute duration. On the long fade, Slater muses ironically on 'The beauty of it all', as some distant floating flute improvisation sketches languidly over rising church-like organ chords, until eventually everything fades out except the organ, left alone, moving through atmospheric chords before settling on a final resolution. It's a stunning end to the album, and is one of Slater's best solo compositions in my view.

Desire Lines – Andrew Cresswell Davis (2015)

Personnel:
Andy Davis: vocals, guitar, ukulele, mandola
Clare Lindley: violin, ukulele, vocals
Brian Mullen: cello, backing vocals
Pete Brandt: bass, guitar, cuatro, lap steel, backing vocals
Eddie John: percussion
Leon Hunt: banjo
Pete Rosser: accordion
Jamie Matthews: harmonica
Will Gregory: whistle
Michael Padron: trumpet
Recorded: Bassic Studios, Bristol, 2015
Producers: Pete Brandt, Andy Davis
Label: Angel Air
Release date: 2015

As Stackridge's long career began to point to a conclusion, Andy Davis released two solo albums simultaneously – an unusual move, but both albums reflected a different side of his musical interests. They were both made available from the band's merchandising stall at gigs before being released by Angel Air, and both featured his full moniker Andrew Cresswell Davis on their covers. *Desire Lines* was more acoustic-based, and *Emergency Love* felt more like a full band album.

Both were artistic peaks for his songwriting, with *Emergency Love*, in particular, hitting some real highs with many powerfully emotional compositions. I will deal with *Desire Lines* first, an album which also had its moments of deep feeling.

'The Chrysler Girl' (Davis, Ferguson)

This song always appeared to be highly regarded by its composer. It was first recorded on the live *Andy Davis Band* album in 1994, and in 2009 it was shortlisted for possible inclusion on the Stackridge album *A Victory for Common Sense*, though in the end, it wasn't selected for that album. The version that opens *Desire Lines* is very different from the more-rocking live version from 1994 and is performed acoustically with some delicate guitar from Davis.

The lyrics imagine the art deco New York skyscraper, the Chrysler building as a beautiful woman, and it's a song in fulsome praise of this structure and all things feminine. Decorated with subtle violin and harmonica, it's a strangely moving experience to listen to, and the key lines are the sober reflection 'One day we'll all return to dust/Just like the Chrysler girl' – a less-than-cheery thought for some people, but I've always found this kind of *terminal* song rather comforting.

'Dirty Nightingale' (Davis, Ferguson)
Released in a different version on the 2005 Stackridge compilation *Sex and Flags*, this is a similar reading to thc previously released recording, and has effectively been dealt with already. A strong feature of Davis' solo output is the amount of re-recording of songs that are already available. Whether this is the composer's quest for the perfect version or a space-filling exercise in the absence of new material remains a moot question.

'Emily' (Davis, Ferguson)
This up-tempo song crosses a hoedown feel with an accordion-led jig and is something of a good time rave-up that will appeal if you enjoy that style of music (I do!). With a lyric about a girl who is always the bridesmaid but never the bride, this is an irresistible feel-good tune with the instrumental jig sections nodding to the bridging violin riffs from the 1973 Stackridge song 'The Road To Venezuela'.

'All I Do Is Dream of You' (Davis)
A conscious attempt to write in the style of the 1940s, this is a case of ukuleles at dawn and the first of several tracks to feature this instrument. During the period covered in this chapter, both Davis and Clare Lindley heavily revived the ukulele both in and out of Stackridge, to good effect. With its period references perfectly observed, you do indeed get the feeling that this song could've been around for the last 70 years or so. Featuring beautiful harmony vocals by Lindley and Davis, this laid-back song had also graced the live Stackridge set since 2012, where it sported an amusing trombone solo by Glenn Tommey, which on this version is superseded by Pete Brandt's gently-swooping lap steel.

'Marching Down The Road' (Davis, Menage)
This is one of those songs that's so steeped in irony, it could easily be prone to misinterpretation, much like some of Randy Newman's more ironic songs were (for example, 'Short People' from the album *Little Criminals*). A song about how religion is often usurped to make excuses for waging war, Davis performs this in the character of a religious zealot stirring up hate against what he views as the 'unbelievers', and as such, it makes a chillingly uncomfortable listen for the most part. Taken at face value, this is indeed scary stuff, as the protagonist is 'Marching in the name of love, with nobody left alive'. As Davis has explained regarding this song, 'Some people just love to hate'. With an unrelenting minor key, and accompanied by gentle guitar and keening violin lines, the overall effect is a touch depressing.

'How Many Tears' (Davis, Lindley)
Providing a lead vocal for Clare Lindley, this co-write with Davis is back in ukulele territory and is another minor-key number with a bluesy feel. The lyric thrust is described by Davis as 'You made me suffer, now it's your turn'

– a slightly selfish but perhaps understandable attitude if you've been done a grievous wrong. It plonks along at a slow tempo, and the chorus turnaround is reminiscent of the 1932 Jimmie Rodgers song 'Gamblin' Bar Room Blues' (also covered by The Sensational Alex Harvey Band in 1975).

'Hothouse Party' (Davis, Brandt)

The tempo picks up for this Brazilian-flavoured samba-like tune with a real Rio carnival feel and is written with long-term writing partner Pete Brandt. An enjoyable feel-good track with a great percussive drive, this is redolent of sand, sea and surf, with more ukuleles and violin to the fore, making a refreshing change of pace.

'The Airs Of Selivoe' (Davis, Brandt)

With the first of several references to Shetland displayed on the recent Andy Davis albums, this is a story song of a fisherman at sea, longing to return to the airs of Selivoe on the west coast of Shetland and to the welcoming harbour of his woman's arms. Davis' grandparents were from Shetland, so a kinship with the islands runs in his blood. With a lilting folk melody and a salty wind-whipped feel, this tune continues the acoustic bias of *Desire Lines* with its picked guitars and plaintive violin arrangement. It's a lovely melody.

'Desire Lines' (Davis, Menage)

There's a laid-back end to the album, with a track driven by just gentle fingerpicking from Davis. This is another co-write with Sarah Menage, and reflects on memories of happy days in the sun with a past love.

Emergency Love (2015)

Personnel:
Andy Davis: vocals, guitar, organ, piano, harmonica, ukulele
Clare Lindley: violin, backing vocals
Brian Mullan: cello, backing vocals
Valere Speranza: bass
Eddie John: drums, percussion
B.J. Cole: pedal steel guitar
Paul Godden: dobro
Stig Manley, Andy Latimer: guitar
Greg Cordez: double bass
John Griffiths, Gina Griffin, Alun Thomas, Andy West, Ben Winship: backing vocals
Recorded: The Brown Ratio Studios, Bath, 2015
Producers: Leon Hunt, Andy Davis
Label: Angel Air
Release date: 2015

'Rain, Rain, Rain' (Davis, Ferguson)

This paean to precipitation first appeared on the live *Andy Davis Band* album 21 years earlier, and here it's making its long-delayed studio debut. Gently driven by a laid-back, funky groove, it's an ideal opening track.

The lyric employs the analogy of a car journey to represent the course of a love affair, with a great line describing the building passion of the early blooms of romance, invoking the 'Love Train', giving a nod to The O'Jays' 1972 hit single of the same name. By the time the chorus arrives, an almost inevitable run into stormy weather eventually brings the metaphorical rain. Mainly built on a durable guitar riff that runs through both verse and chorus, this is a disarmingly simple song. It never really develops much, but if you just sit on the groove and ride along, the journey still proves to be an enjoyable one.

'Nightfishing' (Davis)

Andy Davis describes the thrust of this song as 'resisting temptation in Havana'. The music has an irresistible Cuban/Creole feel running through the sensual rhythm, and the kind of nightfishing that Davis is on about here doesn't involve boats but rather the dusky Cuban ladies of the night. It's a wonderful example of his mature songwriting style, which became increasingly influenced by Americana as the years went by. The evocative lyric paints a picture of a nighttime Caribbean scene as Davis sings in a rich baritone, of a 'deep blue moon' and that he's going to be 'leaving for Havana soon'. Lucky chap!

'Baby Good For You' (Davis, Ferguson)

Another remake from the *Andy Davis Band* album, this track evokes a panorama of wide-open spaces as the American influences come through strongly. You can almost imagine David Lindley playing the pedal steel alongside Jackson Browne, although it's actually legendary steel guitarist B. J. Cole playing alongside Andy Davis. I first witnessed B. J. Cole – the go-to steel player of choice for a huge proliferation of artists over a period of more than four decades – playing live when he was in the band Cochise back in 1971, so he has certainly been around as long as Davis.

Another song with an extremely relaxed tempo, 'Baby Good For You' carries a subtle undercurrent of resignation that's a strong feature of this entire album. With country rock stamped all over it, this is a more-than-worthwhile remake.

'Magdelene' (Davis, Ferguson)

Yet another song in praise of a lady of the night, but this time set in Putney rather than Havana. Buoyed up with acoustic guitars and creamy, rich vocal harmonies, this is a beautiful performance, and is again high on emotional content. There's an almost gospel music feel to the fore: an influence that pervades much of this album. The deep feelings so-well-expressed are also magnified by the slow-to-medium tempos employed on the majority of *Emergency Love* tracks.

'Peacock Of The Universe' (Davis)

Inspired by a real-life event in which Andy Davis' sister chased a Jehovah's Witness down the road after he repeatedly knocked on her window, we find the author in belligerent mode as he rails against those who have 'got religion and think they have all the answers'. With pounding piano and a faux-sanctified feel, this track is the first to lift the tempo on a fairly laid-back album. There's an amusing guitar part in the middle section, where the music slows down as Davis picks a quote from the old 1927 Jerome Kern/Oscar Hammerstein standard 'Ol' Man River'(from the musical *Show Boat*), before the tempo again picks up for the final verse and chorus.

'Charlie's Dead' (Davis, Menage)

Emergency Love proved to be Andy Davis' most autobiographical album so far, as this rock-'n'-rolling nod to one of his early 1960s teenage romances reveals. Recalling the time he used to cycle to his prospective beau's house with his trusty 'Dansette' record player balanced on the handlebars, this tale unfolds to a country rock accompaniment with some fabulous James Burton-style guitar. Cutting a rug in her kitchenette, Davis and his girl were jiving to Elvis, but 'When we got to Bobby Vee, she said 'Charlie's dead''. The mysterious title is based on slang of the period – if a girl's petticoat was showing, it often brought forth the quote 'Charlie's dead'. The sad tale ends for him when his rival – wonderfully described as the guy with 'the chisel toes, blue jeans and Marlon Brando's nose' – woos his girl away.

A great little rock-'n'-roll tune, 'Charlie's Dead' is a wonderful distillation of a more innocent era, and is a real slice of Davis history to boot. Interestingly, it's also another co-write with Sarah Menage, who also co-wrote with Davis' sparring partner James Warren on occasion.

'Emergency Love' (Davis, Ferguson)

As an example of the refined art of a master songwriter, this track takes some beating. The underrated Davis larynx just drips with soul and feeling on this gospel-powered love song of uplifting beauty. This album sports some of Davis' finest singing of his career: perhaps enhanced by the more-personal tack of the songs featured. With what sounds like a substantial choir backing him up, Davis provides perfectly-judged sanctified piano and organ on this hymn-like creation in praise of a girl who he would do anything for: even down to providing '24-hour emergency love'. Exquisitely arranged, with dynamics in all the right places and a perfectly-weighted musical turnaround ending, this is a song of gospel dimensions musically, and unabashed adoration lyrically, and is a slice of picture-perfect songwriting.

'Downtown Lights' (Buchanan)

The only cover version on this album, Davis makes this Paul Buchanan song his own with a truly soulful rendition. Originally a number-67 UK single for The Blue Nile in 1989 (as 'The Downtown Lights'), the tempo is slow and measured, generating a considerably emotional and tense atmosphere during the verses that's only partially resolved with the arrival of the chorus. It's another masterful performance on an album chock-full of tracks brimming with pathos and deep feeling. Listening to this, you really feel you're 'Walking down an empty street' with Davis under those 'downtown lights'. This is a superb cover version.

'Loving You Too Long' (Davis)

A song about contemplating throwing yourself off a cliff, the lyric actually mentions two such places (Marloes in Pembrokeshire and The Kame in Shetland), and you're left in little doubt that this is another very personal song. By the sound of it, love turned Davis around, and thank goodness for that. With a verse melody following a folk song structure, this track has some rhythmically tricky punctuation around its choruses. On his journey of redemption, Davis asks his loved one if her love is 'The milk of human kindness', or whether she's 'The beauty or the beast', as his ever-questing heart continually throws up doubts. With love, it all so often ends in tears, and so it is on the final track of this emotional roller-coaster of an album.

'The Ghost Of Love' (Davis, Brandt)

In many ways the album's most passionately powerful track, 'The Ghost Of Love' finds Andy Davis sitting alone, staring into his glass of beer and dealing with the pain of loss. As he himself has described this song, on the first verse he's 'sore and sober'; on the second verse 'mellow and maudlin', and by the third verse, 'pie-eyed and pitiful'! It's another lovely song, but so full of intensity it's likely to leave the listener emotionally drained by the end of it.

Wonderfully arranged and orchestrated, the rising tension of the beautiful melody is truly heart-wrenching as Davis invites you to raise a glass and 'Toast the ghost of love' so you 'Won't feel lonesome anymore'. Another co-write with his long-term collaborator Peter Brandt, the track drifts then coasts with myriad strings, pizzicato violins and an ending that falls back to just Davis alone playing a plaintive harmonica melody that has the atmosphere of a soldier stuck in a trench in no man's land, with only his mouth organ for company. Like much of this album, the final song appears to address some of Davis' ghosts and relationships and closes an album of startling honesty, and, hopefully, in the end, redemption.

Following the break-up of Stackridge at the end of 2015, Andy Davis and Clare Lindley remained together to continue with their side project DLM, and had already been playing the odd gig or two with this outfit between previous Stackridge commitments. The initials stood for Davis Lindley Mullan: the last-named being cellist Brian Mullan, who'd featured on Davis' brace of solo albums in 2015. DLM dealt in a kind of chamber folk/rock with echoes of Tin Pan Alley in some of the songwriting, and their guitar/violin/cello lineup would turn out several albums going forward. Their eponymous debut album – sold at 2018 gigs – was largely a recycling job, as 11 of the tracks were remakes of previously-available Andy Davis songs. The second album *Nightfishing* followed in 2019, and also had a handful of remakes, including a cover of the Stackridge instrumental 'Who's That Up There With Bill Stokes?' and one other notable cover that DLM recorded – a version of Roger Waters' 'Brain Damage' from the multiplatinum 1973 Pink Floyd album *Dark Side of the Moon*.

The Final Bow, Bristol 2015 (2017)

Personnel:
Andy Davis: guitar, keyboards, vocals
James Warren: bass, vocals
Glenn Tommey: keyboards, trombone, flute, vocals
Clare Lindley: violin, guitar, keyboards, vocals
Eddie John: drums, percussion
Mutter Slater: flute ('Purple Spaceships Over Yatton', 'Slark'), vocals ('Slark')
Recorded live at The Fiddlers, Bristol, 19 December 2015
Label: Angel Air
Release date: 2017

After the 2011 tour, there was a further band defection when Crun Walter decided to hang up his bass and quit music altogether. Being a founder Stackridge member with Andy Davis, Walter had served five separate spells as Stackridge bassist since 1969. He acquired a farm in Herefordshire and settled down to a more agricultural lifestyle. In the same way as Mutter Slater in 2010, he was sorely missed by hardcore Thrashers, and was viewed by many as the life and soul of the band by this juncture, with his earthy humour always an essential ingredient of every Stackridge gig. In his absence, the band decided to remain a five-piece and just reshuffle, with James Warren returning to his bass role as had been the case on their very first album in 1971.

With no further recording dates in evidence, Stackridge settled into a long-term pattern of annual tours. The 2012 tour showed off the new five-piece for the first time, and featured many of the old favourites plus the newer compositions 'Beside The Sea' and 'Dummies', plus two additions to the set: the 1926 Billy Rose/Lee David song 'Tonight You Belong To Me' and a traditional encore jig or two. The 2013 and 2014 tours followed a similar pattern, as the set remained virtually static aside from a new opening number called 'Over The Horizon' and Andy Davis' new 1940s-style song 'All I Do Is Dream Of You'. Although it was always a great experience to see the band live, they appeared to be drifting into a nostalgia-tour pattern, with very little creative forward momentum. No new recording projects materialised going forward, and it was somewhat inevitable when in 2015, the band announced *The Final Bow* tour, as they finally decided to call it a day.

'Over The Horizon' (Lindley, John)

This writing collaboration between Clare Lindley and Eddie John had been the set opener for a few years at this point, but it's an odd song to start a set with. Laid-back in the extreme and underpinned by keyboard arpeggios across its triple-time rhythm, there's not a lot else going on apart from Lindley's lead vocal, some harmonies from the band on the 'Yeah, yeah, yeah' choruses, and a lonely synthesizer solo from Glenn Tommey. Constructed on a rather cold-sounding sequence with some perplexing chord choices, the melody doesn't quite go where you expect it to – not always a bad thing, but in this case, it evinces an uncertain atmosphere that has always sounded a touch emotionless to my ears.

Probably influenced by Lindley's folk-club background, it has something of the air of plainsong about it, but it does feel rather like the work of less-experienced writers compared with the high-calibre material from the bulk of the Stackridge set.

'The Road To Venezuela' (Davis, Smegmakovitch)

This old warhorse is rendered once more by Andy Davis, and it's nice to have a version where you can hear the audience participation, with chants of 'Oi!' aplenty after each two-bar phrase of Clare Lindley's jigging violin solo and some impressive synchronised percussive clapping between the gaps of the quiet guitar-harmonics passage. Who said a British audience can't clap in time?

'The Last Plimsoll' (Davis, Smegmakovitch)

James Warren takes over the lead vocal from Andy Davis on this version which is dispatched with the usual aplomb and no real surprises. It's the abridged arrangement that shortens the instrumental sections by half, and it kind of works but feels less impelling than the longer version that builds up more tension for explosive release at crucial points. The five-piece Stackridge, though, are by this time watertight in their arrangements, having gigged for four years with this lineup.

'Red Squirrel' (Davis)

Over the last few years, 'Red Squirrel' had evolved into a more acoustic-slanted arrangement as opposed to the more-electric original on *A Victory For Common Sense*, although it still retained its rather hollow-sounding noisy climax. To my ears, it still seems like five minutes of the set that could've been donated to a more worthy cause. But Andy Davis obviously carried a torch for this song, as it was ever-present in the set over the previous six years.

'Syracuse The Elephant' (Walter, Davis)

Commencing with a sampled gong crash and some Eastern-sounding doodling from Glenn Tommey as a preface, a rather weary 'Syracuse The Elephant' begins yet another trek through the steamy jungle landscape. Unfortunately, over the last four years of their gigging career, Stackridge had virtually ceased to move forward creatively, and hardly any new material had appeared in the set. Consequently, some of the old tunes were becoming hammered to death on each tour, with the band sounding more akin to a nostalgia act than a still-developing band: 'Syracuse' being one of the songs that underlines this fact.

The central violin solo, though, was always the most impressive part, and here Clare Lindley adheres to the carefully-learnt classic Mike Evans' arrangement circa 1972 – a piece of work that has certainly stood the test of time – and she does it proud as usual, providing the most affecting passage of the whole piece.

'Fundamentally Yours' (Davis, Smegmakovitch)

The evergreen pop of 'Fundamentally Yours' retains its verve as it rocks along agreeably, and was one of the tracks from *The Man in the Bowler Hat* that drew praise from producer George Martin for its words: 'I wish I could write lyrics like that' exclaimed the great man during one of the studio playbacks.

This version cooks nicely and features some Morse-code guitar from Andy Davis on the final verse, that's reminiscent of The Supremes' 1966 hit 'You Keep Me Hangin' On' (a device also used on David Bowie's 1972 hit 'Starman'). The upward key change for the short instrumental coda is joyous, as Glenn Tommey's swirling synthesizer hammers home this Stackridge classic.

'Highbury Incident' (Davis, Bowkett, Slater)

This song from the *Extravaganza* album had made something of a comeback in recent years, and oddly enough, it was never featured in any 1970s live sets. It first appeared live when James Warren and Friends added it to the set for their 2005/2006 gig schedule. It was duly inducted into the Stackridge set and has featured heavily ever since. Another sturdy pop song, it rattles along with a tight stomping arrangement almost identical to the studio version. Never a major song, it's still always a pleasant listen with a host of Stackridge trademarks, especially the instrumental riff passages that really couldn't be by anybody else but them.

'Teatime' (Walter, Davis)

This song is so synonymous with Mutter Slater's flute that I always missed his presence on later versions. 'Teatime' may be simplicity itself as a composition, but it still somehow carries a profound depth of feeling for most Stackridge fans. Where the flute/violin combination was so fundamental to the original, the song seems to lack a crucial dimension with only the violin present, despite Clare Lindley's excellent playing. As Slater was supporting at this gig but did step up to guest on several numbers, it was a shame he didn't step up one last time for this one, really.

'God Speed The Plough' (Wabadaw Sleeve)

The 2015 farewell tour saw some tasty musical treats returning to the set, and this was the first of them. With the opening piano melody joined by some subtle electric guitar from Andy Davis, the spell is cast, and this beautiful tone poem sweeps us away to the English countryside on a journey through its evocative array of themes. Clare Lindley's expressively-sweet violin on the bridge takes us into the pulsing, upbeat section, as we again feel the storm clouds gather, and the major/minor see-sawing chord shifts bring ever-more passionate improvised violin playing, increasingly stoked by Glenn

Tommey's keyboard strings building a tension that is released by the arrival of the glorious, triumphal main central melody over Eddie John's thumping drums. Suddenly we are descending back into a peaceful post-storm triple-time restatement of the opening theme. A drum roll then takes us into the moving coda, where the opening theme now swells to symphonic proportions, underpinned by Tommey's glowing strings and some fabulous guitar power chords from Davis that lift the violin-led melody that extra notch. It's a performance that raises the hairs on the back of this listener's neck, and as the melody floats into the canon-like minor-chord resolution with its bittersweet pathos, Lindley holds a high violin vibrato on the final chord that's the icing on the cake, concluding a rendition of this ultimate Stackridge epic that is absolutely majestic.

'Long Dark River' (Walter)

The main difference between the earlier and later incarnations of Stackridge is that the later variant were more prone to rocking out. 'Long Dark River' is a great example of this newly-evolved propensity to absorb more direct rock influences, and proves to be the perfect track to provide contrast after the ornate classicism of the previous number. With its brooding buildup, shiny harmonies and riff-laden rock closing section, it provides Andy Davis, in particular, with a chance to cut loose in a rock mode with his expressive lead guitar-playing, which really cooks as the track comes to a climax.

'Purple Spaceships Over Yatton' (Walter, Davis)

For the all-time Stackridge instrumental epic, up steps none other than Mutter Slater for the first of two guest appearances. The magic commences as his pure-toned flute once more graces this towering instrumental, sounding as marvellous as the first time I witnessed it live over 43 years earlier. Built on the revised arrangement that first appeared in 2005 as a bonus *new* track on the *The Best of Stackridge* compilation, 'Purple Spaceships' differs from the 1970s live version by dint of its added keyboard string samples played by Glenn Tommey. The chromatic upward string arrangement – feinting to the flattened 5th – engenders a real sense of menace, and plays off brilliantly against Slater's recurring flute motif during this first section. As the sampled strings build, Davis cuts loose with some guitar improvisation, really racking up the tension until a sinister-sounding upward string glissando breaks the taut atmosphere and all falls ominously quiet again with fabulous employment of dynamics: a lost art in much of today's music. We are left floating in a spaced-out void, with various throbs and ripples of controlled guitar feedback at the edges of our consciousness, with only Slater's occasionally-fluttering three-note flute figures to orient us as we descend to just a lonely S-O-S Morse-code bleep sounding like a desperate message being sent by survivors after some alien invasion. This central tract of 'Purple Spaceships' sounds particularly stunning as some really creepy cello samples from Tommey build a malevolent atmosphere.

Over in the right-hand channel, a faint stage laugh is detectable (probably Slater), but it's not loud enough to break the brooding feel of the music. When Tommey brings in some big orchestral string chords heralding the pounding S-O-S crescendo, it is a truly stunning moment. The music moves via some eastern riffs to a hammering climax before finally releasing into the drifting end section, on which Slater cuts loose for one final time with some articulate flute improvisation as only he can, bringing to a close another album highlight.

'All I Do Is Dream Of You' (Davis)

How can you follow 'Purple Spaceships Over Yatton'? By getting out your ukuleles, that's how! In a nice piece of set programming, Clare Lindley and Andy Davis plunk away on this much-maligned but increasingly-popular instrument. Lindley takes the lead vocal on this Davis exercise in 1940s-style songwriting, as this affecting lighthearted love song proves what fine harmony singers they all are, with massed vocal support on the choruses. An upward key change sees a brief ukulele duet between Davis and Lindley, before another nice key change takes us into an amusing trombone solo from Glenn Tommey. The last verse sees some charming reply vocals by a bassless James Warren along with Tommey, both at one microphone, and the good humour of this song shines through brightly.

By the time this album was released, the studio version on Andy Davis' *Desire Lines* album had long been out, but the arrangement is very similar apart from the trombone solo: only featured on the Stackridge version

'Fish In A Glass' (Walter, Davis)

This is the epic from the *Mr. Mick* album, with its long instrumental introduction perfectly performed by the ensemble, with James Warren sticking rigidly to Crun Walter's bass part to drive it forward. After the overture-like first section, we again fall back to ukulele backing for the song section, as Andy Davis relates the saga of Mr. Mick at the dump. This rearrangement for ukuleles is a nice touch and enhances the dynamics, bringing it right down before the mountainous coda where Davis is back on guitar, playing the two-chord arpeggios that underpin Glenn Tommey's string chords and Clare Lindley's improvising violin.

'Something About The Beatles' (Miller, Warren)

James Warren gets a chance for some lead vocals on his paean to the fab four, as he efficiently manoeuvres the bass with his usual dexterity, while singing an independent vocal melody. The coda gives both Davis and Tommey the chance to get into their respective guitar and organ soloing, and the end section sizzles along satisfyingly, concluding another late-period Stackridge pop classic.

'No One's More Important Than The Earthworm' (Haskell)

The third surprise addition to the 2015 farewell tour was this song from the *Extravaganza* album, on its first live outing since 1975. The number kicks off with Andy Davis' repeated five-note guitar arpeggio playing call-and-response with a koto-like sample from Glenn Tommey, giving the intro a distinctly Oriental feel, before a cooking organ solo establishes the unique ambience of this song of cosmic perspective. Davis sings it really well, changing a few of the lines, but the choruses are glorious, with the band supplying harmonies over the ascending chord sequence. One verse is given over to a guitar solo giving Davis plenty of room to get expressive with his emotional playing, and the whole track evinces a brooding, sustained power, despite its medium tempo. It proves to be a fine addition to the set and still sounds as mightily profound as it did back in the 1970s. After all, in the end, no one really *is* more important than that wiggly creature of the earth, whose heritage goes back millions of years before the likes of humans evolved to wreak havoc.

'Lost And Found' (Davis, Warren, Tommey)

Building up to the climax of the set, a brace of more rock-oriented numbers follows, the first of which sees James Warren back on lead vocals for this enigmatic track from *A Victory For Common Sense*. It's another number that underlines the extra solo space given over to more free playing in the later years of Stackridge's long career. There is much fine soloing around the verses and key changes of this interesting composition – from Andy Davis' guitar, Clare Lindley's violin, Glenn Tommey's keyboard, and even some rarely-heard flute from the Stackridge keyboardist as well. He starts off the final section of featured soloing towards the end with some Ian Anderson-style flute-playing. More electric violin and guitar solos then take home another fine performance of this song.

'Boots And Shoes' (Davis, Warren)

The second rocker in a row, the former Korgis classic from their eponymous debut album, has by now become very much a Stackridge song after the definitive arrangement emerged back in 2008. Warren and Davis sing the lead vocals in harmony, and the latter gets yet another chance to peel off some fluent soloing, especially cooking during his workout on the coda, before the band take it home in classic rock style.

'The Final Bow' (Davis)

To close the set proper, the band go low-key as Andy Davis performs his fitting acoustic ballad from *Lemon 2002*. It's a moving moment as he intones 'So take your seats for the final bow', and this time, it really is. With its folk ambience, 'The Final Bow' has an atmosphere all its own, and makes a beautifully understated addition to the 2015 farewell tour set.

'Lummy Days' (Davis)

For the first of a trio of encore numbers, the band treat us to that inevitable unofficial Stackridge theme tune: the incomparable 'Lummy Days'. It's more guitar-centric than earlier versions, as Andy Davis happily picks away at the first two themes, playing the melody straight, while Clare Lindley negotiates the varied themes of this pocket symphony with aplomb. She is especially impressive on the neoclassical central passage that leads back to that priceless juncture when the strident, staccato violin strokes lead once more into that joyous air-punching moment when the main theme crashes in again: for this Thrasher, always one of the best moments of any Stackridge gig. With a perfect flourish, the band hammer through the double-time section towards the magical closing passage with its nine-note final ascension to its humorous denouement and comical exclamation-mark ending. Unbeatable!

'Slark' (Walter / Davis)
Mutter Slater returns to the stage for one last performance of the iconic 'Slark', as his flute starts up *that* timeless riff and we're away on the tale of the West Country's most celebrated dragon once more. Not the 20-minute epic of old (unfortunately), it adheres firmly to the 1972 single arrangement, although now employing eight bars instead of four between the verses. One lovely little touch from Slater's flute is his trilling flourish before the entrance of the big keyboard-driven modulations that precede the reggae-flavoured middle section. It's a shame the audience microphones weren't mixed higher for the inevitable sing-along finale: as they had been earlier in the album on 'The Road To Venezuela'.

'Dora The Female Explorer' (Stackridge)
The final recorded performance from Stackridge just had to be the song that started their recording career back in 1971, as they chug once more through the traditional end for any Stackridge gig: the tale of the inimitable female explorer that was their very first single. The intro and bridge instrumental sections feel more like a hoedown without Mutter Slater's pumping harmonica, but James Warren turns in a peerless performance on bass and vocals on this song of utter simplicity that I still find nigh-on irresistible.

'Do The Stanley' – Aviator Brass (Wabadaw Sleeve)
This extra track on *The Final Bow* is not a Stackridge performance but a return to the stage of one of the evening's support bands – Aviator Brass – who play out the gig with a rather amateur-sounding brass-band version of Mutter Slater's dance-craze number. At least it gives the assembled Thrashers a final sing-along: audible but low in the mix. I personally think they should've turned the audience mics up full and let the fans take the lead, as it would've been much more fun. This track is a non-essential add-on, really.

The Champ – Mutter Slater (2016)

Personnel:
Mutter Slater: vocals, flute, guitar
Chris Cleaver: guitar, backing vocals
Clive Ashley: tenor saxophone, backing vocals
Tom Hughes: organ
Ian Olliver: bass
Dan Wheeler: drums, percussion, backing vocals
Recorded: Olive Tree Studios, Beaminster, Dorset, 2016
Producers/Engineers: Chris Cleaver, Tom Hughes (Production assistance by MSB)
Label: Angel Air
Release date: 2016

The first ex-member of Stackridge to release a new studio album in the era after the band had called it a day was Mutter Slater. In many ways, he'd become the most prolific writer of the lot in the 21st century, as his new 2016 release, *The Champ* was his fourth album of original songs in the last ten years.

'Even Love?' (Slater)

The silver-toned sound of Slater's flute treated with liberal doses of reverb opens his latest outing in fine style. With a spacey, cavernous vibe and a widescreen production, this is a huge-sounding track; the slow pace invoking echoes of Pink Floyd as Tom Hughes' organ and Clive Ashley's echo-laden sax generate an atmosphere of apprehension, backed up as always by the telling and subtle guitar of the amazing Chris Cleaver.

Always one to tackle the big topics, Slater's lyric here deals with nothing less than that cosmic conundrum, the heat-death of the Universe, juxtaposed against more-earthly concerns like human emotion and the power of love to transform our future. With an assumption that some distant descendant of homosapiens will even be around in that far distant epoch when the universe reaches the limits of its expansion (an unlikely prospect), he poses that enigmatic question: 'When every atom dies, how can love survive?'.

With a clear lineage stretching back to 'Beating A Path To Your Door' from Stackridge's *Lemon 2002* mini-album, it's great to hear Slater in a more-expansive mode like this again, and it makes for a powerful opening track.

'Love Affair With Pain' (Slater)

From the cosmos down to some earthy funk, as 'Love Affair With Pain' returns to one of those other Slater preoccupations: the love/hate dichotomy. The soul-music influences are well on display in Chris Cleaver's funky chording and even funkier guitar solo. The guy's playing is so natural that it feels as if he's initiating a conversation with his guitar. Clive Ashley's sax, chips in with some tasty licks, and the chorus of 'Down, down, down' over descending chords is catchy in the extreme, making for a tidy track.

'I May Not Be An Angel' (Slater)

Slowing down the pace once more, Slater again conjures up another dose of angel/Devil iconography as the band sparingly back him up both instrumentally and, on the choruses, vocally. It's a subject he returns to time and again, but whether it reflects an ongoing inner conflict or not remains uncertain, and it's the songwriter's prerogative to either write from the first person or take on a persona to illustrate a certain perspective. Whatever, the results are quite touching as he muses that he may not be an angel, before concluding, 'But could we pretend for a while?'. The chorus melody is memorable and sticks in the mind, and Clive Ashley plays out the track with an effective tenor sax solo.

'Icing On The Cake' (Slater)

Raising the tempo once more, the band rock solidly on this ode to a night on the town in London, as cash is splashed on a spree through the capital with a female companion, no expense spared. The choruses are thumped out by drummer Dan Wheeler, and with another hot sax solo raising the aural temperature, this track proves to be an enjoyably bracing romp.

'A Day On The Town' (Slater)

After a frantic night of debauchery, the next song describes a more-relaxing day out on the town, accompanied by tremolo guitar and some really nice reverb effects on the percussion: especially on the rimshots. Chris Cleaver adds some cool guitar licks, and the sax solo brings to mind David Sanborn's work on David Bowie's 1975 *Young Americans* LP.

'The Champ' (Slater)

The title track is another of Slater's dead-slow 6/8 blues songs and lyrically employs boxing phraseology to describe the feeling of a former champ now feeling down and out. It has a definite soulful gospel flavour, with some excellent organ interjections and another sax break. This track effectively adds to the album's overall light-and-shade.

'Jesus In The Backyard' (Slater)

This is a lowdown, dirty, blues stalker, with its killer riff delivered by Chris Cleaver as only he can. It's one of Slater's edge-of-doom-evoking creations, with a lineage back to 'The Old Dog' from his previous album. He's so good at this type of riff-driven tense groove, and this one is loaded with memorable imagery as we ponder the backyard creeper 'Picking through the bins' and 'Chewing on some skins', while later in the song, he's 'Fighting for survival' and 'Kicking in some shins', as an apocalyptic feel supercharges the atmosphere.

The track ends on some marvellously-controlled guitar feedback, concluding one of the album's best songs.

'Why Are You Talking To Me?' (Slater)

Time for some upbeat, funky rock, as Slater employs humour in this lighthearted message to his woman. Sounding remarkably like Elvis Costello and the Attractions circa 1978, the organ playing is a dead ringer for Steve Nieve's distinctive style and also includes a quick saxophone quote from composer Julius Fucik's march 'The Entry Of The Gladiators'. With melodic guitar and organ solos between the verses, the track cooks along in a great groove. Slater's follow-on from the title question is a terse 'Does it look as if I care?', and there's an amusing tongue-in-cheek rap on the coda and fade that leaves this listener with a smile on his face.

'I'm Not The Man' (Slater)

Ending the album with another 6/8 slow blues probably isn't the best idea, but Slater's sincerity shines through as he testifies mightily on this slightly long song. There's even a touch of his famous flute on the coda to play the track out.

Innocent Bystander – James Warren (2017)

Personnel:
James Warren: vocals, guitar, bass, string and brass arrangements
Andy Davis: piano, organ, drum programming, guitar
Glenn Tommey: piano, organ
Tim Petherick: slide guitar
Nigel Hart: synthesizer
John Baker, Bea Warren, Lyn Ritchie, Steve Robinson: backing vocals
Al Steele: guitar, string and brass arrangements
Richard Mainwaring, Korine Coleborn, Claudine Cassidy: string section
Phil Jarvis, Jon Mainwaring, Ceri Rees: brass section
Recorded: Glenn's Garage, Andy's Place, The Brown Ratio, Inner State, Shabbey Road Studios, Bath, 2016-2017
Producers: James Warren, David Lord
Engineers: James Warren, Leon Hunt, David Lord, Al Steele, Andy Davis
Label: Angel Air
Release date: 2017

Following the dissolution of Stackridge, James Warren continued to do occasional low-profile gigs with cover bands, usually in cahoots with Glenn Tommey – his fellow bandmate in The Blue Meanies: a band that had operated alongside other projects on and off since the 1990s. Between this and bouts of sitting atop Glastonbury Tor with his acoustic guitar, he also ploughed on with his more commercially-slanted songwriting and would continue to be productive going forward.

The first fruits of this emerged in 2017 as a solo album along with Glenn Tommey and his newly-favoured guitar buddy Al Steele. It proved to be something of a mixed bag, with a few of Warren's new ballads providing the highlights.

'The First Time' (Warren, Tommey)

James Warren returns with another dose of his predictably-shiny pop music, opening with this Korgis-like confection. The production is top-notch, and the music perfectly played with the sort of melodic/harmonic tricks of the trade he could churn out in his sleep. Like much of this album, it comes over very much as James Warren having fun recreating a 1960s feel with his perfect craftsmanship, rather than the more-focussed inspiration he's capable of at his best.

Half-intended as a shop window for *Warren the songwriter* in the hope of attracting a high-profile cover version, this generally cheery collection of pop tunes didn't end up doing the business in that department and also divided Thrasher opinion. 'The First Time' sports a busy arrangement building from acoustic guitar to the full works, with keyboard samples and vocal harmonies aplenty, and is certainly catchy.

'Set Me Free' (Warren, Tommey)
Not a cover of the 1965 Kinks single, but another fairly lightweight Warren creation that bounces along in pop mode with a streamlined production expertly guided by David Lord. There is a three-piece string section arranged by James Warren and Al Steele that enhances this madly catchy track.

'That's What You Do To Me' (Warren, Davis)
Coming on like a bargain-basement Spencer Davis Group, this shot at 1960s-style rhythm and blues, unfortunately, doesn't quite conjure the magic of 'Gimme Some Lovin'' or 'I'm A Man', but you can see where the influence is coming from. To be fair, it seems that Warren is having fun, but it all ends up sounding closer to his cover band The Blue Meanies, than anything else. Oddly enough, I recall going to two gigs in quick succession in 1973 where Stackridge were sharing the bill with a reformed Spencer Davis Group, so I'm sure the two bands met and mingled back in the day.

'You've Got The Love That Matters' (Warren, Tommey, Baker)
An interesting remake of a fine track first featured on the superior *Jim's Easy Listening Album* in 2006, this easily trounces almost everything else on this album for sheer quality songwriting. Rather than a straight re-recording, though, this has a whole new arrangement that stands up well against the original version, with wonderful vocal harmonies and a new counterpoint vocal melody on the linking sections that connect the verse/chorus/middle eight, making this the definitive version of this fine tune, standing head-and-shoulders above nearly everything else on *Innocent Bystander*.

'High Time' (Warren, Tommey)
Much of this album feels like 1960s influences filtered through a 1980s sensibility, as with this Beatles-inspired turnout that crosses the fabs' 'I Am The Walrus' with The Rutles' 'Cheese And Onions' to bathetic effect. Again, the tune is catchy enough, but a pop-by-numbers feel predominates, and despite having a few interesting Warren word games thrown in and another infectious melody, it ends up sounding a bit like an amiable Beatles parody.

'Everybody Needs Somebody' (Warren, Siefert)
An attempt to cross Solomon Burke with The Supremes via Phil Collins and The Blues Brothers, this really does feel like a bolted-together construction, with authentic brass stabs exactly where you expect them to be, and a 'You Can't Hurry Love' rhythm carrying the track along. It's probably one to make you dig out the originals for another listen, though.

'That's How I'm Loving You' (Warren, Tommey)
Sounding a bit more like his own man here, Warren offers this plaintive Korgis-style ballad that does manage to generate an atmosphere with its slow drift and

gives the album a welcome change of pace. There is a charming middle eight and a well-judged key change that lifts proceedings for a short guitar solo. You can't really fault his craftsmanship on this yearning opus.

'Have You Seen The Colours?' (Warren, Davis)
Cod-psychedelia is the order of the day on this attempt to return to the paisley era of the late-1960s – although it just about makes it to the mid-1980s, recalling the mock-psychedelia of The Dukes Of Stratosfear, but minus the amusing lyrics and the period *nous* possessed by that intrepid band of musical explorers. This collaboration with Warren's old sparring partner Andy Davis is closer to some of The Move's more lysergic moments. It even quotes that band's 1967 hit single 'I Can Hear The Grass Grow' in the lyric at one point, but I'm not sure if Roy Wood would've let this one through.

'I Just Want You To Tell Me' (Warren, Tommey)
Ending the album in a low-key way, this is another lovelorn Warren ballad where he pleads with his loved one to show they care. The gently affecting verse supported by acoustic guitar has a simple beauty, and the floating chorus has a lovely little melody. I'm a sucker for Warren in ballad mode, and along with 'That's How I'm Loving You' and the sublime 'You've Got The Love That Matters', this tender soliloquy completes the best trio of tracks on *Innocent Bystander*.

It's been one of those albums with a handful of good ideas sprinkled through more-workmanlike compositions and is in no way comparable to the sophistication on display on his previous solo outing *Jim's Easy Listening Album*. Then again, it's a cut or two above his 1980s debut album *Burning Questions*, for which we can be thankful. We would have to wait another four years for a spectacular return of the Warren pop muse in full focus on the excellent Korgis' album *Kartoon World*.

Field of Stone – Mutter Slater Band (2018)

Personnel:
Mutter Slater: vocals, guitar
Chris Cleaver: guitar, backing vocals
Clive Ashley: tenor and soprano saxophones
Tom Hughes: Hammond B3 organ
Ian Olliver: bass
Laurie Higgins: bass, upright bass
Dan Wheeler: drums, percussion, backing vocals
Matt Barge: trumpet
Recorded: Vale Studios, Worcestershire; Olive Tree Studios, Dorset, 2018
Producer: Mutter Slater Band
Engineers: Chris D'Adda (Vale); Chris Cleaver, Tom Hughes (Olive Tree)
Label: Angel Air
Release date: 2018

'Something We Knew As Love' (Slater)

A crackly vinyl effect announces the opening track on Mutter Slater's latest opus, accompanied by a trebly, filtered electric guitar that soon moves into a solid mid-tempo as the man himself launches into a lyric mourning his latest love-gone-sour scenario. The production is crisp and well-panned across the stereo picture, with Chris Cleaver's guitar solo cutting through in the right-hand channel along with Tom Hughes' organ, while Clive Ashley's sax interjections sit out to the left. It makes for a solid opening track.

'Field of Stone' (Slater)

We are back in epic territory with the title track, which follows a line drawn through earlier widescreen Slater compositions such as 'The Unforgiving Man' and 'Even Love?'. In full, slow portentous mode, this opens with a repeated bass riff, as three slow chord strikes on acoustic guitar, play off it.

With the Grim Reaper again on his tail, Slater paints a picture of utter helplessness in the face of impending demise as the tense atmosphere ratchets up via Chris Cleaver's amazing edge-of-feedback guitar machinations. Slater invokes the mythology of the *corvid* genus representing a portent of doom with the line 'That old black crow is laughing', as he metaphorically stumbles through an unforgiving landscape.

As a portrait of utter desolation, this six-and-a-half-minute track is the business, and as Chris Cleaver embarks on a feedback-drenched guitar solo that even invokes a Pete Townshend-style pop-art approach in places (albeit slow and controlled), the tension reaches breaking point. Clive Ashley's twisting and turning sax solo explodes into the aural mix to bring the track to a climax before it all falls back to the bass riff that started it all, with fading guitar feedback closing out this bleak-sounding but enthralling performance.

'Caroline Motion' (Slater)
Now we are plunged back into upbeat territory with a song that sounds like a tribute to the brand of 1960s soul promoted by Stax Records: who gave us the likes of Otis Redding, Sam and Dave, and the influential Booker T. & the M.G.'s. The brazen brass riffs that open it sound akin to the famous Memphis Horns, as Slater's love of sweet soul music comes to the fore. Funky guitar chords provide the bedrock as a cowbell drives the beat and staccato organ chords interject, creating a funky stew. Slater serenades the titular Caroline, and there's some nifty wordplay. I particularly like the line 'But your feet are as heavy as a doorman's *bonhomie*'. A greasy tenor sax solo with jazzy squeaks and judicious use of reverb completes the picture, as the track closes with some stop-time dynamics to take it home in grand style.

'Losing It' (Slater)
Sporting a sparse arrangement of bass drum, moody sax and some clever organ glissandos, this track slowly moves through its paces, while Slater's lyric uses the passing days of the week as an analogy for killing time. His vocals shift suddenly from high to low on this mournful creation that sounds like someone at the end of their tether. There is a tremolo effect on the guitar and a touch of sax soloing, but the most telling feature is Tom Hughes' expressive organ-playing: a masterful demonstration of how to use the instrument as a perfect foil to the vocals.

'Love Is The Stranger' (Slater)
Slater's lazy acoustic strum on a couple of chords sets up the mood of this laid-back song, accentuated by some casual dobro picking from Chris Cleaver. The addition of a string bass gives it a kind of early-1970s Lou Reed feel, as Slater continues to wallow in melancholia, and this less than cheerful but still impelling album moves into a run of slow downbeat songs.

'Folding' (Slater)
We're back to 6/8 soul-influenced blues with this slightly gospel plod through a lyric that equates life to a game of poker. Sounding less than happy, Slater's vocal moves its way through this deadly-slow piece, edged on by some laconic sax and guitar. But you definitely need to be in one of those moods to get the full benefit, and if you're not in that kind of mood, it's difficult to not yearn for something a bit more uplifting.

'Weird Kid' (Slater)
Although sticking with a slow tempo, 'Weird Kid' proves to be an interestingly different song, and Slater revisits his *outsider* observations as he narrates his tale of 'The fat man in the sunshine' who was apparently once 'that weird kid on the hill'. With acoustic guitar supported by tremolo guitar, it moves into a touching middle eight that breaks into a sax solo. There's a key change before

some more dobro from Chris Cleaver, as he picks over a chord pattern that again recalls Lou Reed: particularly 'Sweet Jane'. A sax glissando then brings us to the end of a worthwhile track.

'You're The Reason' (Slater)

As this track starts, it at first appears we are moving back into slow triple-time, until suddenly the tempo ups to something more upbeat as we again revisit a Stax Records vibe. There's a soulful verse with a snare drum thumping out its 4/4 rhythm, and in an adventurous arrangement, the band negotiate a swing back into 6/8 for the sax solo before spinning on a sixpence back into common time for a walloping finale. On this section, Slater sounds like a dead ringer for Otis Redding as his 'Gotta-gotta-gotta-gotta' testifies, brings the track to a fade.

'There's A Wall...' (Slater)

Opening with some solo organ that recalls Jon Lord's work for Deep Purple, the album closer soon moves back into a slow 4/4 groove as Slater returns to the doldrums, but this time in defensive mode as he invokes a 'fortress mentality' against the brickbats of the outside world. Moving at a stately pace, this track builds into a kind of lugubrious power ballad, with imagery of walls, minefields and bastions to keep out the unspeakable evils of the world. Cupping a 'candle of resolve', Slater declaims ', It's all we'll have against the cold', and it's all down to survival of the fittest as the spectre of doom-and-gloom hovers ominously once more. Some warbling soprano sax from Clive Ashley plays the track out, bringing another fine Mutter Slater Band album to a close.

Kartoon World – The Korgis (2021)

Personnel:
James Warren: vocals, bass, guitar
John Baker: vocals, acoustic guitar
Al Steele: vocals, guitars, keyboards, bass
Nigel Hart: keyboards
Paul Smith: drums
Chris Hopkins (Exhibit-1): guitars, keyboards, vocals ('Magic Money Tree', 'This Is A New Low')
Peter Karrie: vocals ('This Is The Life')
Seye Adelekan, Laura Prince: vocals ('The Best Thing You Can Do Is To Love Someone')
Jay Marshall, Ava Volante, Emmy Rivers: backing vocals
The Welsh Television Orchestra:
Richard Mainwaring: violin and viola
Korine Colborn: violin
Claudine Cassidy: cello
Ceri Rees: flute, clarinet
Phil Jarvis: trombone
Julian Tucker: alto and soprano saxophones
Recorded during lockdown at various remote locations in Liverpool, Wales and Bath, 2020-2021
Producer: The Korgis
Label: Angel Air
Release date: November 2021

James Warren and John Baker were gearing up for a tour under the banner '40 years of The Korgis' when the Covid-19 pandemic hit the UK and we all went into the first of several lockdowns in 2020. This scuppered the band's live plans, as all gigs were cancelled, so The Korgis stayed in touch with their fan base via a series of cartoons by Cardiff artist Leah Darknell, titled *Keeping Up With The Korgis*. This proved to be the seed that germinated into a new Korgis recording project for 2020, as Warren and Baker were in touch with guitarist Al Steele who'd featured on Warren's *Innocent Bystander* album, and he was communicating with Chris Hopkins of Liverpool unit Exhibit-1.

Remote songwriting via the internet ensued, and Darknell's cartoon idea blossomed into what eventually became a pop concept album. The concept album was one of those terminologies that always seemed to attract a fair amount of flak, especially from the music press. Most concept albums were designated as such because they displayed an overarching theme that linked the tracks together – be it a story or a set of related lyrical topics, and generally, most of these kinds of albums were firmly in the progressive rock mode rather than pure pop. A couple of examples are *The Lamb Lies Down on Broadway* by Genesis (1974) and *Tales from Topographic Oceans* by Yes (1973). The

Korgis decided to head down this route, and when the album was revealed in 2021, the results proved to be spectacular.

One of the strengths of *Kartoon World* is the collaborative band feel of the album, with the tight five-piece unit of James Warren, John Baker, Al Steele, Nigel Hart (keyboards) and Paul Smith (drums). The extensive employment of live drums rather than the programmed variety brings the music alive; there is much hot playing from all involved, and best of all, some truly exceptional pop songwriting. The group vibe really pulls this album together, pretty much ensuring there are no truly weak moments on what must rate as the most consistently good album to emerge under the Korgis moniker. An inspired choice of guest musicians provided that extra sheen of quality, which proved to be the final flourish on this highly addictive set of recordings.

'Kartoon World Overture' (Steele, Baker, Warren)

The action opens with the first of two short orchestral chamber pop instrumentals. The harmonic material for this short overture is derived from the song 'Cartoon World', which appears much later on the album. This 38-second prelude is beautifully orchestrated, and brings to mind the style of George Martin's score for the animated film *Yellow Submarine* in its 'Pepperland' feel. The superb orchestral arrangements on *Kartoon World* are performed by The Welsh Television Orchestra and really add to the extra sonic depth on display throughout.

'Bringing Back The Spirit Of Love' (Steele, Warren)

One of the joys of this album is the way the tracks link into each other, utilising a similar method to that on the excellent 2005 Stackridge compilation album *Sex and Flags*. This gives *Kartoon World* a beautiful flow, and this song is one of the album's signal tracks, dealing as it does with a central theme of the entire work, as The Korgis resurrect the universal-love motif so redolent of much of The Beatles' work. The inspiration for this theme was driven by the countless examples of selfless expression and community spirit that proved to be one of the most heartwarming by-products of the 2020 pandemic lockdown. The album is in effect holding a mirror up to the struggles of the new decade, and the songs herein are very much linked to the events we all lived through in this period.

What of the music, you may ask – well, if you like pure pop in the classic style, you'll find it here in spades, and this album really appeals to the eternal pop fan in me. This song opens on a mid-tempo shuffle before James Warren enters the fray with the line 'We're gonna start a revolution', as the music recalls the feel of 1990s Britpop, displaying a huge degree of pop thrill as the verses run into the anthem-like chorus that – not for the last time on this album – recalls the work of 1970s pop innovators 10cc. Positive vibes abound, and the glorious sound is highly addictive as we get the first of many Al Steele guitar cameos over the chorus chords. As on the rest of the album, guitar solos are kept brief and to the point, as are other instrumental breaks. The coda sees Warren getting out his megaphone for a positive rallying speech to the troops of love, and the whole caboodle ends with what sounds like someone turning off the power to the recording console as everything grinds to a halt.

'Back In The Eighties' (Baker, Warren, Steele)

Grabbing our time machine, we are next whisked back to the 1980s, as this John Baker-led confection raises the ghost of Yazoo with a suitably electro-pop soundtrack to accompany our temporal journey. Power chords from Al Steele, tuck under a chorus that climaxes in a huge harmonised suspended chord before whipping back to the nifty electro-pop synthesizer verse riff. It's a hugely catchy affair, and there's a driving middle eight to round it off, with lyrical mentions of Madonna, VCRs, Rubik's cubes and other 1980s paraphernalia, until it falls back to a sequenced synthesizer bass note: a symbol of the era in question.

'All Roads Lead To Rome' (Baker, Warren, Steele)

The sweeping eclecticism that is a hallmark of this album leads us next into a superbly atmospheric slow gospel blues tune, tied to a bar of 6. James Warren here sounds uncannily like John Lennon – his voice slavered in Phil Spector-style reverb recalling the *Imagine* album that Warren's former writing partner Andy Davis contributed to 50 years earlier. There's even a lyrical nod to Lennon's 'Norwegian Wood' with the line 'Then you fall asleep in the bath'. The seductive bass line sounds like Warren is playing fretless, and the gospel organ and piano add that sanctified feel to a track that's brilliantly arranged and a joy to listen to.

There's a subtle emotion that runs through this entire album that many of the tracks share, giving the feeling that much of this material was written from the heart. The chorus on this track evinces a warming glow as the classic imagery of the bold knight riding to the rescue of a maiden is reversed to the woman emotionally rescuing the man. It's a fascinating relationship song in which the music and lyrics compliment each other perfectly. A nicely understated slide guitar solo rounds things off before a final chorus where Warren's passionate vocals extemporise on the melody with an upward skim that brings out the emotion in the lyrics, and it closes with a perfectly-formed classic blues ending followed by some organ doodles to take it home.

'This Is the Life' (Steele)

On a song about the crazy lifestyles so many of us lead in this modern world, the verses take the form of a funky rap in a style that Godley & Creme explored back in the 1980s on tracks such as 'Snack Attack' from the 1981 album *Ismism*. It's even sung in a style similar to that song, with edgy lyrics giving the track some serious bite. The line 'Just a breath away from a panic attack' really sums up how many of us have felt during the first two years of the Covid-19 pandemic. We abruptly change style for the memorable choruses, to a swaying sing-along of the song title, and this is followed by a theatrical rap from actor Peter Karrie (West End star of *The Phantom Of The Opera*), whose strident Scottish accent declaims a string of ills of the modern world, punctuated by group chants of the title. After a final chorus, an unexpected frantic free-form jazz piano interlude suddenly appears, sounding for all the world like Mike Garson's playing on David Bowie's 1973 track 'Aladdin Sane' – so much so that it almost feels as if it's in aural inverted commas (if that's possible!). The final verse brings it all back to the underlying album theme – to stand up for love in the face of the daunting tide of craziness that constitutes modern society.

'Time (Song for Dom)' (Warren, Steele)
This is a track that starts in triple time, driven by a fetching minor-key harpsichord arrangement as James Warren sings a lyric inspired by the antics of a certain Mr. Cummings, in effect recording a slice of our recent social history in song. Cleverly sung from the point of view of the turncoat Tory, it's an amusing episode with several musical twists and turns to keep us on our toes. The choruses have a light jazzy swing with some nimble in-the-groove playing that impresses with a bigger surprise after the second chorus when the track rocks into 4/4 for a positively scorching Hammond organ solo followed by a rocking up-tempo verse punctuated by wailing guitar licks. This all eventually resolves into a return of the swinging chorus music for a neat jazz guitar solo before collapsing into a harpsichord coda for the closing verse.

'La La Land' (Baker, Warren, Steele)
This guitar intro reminds me of a T. Rex boogie as it charges into a pop/rock verse and the lyric expands on the chaos of a Los Angeles lifestyle. The chorus is ultra-catchy and brings to mind Billy Joel in up-tempo style, and police siren effects adorn the second verse to illustrate the gridlocked highways leading into the city. After a second chorus, a middle eight takes us to the beach, as the ghost of surfing Beach Boy Dennis Wilson and his crew are evoked with some gorgeous harmony vocals in classic Beach Boys style. It's a highly contagious track with a short reverb-soaked vocal link at the end that cleverly leads into the next selection.

'Magic Money Tree' (Steele, Warren, Hopkins)
One of a pair of tracks on the album that include the band Exhibit-1 and Chris Hopkins of that outfit is featured on a co-write with Al Steele and James Warren. The title was inspired by a Theresa May quote a few years back about having 'no magic money tree'. It's a real funky affair, with the choppy rhythm guitar, bass and drums kicking up an impressive groove on the verses. This slides into a streamlined chorus that you definitely won't get out of your head once you've heard it, where the bass marches effortlessly up and down the scale, and the vocals soar in a watertight band performance. The

harmonies on the middle section are a dead ringer for the style of Australian band Crowded House and sound fabulous. The lyrics scan brilliantly and raise a vision of a modern society that's in danger of completely losing its moral compass, with images of the chasm separating the rich from the poor and the lack of compassion displayed by a society that constantly elevates money above people.

'Space' (Warren, Steele)
A point of stillness in the midst of the album, 'Space' finds us floating weightlessly, looking down on the myriad creatures scrambling to and fro across the surface of this planet (including the human race) while this small world circles its fairly ordinary yellow dwarf star, itself in a huge galaxy that is one of a billion other galaxies in this ever-expanding universe. It is a song invoking a cosmic perspective on the crazy goings-on on Earth below. With James Warren's disembodied vocals floating in the ambient ether – with only the occasional Pepperland-style cello interjection playing wobbling two-note phrases – we are at peace. The second verse brings an intermittent piano as Warren sings, 'I feel like I've never been so high' and we go into the floating chorus preceding a middle section of synthesizer and drums playing some triple-time riffs. To close the track, the last chorus enters, this time with a backbeat, before it finally falls back to the disembodied vocal, followed by a lonely Morse-code signal, recalling those purple spaceships first encountered half a century earlier.

'This Is A New Low' (Hopkins, Steele, Warren)
Chris Hopkins' outfit Exhibit-1 return for the first track on the album to feature an overdriven electric guitar, and this has a touch of that 1980s Toto/Journey feel as the verses are punctuated by a punchy guitar with bass and drums following suit. This is the closest the album comes to a more hard rock style (but not *that* hard!) with that galloping rhythm so redolent of the genre.

The lyrics are portentous, and berate that 'we could have seen the signs, but we weren't listening', bringing to mind the impending climate emergency we all now face in these desperate times, as well as unheeded early warnings about preparing for possible pandemics before they come upon us. Towards the end, the voice of the Shabbey Road Mainframe Computer enters the fray with a creepy futuristic feel, coldly stating 'This is not a high' and 'This is a new low', broken with the words 'I repeat'. It's a disturbing interlude; brilliantly put together. The track then rocks into the sunset with a guitar solo on heavy sustain as it fades away.

'Broken' (Parry, Warren, Steele)
A typical love-gone-wrong ballad in classic Warren mode, this is actually a co-write with Darren Parry and Al Steele. With its signature Korgis feel and swelling orchestration, it's built in an archetypal Warren-style. There's a more

up-tempo middle eight with orchestration very reminiscent of mid-period Beatles, before it transforms into a power ballad when the sustained guitar solo arrives, sounding like Al Steele wringing emotion from every last note he plays.

'The Ghost Of You' (Warren, Steele)

On a track that is simplicity itself, the upbeat verses perch upon pretty much a single chord with a second implied one. This builds up a musical tension that eventually finds its release in a euphoric rush when the elevated chorus arrives as James Warren's vocals head for a higher octave. There follows a cascading, brain-permeating melody that curls deliciously downward in sinuous waves. Simple it may be, but it carries a potent emotional depth charge as the lyrics deal with that profound kind of loss we all suffer at some point in our life when all we are left with are the ghosts of our memories of a departed loved one. The very definition of pop songwriting, this song itself proves to be a ghost, set to haunt the jukebox of the mind when you least expect it.

'Bringing Back The Spirit of Love – Reprise' (Steele, Warren)

This short 16-second orchestral arrangement is another instrumental chamber pop snippet; this time, a reprise of the earlier paean to love that followed the opening prelude, and is a brief but wonderful interlude that leads us perfectly into the title track.

'Cartoon World' (Steele, Baker, Warren)

The title track (with the correct spelling of 'cartoon' this time) is a sublime creation. With a gentle rhythm, it starts in an understated style with acoustic guitar and vibes, until a lead guitar appears, playing a prelude of the chorus melody and strongly bringing back the sonic feel of the 1964 Beatles' album *Beatles For Sale*. The collaborative writing really comes to the fore with John Baker being the principal architect of the verses, Al Steele coming up with the sing-along but moving choruses, and James Warren contributing a perfect middle eight that takes the song to another level.

The verses have an almost confidential, conversational feel and really nail the feeling that many of us experience in these troubled times – that society has virtually become akin to living in an exaggerated cartoon with its sound-bites and pick-and-mix cultural landscape where the old certainties appear to no longer apply, as everything is constantly channelled toward the lowest common denominator. Unfortunately, although 'There's not too much to shout about' as the lyric says, there's no one to say 'cut'. The chorus aims for its target audience with deadly accuracy, and is liable to hit those in their second half-century firmly below the ribs with the final chorus couplet, 'Maybe it's just me/I liked it how it used to be in the seventies' (It brought a tear to my eye anyway). After two verses and choruses, Warren's middle eight hits it on the button with the line 'To the money god, we are cartoon slaves', as the music elevates to another plateau with the allegory of the human race trapped in a self-made, rapidly deteriorating 'cartoon world' where 'The story won't allow us to go back'. Poignant and moving, 'Cartoon World' is the first of a pair of world-beating songs that close this fine pop album.

'The Best Thing You Can Do Is To Love Someone' (Steele, Warren)

With the closing track, we finally come full circle as the universal-love motif is enshrined in a song as simple as it is beautiful. Working together, Al Steele and James Warren combine to create an anthem-like denouement to the album. Steele's inspired, gentle acoustic verses are perfectly complemented by Warren's lush, floating, string-cushioned middle section. The final touch that lends this track its overpoweringly soulful emotion is the addition of Seye Adelekan (bass player with Gorillaz) and the wonderful vocals of Parisian singer Laura Prince. The lyric strongly reflects the difficult times many of us have lived through, and the deep loss felt by so many, but still comes across with an overwhelmingly positive message that despite all the despair and loss, we all need to hold onto and share love. It's a moving performance and liable to bring a tear to the eye of the more sensitive listener.

Seye Adelekan's vocals are remarkable, displaying a wonderful occasional catch in his voice where a note suddenly flips up an octave in such an expressive way: very soulful. Laura Prince is likewise a brilliant vocalist, and the three-way vocal combination of Warren, Adelekan and Prince gives the track something really special.

This is a sort of modern campfire song that would sound as good performed with acoustic guitar in a folk club as it would in a packed stadium with the crowd swaying from side to side, singing along, which is easy to imagine. It brings to a close a perfect pop album that I would say is about as close as it gets to a perfect pop classic in this day and age, and it just may be The Korgis' finest artistic achievement to date.

50th Anniversary

To celebrate 50 years since the first Stackridge album was unleashed on an unsuspecting world, 2021 saw the release of a three-CD compilation selecting 50 tracks from their back catalogue. These are arranged in a somewhat higgledy-piggledy fashion, completely ignoring chronology, but it does serve to demonstrate the abrupt changes in style that were part of their *modus operandi* from day one. David Bowie may have adopted a different style for every album, but Stackridge pretty much did the same for every song! It's one of the many reasons why I love them so much.

The eagle-eyed will notice one unfamiliar title in the shape of the track that kicks off this compilation: namely 'Overture'. This is not a brand new recording, though, but rather a mash-up of instrumental excerpts drawn from various compositions and edited into a kind of overture to the album. There are a few new brief orchestral flourishes added *en route*, but 99% of the track consists of sections of 'Coniston Water', 'Humiliation', 'Essence Of Porphyry', 'God Speed The Plough', 'Do The Stanley' and 'Happy Ending Music', pasted together in a 4:39 collage via a few jarring edits. It's pretty much non-essential stuff for the lay person, but is obviously one for complete Stackridge nuts, like me! There is also an unexpected treat included in the shape of a previously unreleased version of the band's live *Old Grey Whistle Test* performance of 'Dancing On Air' from February 1975.

50 years is a long time to sustain a recording career, but three of the core four Stackridge songwriters have all achieved this, both with and without the parent band. James Warren ended up having the most commercial success of the four, having penned a simple haunting ballad that became a pop standard in 'Everybody's Got To Learn Sometime'. Although his writing could occasionally skim the pop surface, there were still many of those deeper moments when his best compositions hit stunning artistic arcs – 'The Three Legged Table', 'Friendliness', 'Father Frankenstein Is Behind Your Pillow', 'It Must Be Time For Bed' and 'The First Name Of Love' to name but a few of the Stackridge examples. Along with the best of his Korgis and solo output, they all testify to an enduring talent. Andy Davis, who had guided Stackridge through so many different variants, consistently ploughed a deep emotional furrow and reigned supreme in the arena of inspired instrumentals, such as 'Lummy Days', 'February In Shropshire' and 'Charles Louis Dance'. His late-period lyrics revealed a troubled soul that poured forth into his music to produce real tearjerker moments like 'The Chrysler Girl', 'Emergency Love', the sublime 'The Ghost of Love' and many more. He and Crun Walter turned out timeless Stackridge classics like 'Slark', 'Purple Spaceships Over Yatton', 'Fish In A Glass', and the magnificent 'Teatime'.

Crun Walter's earthy lyrics went hand-in-glove with Andy Davis' imaginative melodies, and the bearded one's solo compositions, although rarer, were more often than not full of charm and good humour. He showed his deeper side too with 'Long Dark River' from the Stackridge comeback album *A Victory for Common Sense* in 2009, and his writing talent spanned 40 years before he decided to finally call it a day in 2011.

Then there was the one and only Mutter Slater – a man possessed of a natural charisma that could charm the birds off the trees; a ready talent for an original tune, and best of all, he had the most sublime pure-toned flute sound of any era. His writing contribution to the Stackridge canon was initially sparse, but from *The Man in the Bowler Hat* onwards, was ever-more telling. These ranged widely from the fun of 'Do The Stanley' and the deceptively clever 'The Galloping Gaucho', to the melodic nous of tunes like 'Pinafore Days', 'God Speed The Plough', 'The Slater's Waltz', and his later notable contributions to the band: the more-collaborative 'The Old Country' and 'North St. Grande'. His solo work, too – though more genre-specific than his wide-ranging Stackridge work – was often thoughtful, displaying a ready wit and a way with words that resulted in many a memorable couplet throughout the career of his own Mutter Slater Band. Also, let's not forget his questing experimental spirit as well, starting low-key with the ambient 'Story Of My Heart' in 1972, through to the likes of 'Coniston Water' and 'Beating A Path To Your Door'. His Mutter Slater Band albums also display this admirable trait on the more expansive epics such as 'The Unforgiving Man', 'Even Love?' and 'Field Of Stone'.

Although it seems exceedingly unlikely at this point that we'll see another Stackridge reunion, in many ways, they've done more than enough for us already. They certainly changed my life forever, and profoundly influenced my own musical career over the last 50 years since that magic moment on 3 July 1972 when I walked into the Marquee Club in London's Soho to witness my very first Stackridge gig. On that day, I was stunned by the eclectic sweep and versatility of their spellbinding performance, and was especially entranced by Mutter Slater's incredible flute-playing on epics like 'Purple Spaceships Over Yatton' and 'Slark'. The band's dedicated followers – the ranks of Rhubarb Thrashers who continued to support this remarkable band through thick and thin – proved to be a tenacious bunch. The journey from the early-1970s through to well into the next century took many of us from teenagers at our first Stackridge gigs to thinking about our pensions by the time of their 'Final Bow' in 2015. For many of us, it really has been the journey of a lifetime. None of us will ever forget them, and most of us have had our lives changed by them.

Many admirers of the band became musicians themselves, and a plethora of Stackridge-influenced bands and solo artists followed in their wake – including The Alsatians, The High Llamas (Wonder where their name came from – 'The Road to Venezuela' anyone?), The Divine Comedy (Neil Hannon professed to being a fan), The Valuable Fools, LAF, Tim Moon, The Brighton Peers, The Dolphin Post and many others. Hopefully, due to the magic of recorded sound, many more will have the chance to freshly discover the band's music in years to come, and in my mind, there is no doubt that there will indeed be a small corner of England that is 'Forever Stackridge', along with a large corner of my heart!

Roy Harper - *on track*

every album, every song

Opher Goodwin
Paperback
160 pages
50 colour photographs
978-1-78951-130-6
£14.99
$21.95

Every album and every song by this legendary troubadour.

Roy Harper must be one of Britain's most undervalued rock musicians and songwriters. For over fifty years, he has produced a series of innovative albums of consistently outstanding quality, putting poetry and social commentary to music in a way that extends the boundaries of rock music. His 22 studio albums and 16 live albums, made up of 250 songs, have created a unique body of work.

Roy is a musician's musician. He is lauded by the likes of Dave Gilmour, Ian Anderson, Jimmy Page, Pete Townsend, Joanna Newsom, Fleet Foxes and Kate Bush. Who else could boast that he has had Keith Moon, Jimmy Page, Dave Gilmour, John Paul Jones, Ronnie Lane, Chris Spedding, Bill Bruford and Steve Broughton in his backing band? Notable albums include *Stormcock*, *HQ* and *Bullinamingvase*.

Opher Goodwin, Roy's friend and a fan, guides the reader through every album and song, providing insight into the recording of the songs as well the times in which they were recorded. As his loyal and often fanatical fans will attest, Roy has produced a series of epic songs and he remains a raging, uncompromising individual.

Fairport Convention - *on track*

every album, every song

Kevan Furbank
Paperback
176 pages
44 colour photographs
978-1-78951-051-4
£14.99
$21.95

Every album by these legends of British folk rock.

Fairport Convention are a great British institution – or, at least, they should be. For more than 50 years they have helped to keep traditional music alive and kicking by injecting it with a healthy dose of electric rock 'n' roll. Their finest albums – including *What We Did On Our Holidays* and *Liege And Lief* – are landmarks is the development of British music.

In this exhaustive and illuminating book, Kevan Furbank looks at all the studio albums in detail – from their uncertain debut in 1968 to their most recent release, celebrating half a century of music-making. He chronicles the stories behind each recording, touching on the highs and lows, the successes and tragedies, the pleasure and pain, and examines the songwriting, arrangements and traditions that inspired each track. In doing so, he also looks at the contributions made by the many great musicians who have passed through Fairport's 'revolving-door' line-ups, including guitar wizard Richard Thompson, angel-voiced Sandy Denny, demon fiddler Dave Swarbrick and the 'guv'nor' of British folk-rock, Ashley Hutchings. Fairport Convention's musical story is as dramatic as any soap opera. If you have never heard any Fairport this book is the perfect introduction. If you have, you will want to go back and revisit the music this band has made over the last 50 years.

Because, in the words of Richard Thompson, it all comes round again.

The Hollies - *on track*

every album, every song

Andrew Darlington
Paperback
160 pages
48 colour photographs
978-1-78951-159-7
£14.99
$21.95

Every album by these British pop legends.

'The road is long, with many a winding turn, that leads us to who knows where? Who knows where?'

Everyone loved The Hollies. They were the 'group's group'. Never confrontational or rebellious, always smartly suited, always smiling. The band had an unbroken run of immaculate pop singles which, while they seldom had that must-buy factor of the latest Rolling Stones or Beatles record, were hallmarked by tight harmonies and an almost unfailing chart sensibility. Throughout the sixties and well into the seventies, everyone had at least one or two Hollies singles in their collection and nobody begrudged The Hollies their hits.

When 'He Ain't Heavy, He's My Brother' and 'Long Cool Woman In A Black Dress' became global million-sellers, The Hollies were inducted into *The Rock 'n' Roll Hall Of Fame*. Graham Nash – by then deep into his second career as part of Crosby, Stills and Nash - was reunited with other members of the outfit on stage together in the March 2010 ceremony.

This book tells the full story of the band's music, from the band's origins in Manchester, through the full arc of hits, and the albums – track-by-track, into the twenty-first century, then... now... always.

On Track series

Alan Parsons Project – Steve Swift 978-1-78952-154-2
Tori Amos – Lisa Torem 978-1-78952-142-9
Asia – Peter Braidis 978-1-78952-099-6
Badfinger – Robert Day-Webb 978-1-878952-176-4
Barclay James Harvest – Keith and Monica Domone 978-1-78952-067-5
The Beatles – Andrew Wild 978-1-78952-009-5
The Beatles Solo 1969-1980 – Andrew Wild 978-1-78952-030-9
Blue Oyster Cult – Jacob Holm-Lupo 978-1-78952-007-1
Blur – Matt Bishop – 978-178952-164-1
Marc Bolan and T.Rex – Peter Gallagher 978-1-78952-124-5
Kate Bush – Bill Thomas 978-1-78952-097-2
Camel – Hamish Kuzminski 978-1-78952-040-8
Caravan – Andy Boot 978-1-78952-127-6
Cardiacs – Eric Benac 978-1-78952-131-3
Eric Clapton Solo – Andrew Wild 978-1-78952-141-2
The Clash – Nick Assirati 978-1-78952-077-4
Crosby, Stills and Nash – Andrew Wild 978-1-78952-039-2
The Damned – Morgan Brown 978-1-78952-136-8
Deep Purple and Rainbow 1968-79 – Steve Pilkington 978-1-78952-002-6
Dire Straits – Andrew Wild 978-1-78952-044-6
The Doors – Tony Thompson 978-1-78952-137-5
Dream Theater – Jordan Blum 978-1-78952-050-7
Electric Light Orchestra – Barry Delve 978-1-78952-152-8
Elvis Costello and The Attractions – Georg Purvis 978-1-78952-129-0
Emerson Lake and Palmer – Mike Goode 978-1-78952-000-2
Fairport Convention – Kevan Furbank 978-1-78952-051-4
Peter Gabriel – Graeme Scarfe 978-1-78952-138-2
Genesis – Stuart MacFarlane 978-1-78952-005-7
Gentle Giant – Gary Steel 978-1-78952-058-3
Gong – Kevan Furbank 978-1-78952-082-8
Hall and Oates – Ian Abrahams 978-1-78952-167-2
Hawkwind – Duncan Harris 978-1-78952-052-1
Peter Hammill – Richard Rees Jones 978-1-78952-163-4
Roy Harper – Opher Goodwin 978-1-78952-130-6
Jimi Hendrix – Emma Stott 978-1-78952-175-7
The Hollies – Andrew Darlington 978-1-78952-159-7
Iron Maiden – Steve Pilkington 978-1-78952-061-3
Jefferson Airplane – Richard Butterworth 978-1-78952-143-6
Jethro Tull – Jordan Blum 978-1-78952-016-3
Elton John in the 1970s – Peter Kearns 978-1-78952-034-7
The Incredible String Band – Tim Moon 978-1-78952-107-8
Iron Maiden – Steve Pilkington 978-1-78952-061-3
Judas Priest – John Tucker 978-1-78952-018-7

Kansas – Kevin Cummings 978-1-78952-057-6
The Kinks – Martin Hutchinson 978-1-78952-172-6
Korn – Matt Karpe 978-1-78952-153-5
Led Zeppelin – Steve Pilkington 978-1-78952-151-1
Level 42 – Matt Philips 978-1-78952-102-3
Little Feat – 978-1-78952-168-9
Aimee Mann – Jez Rowden 978-1-78952-036-1
Joni Mitchell – Peter Kearns 978-1-78952-081-1
The Moody Blues – Geoffrey Feakes 978-1-78952-042-2
Motorhead – Duncan Harris 978-1-78952-173-3
Mike Oldfield – Ryan Yard 978-1-78952-060-6
Opeth – Jordan Blum 978-1-78-952-166-5
Tom Petty – Richard James 978-1-78952-128-3
Porcupine Tree – Nick Holmes 978-1-78952-144-3
Queen – Andrew Wild 978-1-78952-003-3
Radiohead – William Allen 978-1-78952-149-8
Renaissance – David Detmer 978-1-78952-062-0
The Rolling Stones 1963-80 – Steve Pilkington 978-1-78952-017-0
The Smiths and Morrissey – Tommy Gunnarsson 978-1-78952-140-5
Status Quo the Frantic Four Years – Richard James 978-1-78952-160-3
Steely Dan – Jez Rowden 978-1-78952-043-9
Steve Hackett – Geoffrey Feakes 978-1-78952-098-9
Thin Lizzy – Graeme Stroud 978-1-78952-064-4
Toto – Jacob Holm-Lupo 978-1-78952-019-4
U2 – Eoghan Lyng 978-1-78952-078-1
UFO – Richard James 978-1-78952-073-6
The Who – Geoffrey Feakes 978-1-78952-076-7
Roy Wood and the Move – James R Turner 978-1-78952-008-8
Van Der Graaf Generator – Dan Coffey 978-1-78952-031-6
Yes – Stephen Lambe 978-1-78952-001-9
Frank Zappa 1966 to 1979 – Eric Benac 978-1-78952-033-0
Warren Zevon – Peter Gallagher 978-1-78952-170-2
10CC – Peter Kearns 978-1-78952-054-5

Decades Series

The Bee Gees in the 1960s – Andrew Mon Hughes et al 978-1-78952-148-1
The Bee Gees in the 1970s – Andrew Mon Hughes et al 978-1-78952-179-5
Black Sabbath in the 1970s – Chris Sutton 978-1-78952-171-9
Britpop – Peter Richard Adams and Matt Pooler 978-1-78952-169-6
Alice Cooper in the 1970s – Chris Sutton 978-1-78952-104-7
Curved Air in the 1970s – Laura Shenton 978-1-78952-069-9
Bob Dylan in the 1980s – Don Klees 978-1-78952-157-3
Fleetwood Mac in the 1970s – Andrew Wild 978-1-78952-105-4
Focus in the 1970s – Stephen Lambe 978-1-78952-079-8
Free and Bad Company in the 1970s – John Van der Kiste 978-1-78952-178-8

Genesis in the 1970s – Bill Thomas 978178952-146-7
George Harrison in the 1970s – Eoghan Lyng 978-1-78952-174-0
Marillion in the 1980s – Nathaniel Webb 978-1-78952-065-1
Mott the Hoople and Ian Hunter in the 1970s – John Van der Kiste 978-1-78-952-162-7
Pink Floyd In The 1970s – Georg Purvis 978-1-78952-072-9
Tangerine Dream in the 1970s – Stephen Palmer 978-1-78952-161-0
The Sweet in the 1970s – Darren Johnson 978-1-78952-139-9
Uriah Heep in the 1970s – Steve Pilkington 978-1-78952-103-0
Yes in the 1980s – Stephen Lambe with David Watkinson 978-1-78952-125-2

On Screen series

Carry On… – Stephen Lambe 978-1-78952-004-0
David Cronenberg – Patrick Chapman 978-1-78952-071-2
Doctor Who: The David Tennant Years – Jamie Hailstone 978-1-78952-066-8
James Bond – Andrew Wild – 978-1-78952-010-1
Monty Python – Steve Pilkington 978-1-78952-047-7
Seinfeld Seasons 1 to 5 – Stephen Lambe 978-1-78952-012-5

Other Books

1967: A Year In Psychedelic Rock – Kevan Furbank 978-1-78952-155-9
1970: A Year In Rock – John Van der Kiste 978-1-78952-147-4
1973: The Golden Year of Progressive Rock 978-1-78952-165-8
Babysitting A Band On The Rocks – G.D. Praetorius 978-1-78952-106-1
Eric Clapton Sessions – Andrew Wild 978-1-78952-177-1
Derek Taylor: For Your Radioactive Children – Andrew Darlington 978-1-78952-038-5
The Golden Road: The Recording History of The Grateful Dead – John Kilbride 978-1-78952-156-6
Iggy and The Stooges On Stage 1967-1974 – Per Nilsen 978-1-78952-101-6
Jon Anderson and the Warriors – the road to Yes – David Watkinson 978-1-78952-059-0
Nu Metal: A Definitive Guide – Matt Karpe 978-1-78952-063-7
Tommy Bolin: In and Out of Deep Purple – Laura Shenton 978-1-78952-070-5
Maximum Darkness – Deke Leonard 978-1-78952-048-4
Maybe I Should've Stayed In Bed – Deke Leonard 978-1-78952-053-8
The Twang Dynasty – Deke Leonard 978-1-78952-049-1

and many more to come!

Would you like to write for Sonicbond Publishing?

We are mainly a music publisher, but we also occasionally publish in other genres including film and television. At Sonicbond Publishing we are always on the look-out for authors, particularly for our two main series, On Track and Decades.

Mixing fact with in depth analysis, the On Track series examines the entire recorded work of a particular musical artist or group. All genres are considered from easy listening and jazz to 60s soul to 90s pop, via rock and metal.

The Decades series singles out a particular decade in an artist or group's history and focuses on that decade in more detail than may be allowed in the On Track series.

While professional writing experience would, of course, be an advantage, the most important qualification is to have real enthusiasm and knowledge of your subject. First-time authors are welcomed, but the ability to write well in English is essential.

Sonicbond Publishing has distribution throughout Europe and North America, and all our books are also published in E-book form. Authors will be paid a royalty based on sales of their book. Further details about our books are available from www.sonicbondpublishing.com. To contact us, complete the contact form there or email info@sonicbondpublishing.co.uk